AIDS CRISIS IN AMERICA

A Reference Handbook

AIDS CRISIS IN AMERICA

A Reference Handbook

Mary Ellen Hombs
Director, Legal Services Homelessness Task Force
of the National Housing Law Project

Introduction by Virginia Shubert

CONTEMPORARY WORLD ISSUES

ABC-CLIO

Santa Barbara, California
Denver, Colorado
Oxford, England

Library of Congress Cataloging-in-Publication Data

Hombs, Mary Ellen.
    AIDS crisis in America : a reference handbook / Mary Ellen Hombs.
        p.   cm. — (Contemporary world issues)
    Includes bibliographical references and index.
        1. AIDS (Disease)—United States—Epidemiology.   2. AIDS
    (Disease)—Government Policy—United States.   3. AIDS (Disease)—
    United States—Bibliography.   I. Title.   II. Series.
        [DNLM: 1. Acquired Immunodeficiency Syndrome—bibliography.
    2. Acquired Immunodeficiency Syndrome—epidemiology—United States.]
    RA644.A25H655   1992   362.1'969792'00973—dc20   92-48841

ISBN 0-87436-648-8 (alk. paper)

99 98 97 96 95 94 93 92   10 9 8 7 6 5 4 3 2 1

ABC-CLIO, Inc.
130 Cremona Drive, P.O. Box 1911
Santa Barbara, California 93116-1911

This book is printed on acid-free paper ⊖.

Manufactured in the United States of America

To those who died without hope,
to those who fought back.

Contents

List of Tables, xi
Preface, xiii

1 Introduction, 1

Basic Science and the Epidemic, 3
>The Human Immunodeficiency Virus, 3
>HIV-Related Illness, 4
>The Definition of AIDS, 5
>Transmission of HIV, 6
>Treatments, 8

The Demographics of HIV, 9
>The Community Response to AIDS, 11

Shaping AIDS Public Policy, 13
>The Role of the Government, 13
>Other Institutions, 14
>The Role of People Living with AIDS, 14

Public Policy Issues, 15
>Access to Health Care, 15
>Research and the Approval of New Treatments, 16
>Prevention and Education, 17
>Testing and Confidentiality, 18
>Systems of Care, 19

Conclusion, 22

2 Chronology, 27

3 Biographical Sketches, 49

4 Facts and Statistics, 55

Terminology for Understanding HIV/AIDS, 56
    The Importance of Language, 56
    Terms To Understand: Three Mini-Glossaries, 57
CDC Surveillance Case Definition, 66
HIV/AIDS and the World, 81
HIV/AIDS and the Nation, 83
    Funding, 84
    Health Care Costs and Concerns, 87
    Who Gets HIV/AIDS, and How Do They Get It?, 88
    Facts on HIV Testing, 88
    What Diseases Strike People with AIDS?, 90
    HIV/AIDS and Tuberculosis, 90
    How Many People Are Dying from AIDS Each Year?, 92
HIV/AIDS and the States, 92
    How States Are Affected by AIDS, 92
    How Many People Have AIDS in Each State?, 93
    HIV/AIDS and State Law, Selected Years, 93
    Needle Exchange Programs in the States, 93
HIV/AIDS and Specific Populations, 94
    Women and HIV/AIDS, 94
    Pediatric HIV/AIDS, 97
    Racial/Ethnic Minority Groups and HIV/AIDS, 98
    HIV/AIDS and Adolescents, 98
    HIV/AIDS and IV Drug Use, 101
    HIV/AIDS in Correctional Facilities, 102
    HIV Infection and the Military, 104
    HIV/AIDS in Rural Areas, 105
HIV/AIDS and Public Opinion, 106
    What Do Americans Understand about HIV/AIDS?, 106
    Facts on HIV/AIDS Education and Prevention Issues, 108
    Treatment of People with HIV/AIDS, 109

5 Documents and Reports, 113

The Onset of the Epidemic in the United States, 113
    The Opportunistic Infections, 114
    Naming the Disease, 119
    Blood and Blood Products, 121

Perinatal Transmission, 123
Transmission among Heterosexuals and Prison Inmates, 123
Risk Reduction, 125
The Surgeon General's Report, 126
Firsthand Perspectives on the Epidemic, 132
People with AIDS (PWAs), 132
Women and HIV/AIDS, 135
Intravenous Drug Users, 136
Homeless People with HIV/AIDS, 139
The Impact of HIV/AIDS on Other Aspects of Society, 144
HIV Disease in Correctional Facilities: A Model Response, 144
HIV/AIDS and the Workplace, 148
HIV/AIDS and Health Care Workers, 149
Responding to the Epidemic, 151

6 HIV/AIDS and the Law, 157

Chronology of Significant Federal Legislation since 1982, 157
Selected Legal Cases, 159
Discrimination Issues, 160
Testing Issues, 166
Other Issues, 167

7 Organizations, Government Agencies, and Hotlines, 171

Organizations, 172
Federal Programs and Agencies, 188
State AIDS Coordinators and Hotlines, 194
National Hotlines, 203

8 Reference Materials, 205

Print Materials, 206
Reference Books, 206
Monographs, 209
Pamphlets and Newsletters, 215
Government Documents and Reports, 216
Anthologies, 221
Personal Accounts, 224
Photographic Works, 228
Fiction and Poetry, 228

Nonprint Materials, 229
    Films and Videos, 229
Computer Databases and Other Resources, 235
Other Government Information Resources, 237

Glossary, 239
Index, 257

Tables

4-1 Estimated Cases of HIV/AIDS Worldwide, 83

4-2 National Institutes of Health (NIH) HIV/AIDS Funding, 85

4-3 Centers for Disease Control (CDC) HIV/AIDS Funding, 85

4-4 States Ranked by Cumulative HIV/AIDS Caseload, June 1991, 86

4-5 States Ranked by Total Spending of Solely State Funds, 87

4-6 States Ranked by Per Capita Spending of Solely State Funds, 87

4-7 Race/Ethnicity of Reported Pediatric AIDS Cases, 89

4-8 Race/Ethnicity of Reported Adult/Adolescent AIDS Cases, 89

4-9 Diseases Common in Persons With AIDS (PWAs), 91

4-10 Numbers of AIDS Deaths Each Year, 92

4-11 AIDS Cases by State, 95

4-12 HIV/AIDS and State Law, 96

4-13 State HIV/AIDS Laws Introduced and Passed 1983–1990, 96

4-14 AIDS Cases by Ethnic Group, 99

4-15 Percentage of 9th- to 12th- Grade Students Engaging in Risk Behaviors, 100

4-16 Sources of Exposure to HIV for Two Age Groups, 101

4-17 Have You Heard or Read about a Disease Called AIDS?, 106

4-18 Whom do Adults Think Is Most Likely to Have AIDS?, 107

4-19 Whom do Teens Think Is Most Likely to Have AIDS?, 107

Preface

OFFERING A COMPREHENSIVE PICTURE of the history, significance, and future of HIV/AIDS in this country is a formidable task, even though much has already been written on the subject of HIV/AIDS and its impact in the United States. Yet it seems from all the available education surveys that little of this material has had the necessary effect on the public. Perhaps this is because so many people have received their "AIDS education" from the mass media, which offer little depth and a selective showcasing of some aspects of the epidemic. With this as a basis, most people have held fast to the notion that HIV/AIDS has little to do with their lives. Nothing could be further from the truth.

The curious mixture of science and politics that characterizes the U.S. AIDS epidemic is aptly demonstrated by the action of the federal Centers for Disease Control (CDC) that took place as this book went to press. On 22 October 1992, CDC announced an amended proposal to update the AIDS surveillance case definition for the first time since 1987. The proposed expansion, set to take effect 1 January 1993, would add the following to the 23 clinical conditions currently recognized as "AIDS": recurrent pneumonia, pulmonary tuberculosis, invasive cervical cancer, and a CD4 t-lymphocyte count of fewer than 200 cells, when these conditions occur in conjunction with HIV infection. (This proposed expansion is in addition to the material presented in chapter 4.)

Although these conditions have long been recognized as being directly related to the immune compromise resulting from HIV infection, CDC has for years continued to use an AIDS case definition based on the opportunistic infections found primarily in gay men, the first group identified as being impacted by HIV/AIDS in the United States. The result was that other persons, including women and injection drug users, have been systematically excluded from epidemiology, research, and systems of care for persons with "AIDS." By CDC's own calculations, the old definition has undercounted AIDS cases by 40–50 percent.

The proposed change to the definition was the result of over three years of relentless pressure from HIV-positive women, AIDS activists and advocates, and health care providers. The nationwide effort to force this expansion employed a full range of tactics, including street demonstrations, meetings with CDC officials, testimony from HIV-positive women, and a grassroots campaign by a coalition of over 350 community-based organizations. If the expanded definition goes into effect as expected, advocacy by and for people living with AIDS will indeed have forced the medical and scientific establishment to recognize for the first time thousands of Americans who have been living with AIDS for years.

The challenges here are to offer a variety of resources in the hope that every individual can locate a place to connect with this important problem and to present readable information that does not evade the blunt impact of the facts since 1981. It will be obvious from reading this material that the reality of HIV/AIDS is very close to home for most Americans.

The epidemic of HIV/AIDS in our nation has grown dramatically during the last decade; it now reaches into every kind of community: urban and suburban, small cities, rural areas. All sorts of institutions have responded to it, some unwillingly: schools, religious communities, hospitals, offices, and industries. As a result, students at every level, their teachers, writers, and the concerned public have sought further information about the causes of HIV/AIDS and its solutions. Countless school papers and research projects have been undertaken.

For most people, the chief vehicle for understanding the epidemic has been the evening news, weekly magazines, and perhaps a daily paper. Yet, by their very nature, these outlets can give only the most brief and superficial exposure to significant problems, let alone those with so many social, economic, political, and medical consequences. They cannot begin to offer solutions to a problem that is complicated by many national factors.

There have not been any significant information sources available to assist researchers doing other than scientific or technical work. No comprehensive source has offered an organized and selective overview of the wide variety of existing resources and tools for addressing the problem. As a result, researchers have frequently turned to those with the most exposure to the problem—local direct service providers—who unfortunately also have the least spare time to assist individuals.

This lack of resources has also affected the concerned citizen who is seeking some depth of understanding about a widespread and costly human problem. Ordinary citizens, persons working in religious and voluntary organizations seeking to address the problem in their local communities, and policymakers at all levels have sought information that was accessible and organized. Moreover, they have a real need to draw on the experiences of others, and to build on lessons already learned elsewhere.

This book represents an effort to fill that gap. In many ways, a reference book is the perfect answer to the need that exists, because it can provide a thorough introduction and overview with some economy of form. Even so, there is a vast amount of information and resource material available that could not be covered here. I have tried to provide overviews of key aspects and factors wherever possible and to offer access to materials that might not otherwise be found.

Chapter 1 is an introductory essay by attorney and advocate Virginia Shubert of Housing Works, Inc., in New York City, a major service provider to homeless people with HIV/AIDS. Shubert paints a picture of the principal aspects of the epidemic in the United States, ranging from the basic science of the virus to the social, political, and economic questions it raises.

Chapters 2 and 3 include a survey of key events and players in the first decade of the epidemic and offer an initial timeline of significant activity.

Chapter 4 provides a quick reference to facts and statistics on the epidemic. Mini-glossaries define basic terms used here and elsewhere. Tables and overviews of important facts are provided to show how HIV/AIDS affects the world, the nation, the states, and special population groups.

Chapter 5 studies the unfolding of the U.S. epidemic, through the presentation of documents and reports from other sources. These are presented first historically, through excerpts from government reports, and then according to groups of people affected by HIV/AIDS. The latter section attempts to round out the picture often presented in the press by telling the first-person stories of how HIV/AIDS affects various groups of people.

Major efforts to address such problems as discrimination and health care needs through litigation and legislation are covered in Chapter 6.

Because HIV/AIDS represents such a complex problem, there are many professional and voluntary organizations, as well as government agencies, involved in studying it, addressing it, or solving it.

Chapter 7 provides a selective listing of these groups and offers sources for further pursuit of specialized interests and opportunities for personal involvement.

Chapter 8 presents an extensive reference bibliography that includes video and computer database resources. Because of the crucial need to reach adolescents and other communities, video has taken on an important educational role in the fight against HIV/AIDS. It provides an easily accessible vehicle, and one that will capture the attention of those who need to be reached. In addition, with so much information developing so rapidly, computers and computer networks play an important role in individuals and organizations communicating about this problem. A wide variety of non-print resources—including videos, films, databases, and exhibits—is available for education and research use.

The Glossary defines common terms to help unravel some of the vocabulary encountered in reading about the epidemic.

No one attempting to write about this topic could do so honestly without acknowledging the excellent documentary work done by many others writing during the last decade. With these resources, I have usually been able to sort out the scientific and medical competition, the politics, the confluence of events, and the national brokering that went on during the last decade.

In closing, I must acknowledge the contributions made by others to this book. Many of the sources I consulted, and many of the heroic efforts being made by others in advocacy and service, are the direct result, not only of inadequate public responsibility in the face of the epidemic, but also of individual experience and loss in the epidemic. Obviously, these efforts are made at personal cost, and often as a way of putting anger, grief, and loss to a shared and positive use. All of us should be grateful to those so involved, but more, we should not remain bystanders.

I am grateful to the countless overworked and understaffed organizations that responded to my calls and inquiries and sought ways to make more and better information available for this project. Roger, Marie, and Peggy Hombs have all aided my research with information, materials, and leads. Thanks also to my friend and colleague Virginia Shubert, whose advocacy has educated many.

Mary Ellen Hombs

1

Introduction

Virginia Shubert
Attorney and Director of Public Policy Advocacy
Housing Works, New York City

THE HUMAN IMMUNE SYSTEM DISORDER now known as Acquired Immune Deficiency Syndrome, or AIDS, was first identified in the United States in 1981, when physicians in New York City and San Francisco were confronted with the mysterious deaths of a growing number of young men who had illnesses usually held in check by the body's natural defenses. In the decade that followed, over 144,000 American men, women, and children lost their lives due to the Human Immunodeficiency Virus (HIV), the agent that causes AIDS.[1]

A period of delay between HIV infection and the onset of related illness means that the impact of HIV will continue to expand dramatically, regardless of current prevention efforts. The federal Centers for Disease Control (CDC) conservatively estimates that at least 1 million Americans are currently infected with HIV, and most of these persons will develop related illnesses in the next ten years. AIDS is already the leading cause of death for young men and women in some urban centers, and it is expected that the number of cumulative HIV-related deaths that occurred in the first ten years in the United States will double by 1993: The toll will rise from 144,000 to over 350,000 deaths.[2]

The U.S. epidemic is a part of a devastating HIV/AIDS pandemic, or worldwide epidemic. The World Health Organization (WHO) estimates that at least 9–11 million adults have been infected

1

with HIV since the late 1970s, and about 1 million children have been born infected with HIV. In certain parts of the world such as Sub-Saharan Africa, where heterosexual activity is the primary means of HIV transmission, between one-quarter and one-third of all adults aged 15–49 living in large urban centers have become infected with HIV. Globally, over 75 percent of cumulative HIV infections in adults are the result of heterosexual intercourse.[3]

Some analysts believe that these figures are too conservative and that the pandemic's major impacts are yet to come. They predict that the number of people worldwide who develop AIDS in the period 1992–1995 alone will exceed the total number to date; that the number of children orphaned by AIDS will more than double in the next three years, to 3.7 million by 1995; and that by the year 2000 between 38 and 110 million adults, and over 10 million children, will be infected with HIV.[4]

Though heterosexual transmission is rapidly increasing in the United States, HIV/AIDS continues to affect primarily gay men and intravenous (IV) drug users, the first groups infected in this country.[5] AIDS is now known to be the result of the insidious and deadly virus HIV, but it could be said that the U.S. epidemic has been fueled as much by the social factors of political disenfranchisement, homophobia, racism, and sexism as by any infectious agent. HIV struck first and disproportionately at those already disadvantaged in society—gay and bisexual men, intravenous drug users, women, and people of color. The chilling stigma of AIDS has compounded the burdens faced by communities already struggling with discrimination, poverty, a lack of health care, and drug addiction. The resulting marginalization of those affected by HIV/AIDS has led the larger society to apathy and fear rather than to the mobilization of adequate resources for essential medical research and the development of necessary systems of care. Meanwhile, the continuing widespread belief that the spread of HIV is limited to certain groups—as well as societal discomfort in speaking frankly about sexual intimacy and drug use—has delayed or prevented critical efforts to stop continued transmission of HIV. In short, the cultural and political distance between different segments of U.S. society has made it possible for the majority of Americans to believe that their lives will not be touched by HIV/AIDS. But viruses do not respect political, social, or economic differences.

HIV has become part of all of our lives. The tremendous cost in young lives lost already has had a devastating effect on individuals, families, and society at large. Many persons have turned their grief and loss into an unparalleled community response, creating new organizations and new approaches for the provision of medical care and support services. HIV has insinuated itself into the daily life of institutions as well, as schools, businesses, and churches have formulated policies on issues ranging from class participation and employment to the use of communion cups.

Basic Science and the Epidemic

The Human Immunodeficiency Virus

AIDS is caused by the Human Immunodeficiency Virus, a retrovirus that replicates itself by invading and destroying cells of the body. HIV attacks cells of the body's immune system, gradually impairing the ability to fight illness and leaving a person vulnerable to a range of opportunistic infections, which are present in most persons' bodies but require the opportunity of a weakened immune system to flourish.[6]

It can take a few months to many years for HIV to cause identifiable damage to the immune system. HIV gains entry to certain cells of the immune system called T4-cells and macrophages by entering the bloodstream. An exchange of body fluids (such as occurs in sexual intercourse or by sharing syringes in drug use) can allow the virus to pass in blood, blood products, semen, or vaginal mucosa. The body mounts an immune response to the infection and usually develops antibodies to HIV in 3–6 months. It is these antibodies that are detected by an HIV test, not the virus itself. However, the antibodies do not eliminate all of the virus. Typically, over a period of as long as 8–10 years, the virus multiplies and causes gradual damage to the immune function, as it kills T4-cells and causes macrophages to function improperly. This damage may be detected by a decline in the number of T4-cells. A T4-cell count of 1,000 is considered normal, and fewer than 200 indicates severe compromise of the immune system. The appearance of frequent, unusual, or severe infections indicates that the immune system is not operating properly.[7]

> Floyd, a long-term survivor, was diagnosed with HIV-related illness in 1983. He has been aggressively involved in his care and has combined antiviral treatments with a holistic approach to nutrition and stress reduction. His T4-cell count is stable, and he is a volunteer with an AIDS support organization. Floyd works full-time as a teacher.

HIV-Related Illness

Acquired Immune Deficiency Syndrome (AIDS) describes the syndrome of certain opportunistic infections resulting from immune deficiency that has been acquired from another person. AIDS itself is not a disease, and HIV-related illness is more accurately described as a spectrum, or range, of HIV infection. The first stage of the HIV spectrum is described as asymptomatic HIV infection, meaning infection is present without symptoms. A person may be seropositive, meaning they have tested positive for HIV antibodies but have no visible symptoms and remain healthy for a number of years. Several long-term studies of gay men with HIV infection have shown that HIV is a progressive infection that leads to serious illness in a majority of people in 8–12 years.[8] Children born with HIV and people infected through blood transfusion seem to get sick more quickly, and no studies have been done to determine the rate of progression among women.[9] There is no visible physical indicator of HIV infection prior to the onset of related illness.

As the immune system is gradually damaged, the person becomes symptomatic or HIV-ill, experiencing a variety of symptoms that may include lymphadenopathy (chronically swollen lymph nodes), weight loss, fatigue, diarrhea, night sweats, thrush (oral candidiasis, a white plaque coating the tongue), severe skin conditions, and other problems.[10] Women have been found to experience chronic vaginitis, pelvic inflammatory disease, cervical cancers, and chronic sexually transmitted diseases.[11] In children, vague, general symptoms are likely to signal the onset of HIV-related illness, including failure to thrive, developmental delays, diarrhea, and recurrent bacterial infections.[12] This phase of HIV-related illness was formerly referred to as AIDS-Related Complex (ARC) but is now generally described as symptomatic HIV infection.

With the body's defenses substantially impaired, the HIV-infected person becomes unusually vulnerable to serious infectious illnesses such as tuberculosis, endocarditis (an infection of the heart's lining), meningitis, and bacterial pneumonias. These infections also affect the population at large, but they occur far more frequently and are potentially fatal in HIV-infected persons.[13]

The HIV pandemic has been accompanied by a startling worldwide increase in the incidence of tuberculosis (TB), once thought to be a disease of the past. A dramatic resurgence of tuberculosis has occurred in the United States since 1985. After a steady decline throughout the twentieth century, a bona fide TB epidemic now exists in many U.S.

cities, particularly New York City, where the total number of new cases of TB almost doubled between 1985 and 1990.[14] Worsening economic and social conditions, including the growth in homelessness and the scarcity of health care, have contributed significantly to the rise in TB. The increase has also been found to be linked to comcomitant HIV infection, which renders a person extremely vulnerable to TB disease and TB-related death.[15] TB is a disease of poverty and poor living conditions and is readily transmitted in overcrowded, unsanitary, and unventilated environments. Homelessness among persons with HIV infection has also been identified as a major contributing factor to the spread of TB, because crowded homeless shelters provide an optimal setting for the transmission of TB.[16]

Persons with severe immune deficiency may succumb to one or more opportunistic infections (such as *Pneumocystis carinii* pneumonia [PCP] or Kaposi's sarcoma). Many persons with serious immune suppression also develop one of a number of related organic mental disorders such as cognitive impairment (language or movement disorders), which are known as AIDS dementia complex.[17]

The course of illness after the appearance of HIV-related symptoms varies greatly, depending upon a person's access to medical care, psychological and social stability, nutrition, drug and alcohol use, availability of appropriate housing and support services, and other factors bearing on health. The progression of HIV infection in children, who have immature immune systems, is likely to be much more rapid than in adults, although some children have a long, relatively stable course.[18]

> Sarita, age 22, experienced chronic yeast infections and pelvic inflammatory disease that went undiagnosed as being HIV-related until her infant was tested for HIV after recurrent bacterial infections. When Sarita tried to contact the baby's father, she learned that he had died of PCP.

The Definition of AIDS

The federal Centers for Disease Control (CDC) definition of AIDS was developed as an official surveillance tool—specific diagnostic criteria to enable the medical community to track the spread of HIV-illness.[19] CDC initially defined AIDS as HIV infection plus a history of one of a number of opportunistic infections that are extremely rare and unquestionably related to immune deficiency. This definition was increasingly criticized, however, because it excluded other serious infections known to be intimately associated with HIV infection, such as pulmonary tuberculosis and bacterial pneumonias. Moreover, because it was based on HIV-related manifestations in gay white men—the group most studied early in the epidemic—CDC's initial definition of AIDS had the effect of excluding significant numbers of women, persons of color, and persons who contracted HIV through IV drug use.[20] Despite the rapid changes in our understanding of the HIV/AIDS epidemic and the communities affected, CDC's definition has not been revised during the five years from 1987 to 1992.

Although it has been generally acknowledged that CDC's initial AIDS definition included only a small portion of the spectrum of HIV-related illness, statistics based on the definition have been widely used to allocate funding and to set research priorities. Federal disability entitlements, Medicaid, and a variety of other benefits have also been tied to the definition, limiting an individual's eligibility in a manner that has denied assistance to many persons who died without ever achieving a CDC diagnosis. Under mounting pressure to expand the definition, CDC announced in August 1991 that it would implement a new surveillance definition of AIDS in early 1992 that would include all individuals with extremely low T4-cell counts (below 200). The change was criticized as insufficient, however. Many serious HIV-related illnesses experienced by persons with T4-cell counts above 200 would still be excluded, such as the gynecological conditions experienced by women with HIV, and many persons cannot afford or are unable to obtain T4-cell testing.[21]

> Gloria, a Hispanic woman, has been in a long-term monogamous relationship with her husband of eight years, Eduardo. Recently, Eduardo has experienced chronic fatigue, and he has swollen lymph nodes; his doctor suggests that he and Gloria be tested for HIV. Gloria protests that they have both been faithful, but when Eduardo tests positive, he tells Gloria that in the past he had sexual relations with both men and women. Gloria had relied on birth control pills for contraception. She tests HIV positive. Of their two children, Lisa tests HIV positive and Enrique is HIV negative.

Transmission of HIV

HIV prevention education has been hampered by a focus on risk groups rather than on high-risk behaviors. Public attempts to identify groups of individuals as being at-risk of HIV simply because of their sexual orientation, race, or nationality have diverted attention from the risks presented by specific behaviors such as unprotected sexual intimacy and needle sharing. This approach has also resulted in unwarranted public fears, discrimination, and isolation of persons living with HIV/AIDS.

HIV is transmitted only through the direct exchange of blood, semen, or vaginal secretions. Only four routes of HIV transmission have been identified: (1) unprotected sexual conduct, (2) unscreened transfusions or infusions of blood or blood by-products, (3) sharing of intravenous needles, and (4) congenital or perinatal transmission from a woman to her fetus or newborn. The virus lives only a short time when exposed to air, and intact skin acts as a barrier to transmission.[22] Infected blood, for example, poses a threat only if it comes in contact with an open wound or when there is an inoculation. Accidental needlesticks of health care workers have resulted in infection in less than 1 percent of the cases.[23]

HIV cannot be transmitted through the casual contact involved in sharing a household, working together, or attending school. A wide variety of activities have been studied and eliminated as possible means of transmission, including sharing toilets, baths, eating utensils, toothbrushes, and other items and facilities, as well as touching, hugging, or kissing a person with HIV.[24]

Despite the evidence, fears regarding transmission persist. The highly publicized 1991 case of the infection of Kimberly Bergalis and four other persons by a Florida dentist with AIDS is a case in point. That single incident stimulated an active national debate concerning the possible risk to patients posed by HIV-infected health care workers, even though these five cases are the *only* recorded instances of alleged transmission from a health care provider to patients.[25] CDC has estimated that the risk of transmission from an HIV-positive surgeon to a patient during a procedure is only 1 in 416,667—minute when compared to the routine risks associated with health care, such as the risk of death from a pregnancy-related complication (1 in 15,385) or the risk of death from anesthesia (1 in 10,000).[26]

In July 1991, CDC issued new guidelines urging all physicians who perform exposure-prone procedures to learn their HIV status and refrain from performing these procedures if they test positive for HIV.[27] The U.S. Congress and several states are considering legislation making it a felony for some or all HIV-positive medical professionals not to reveal their HIV status to patients. HIV-positive providers feel that they face a difficult choice: either to disclose their status, and thereby risk rendering themselves unemployable due to the threat of publicity or litigation, or to continue to practice without disclosing, and thereby risk going to jail.[28]

> James, a 46-year-old former IV drug user, was homeless and staying in a drug-free shelter. Without a regular source of medical care, he was unable to prove that he had experienced HIV-related weight loss and recurring bouts of bacterial pneumonia, which meant he was ineligible for AIDS services at the public hospital or through local social service agencies.

Treatments

There is, as yet, no cure for AIDS, no vaccine to prevent HIV infection, and no treatment to reverse infection. Until 1992, no animal model had been identified as paralleling the human course of HIV infection, regarded by scientists as a necessity for vaccine research. Efforts to produce a vaccine have failed so far because there are many strains of HIV, and the virus varies too much in appearance for the development of one effective vaccine. Worldwide testing of experimental vaccines on humans will not begin until 1994. Much of the medical research to date has focused on methods of bolstering the immune system and of preventing or effectively treating HIV-related infections.[29] There are essentially three groups of treatments.[30]

Zidovudine (AZT), for years the only drug approved by the Food and Drug Administration (FDA) for the treatment of HIV, is an antiviral medicine designed to slow or stop the deterioration of the immune system and to slow the spread of the virus to new cells. In 1992, FDA approved another antiviral, ddI, before the completion of tests to establish its effectiveness and assess side effects, for use by patients who cannot tolerate or are not helped by AZT.[31] In certain circumstances, FDA also permits distribution of one other antiviral that is in clinical trials, ddC. Also, some herbal and natural products have shown antiviral properties. Antivirals are recommended for use any time the T4-cell count falls below 500. However, some persons have toxic reactions to one or more of the drugs, and the benefits of AZT have been shown to diminish over time for some persons, making antiviral therapy a complex and individualized matter.

Immune modulators such as interferon are intended to restore the balance of the various components of the immune system and to diminish auto-immune activities in which the body attacks its own cells. Unfortunately, little scientific agreement exists on which immune modulators actually work.

A third group of treatments are medications used to prevent the occurrence of common opportunistic infections such as *Pneumocystis carinii* pneumonia (PCP) or to prevent the return of these infections after a first occurrence.

Antivirals, immune modulating medicines, and preventive therapies are used in combination with the goal of improving and extending the good health of the HIV-infected person. Also vital are general health maintenance measures, and many persons use complementary therapies such as yoga and relaxation techniques. In the absence of other effective treatments, the HIV/AIDS epidemic has yielded a strong patient emphasis on holistic health measures that unite the well-being of mind and body. In addition, drugs not yet licensed for use in the United States are often available through buyers' clubs organized to facilitate access to these therapies, and a number of community-based projects have been formed for the collection, analysis, and dissemination of up-to-date treatment information.

For many years, the lack of available treatments meant there was little advantage to learning whether one was infected with HIV. The stigma and discrimination associated with being HIV infected led many persons to make a deliberate decision not to seek testing for HIV. The benefits of knowing one's HIV status have changed, however, with the development of treatment strategies that may delay the onset of HIV-related illness through early intervention, and most health care professionals believe that access to these therapies creates an incentive for testing. Unfortunately, such early intervention remains largely unavailable for many poor persons who have little or no access to health care. For these persons, there continues to be little to gain and a significant risk of HIV-related discrimination or harassment if their HIV-positive status is revealed.

The Demographics of HIV

Though the brunt of the U.S. epidemic to date has been borne by gay and bisexual men, a closer look at the statistics reveals that the face of the epidemic is changing and that it is an epidemic less of risk groups than of communities and intimate contacts.

HIV/AIDS strikes disproportionately at certain communities. As of June 1992, CDC had reported 230,179 cases of AIDS, of which 130,822, or 58 percent, were reportedly the result of men having sex with men; 51,447, or 23 percent, were attributed to IV drug use; and 14,045, or 6 percent, were attributed to heterosexual transmission.[32] African-Americans constitute only 12 percent of the U.S. population but 30 percent of AIDS cases. Hispanics constitute 9 percent of the nation's population but 17 percent of reported AIDS cases.[33] The equally disproportionate effects on these communities of unemployment, poverty, and the lack of drug treatment, health care, and social services make it likely that they will continue to be devastated by HIV/AIDS.

The rate of increase in HIV/AIDS is also significantly higher for some groups of persons at risk. Effective prevention efforts in the gay community have resulted in a leveling of the number of new infections, whereas infection among drug users, women, and adolescents is steadily increasing. Newly reported AIDS cases among IV drug users outnumber those among gay and bisexual men, and approximately 33 percent of AIDS cases are linked to IV drug use. Moreover, HIV infection is increasingly related not only to IV drug use but also to unprotected sexual activity associated with the use of cocaine/crack and alcohol.[34]

Women are the fastest growing category of cases, both as a consequence of IV drug use and as a result of sexual intimacy with HIV-infected partners. As approximately 30 percent of children born to HIV-infected mothers carry the virus, HIV among newborns is also increasing. The proportion of women among reported AIDS cases grew from 3 percent in 1981 to 10 percent in 1991, and because HIV-related symptoms are often overlooked or misdiagnosed in women, these figures are no doubt understated. Women with AIDS are overwhelmingly African-American (53 percent) or Hispanic (21 percent), in sharp contrast with the fact that these groups represent only 12 percent and 6 percent, respectively, of the U.S. population.[35] Over 78 percent of pediatric AIDS cases are African-American or Hispanic.[36]

A report on homeless youth in New York City revealed an HIV infection rate of 6.5 percent among the 16- to 20-year-olds surveyed, and the rate of infection increased to 17 percent among youth who were 20 years old. Often forced to engage in sex for survival, homeless youth are at extremely high risk of infection, and it is clear that the large number of persons diagnosed with AIDS in their twenties were infected while adolescents.[37]

Indeed, poverty itself and residence in certain urban neighborhoods have become risk factors for HIV infection in several urban centers. Homelessness, for example, can be both a cause and a result of HIV infection. One study of homeless men in a New York City men's shelter revealed a 62 percent infection rate among residents who sought health care in the shelter clinic.[38]

Epidemiological evidence has shown that the geographic concentration of drug use in certain parts of the inner city results in geographic concentration of HIV and very high rates of infection in the population of these neighborhoods. In New York City's South Bronx, for example, between 10 and 20 percent of the entire population of 25- to 45-year-old men are infected, as are 5–8 percent of all women in the same age group. In such a community, every sexually active adult faces a significant risk of infection, regardless of sexual orientation or drug use.[39]

A steady flow of infection from these areas to adjacent urban areas and also to distant locations has been shown. For example, social and family relationships may result in the migration of sexual partners and/or relatives between two or more locations that are the basis of an extended family's life, such as the South Bronx and Puerto Rico or Washington, D.C., and South Carolina.[40] Thus, whereas 80 percent of all reported AIDS cases during 1981–1982 were from 6 large cities, the picture was much different in 1991: 31 metropolitan areas, 25 states, and Puerto Rico each reported over 1,000 cumulative cases, and an increasing incidence was noted in rural areas.[41]

Because HIV transmission is based on patterns of intimate contact, and because initial infection is invisible, from time to time HIV transmission has appeared to be limited to certain groups or certain areas of the country. But in fact, we are all at risk, and we are all living with AIDS and HIV.

The Community Response to AIDS

Most AIDS advocates and service providers are based in the middle-class, white, gay community, where the HIV/AIDS epidemic first emerged in this country. With little or no government effort to provide care, these community-based organizations are mostly privately funded and aided by thousands of volunteer workers who have served their communities tirelessly and compassionately. However, as more drug users, persons of color, and women are affected, existing AIDS organizations have not been able to meet the needs generated by the cruel combination of poverty and HIV.

African-American and Hispanic communities face daunting obstacles in their efforts to deal with the HIV epidemic. HIV/AIDS is but one among many pressing priorities in communities already disproportionately affected by massive unemployment, poverty, violence, and addiction. Already blamed and discriminated against for these serious social problems, these communities have been understandably afraid of the added stigma of AIDS.[42]

Community-based organizations in these communities have little access to private resources. Nor do they have the resources to compete with mainstream institutions for large foundation grants or for all-too-scarce public monies. At the same time, the clients they seek to serve have the greatest need for assistance. These organizations often must address hunger, homelessness, or addiction before they can turn to the issue of HIV. The AIDS epidemic has stretched traditional organizations beyond their capacity, and the financial and cultural hurdles to developing new AIDS-specific organizations are often insurmountable in poor communities.

Meanwhile, homophobia, racism, and disdain for anyone addicted to drugs have led many to conclude that persons with HIV are not valuable or deserving of care and have reinforced the view among most Americans that HIV and AIDS are problems of others. The fear engendered by AIDS has even led to such acts of violence as the 1981 burning of the home of the Ray family, whose three young hemophiliac sons were living with HIV.

Certain individuals living with HIV and AIDS have made a significant impact on public perception by placing a human face on HIV/AIDS. Actor Rock Hudson's death from AIDS in 1985 brought the first significant media attention to the issue and caused the first public reaction by President Ronald Reagan, who knew Hudson personally. The education efforts of HIV-infected teenager Ryan White and the public statements of Kimberly Bergalis, a Florida woman who allegedly became infected by her dentist, have had a significant impact on legislative debate regarding HIV/AIDS issues. The 1991 announcement by basketball star Earvin "Magic" Johnson about his HIV infection presented a chance for a new and widespread acknowledgment of risk. Johnson's popularity humanized the epidemic for many people who had never before known someone living with HIV or AIDS.

For the most part, however, society has pervasively denied the terrible toll being taken by HIV—the loss of over 100,000 persons in the prime of their lives—and has exhibited a lack of compassion for persons with HIV/AIDS and their loved ones. This, in turn, has meant (1) a lack of the necessary political will to commit adequate resources to medical research and to the care of persons with HIV-related illness and (2) a lack of attention and openness to crucial education and prevention messages.

Shaping AIDS Public Policy

The Role of the Government

All but the most conservative analysts believe government has failed to provide leadership in formulating an appropriate public response to the health crisis presented by the HIV/AIDS epidemic. At all levels of government, the prejudices and fears surrounding AIDS have shaped the public debate and response to the epidemic. The political will of officials to devise responsible and compassionate public policies has been sapped by the fear and misunderstanding of the public.

Throughout the last decade, an ominous silence has existed on the federal level, as Presidents Reagan and Bush have rarely mentioned the epidemic. There has been much study of AIDS and little action: The recommendations of the 1988 *Report of the Presidential Commission on the Human Immunodeficiency Virus Epidemic* were ignored, and President George Bush did not even respond to the 1991 report of the National Commission on AIDS, even though both reports decried the lack of national leadership on AIDS policy.[43]

In 1990, Congress enacted the first federal legislation directed at providing care for persons with HIV and AIDS. The Ryan White Comprehensive AIDS Resource Emergency (CARE) Act provides for emergency relief to fund prevention, health services, and health care in communities hardest hit by AIDS, and the AIDS Housing Opportunities Act promotes housing options for homeless persons with HIV-related illness. However, both programs were funded at low levels, and there remains no coordinated federal policy regarding HIV/AIDS research, prevention, or care.

Though the inclusion of persons with HIV among those protected by the 1990 Americans with Disabilities Act was a significant step, many federal programs still actively discriminate against persons with HIV/AIDS. HIV antibody testing is required by the military and as a condition of employment with the State Department, and nonresidents may be denied entry to the United States or legalization of their immigration status if they are HIV positive. Finally, in some cases federal policies have actually hampered the efforts of other groups. For example, in 1988 the federal government placed limitations on explicit safer sex and drug-use information in federally funded education materials.[44]

State and local governments, laboring under enormous fiscal burdens, bear responsibility for meeting most of the health care, housing, and social service needs of persons with HIV and AIDS; these governments also have lacked the political will for adequate funding for prevention and care. Even where a high level of need has prompted housing and service development, the lack of federal funding has placed an impossible burden on local governments.[45]

Other Institutions

Although religious institutions have played an important role in calling for and providing compassionate care for persons with AIDS and HIV-related illness, the ability of religious institutions to influence larger public policy issues has been limited by moral judgments and beliefs. For example, religious values have been cited as a rationale for efforts to obstruct such crucial policies as frank and effective prevention education. Some religious leaders and organizations have even argued that persons with HIV and AIDS deserve their illness because of the behaviors that led to their HIV infection.

Remarkably little coverage of HIV and AIDS has appeared in the mainstream media, particularly in the early days of the epidemic when it was thought to be a problem affecting only gay men. Coverage has been sporadic and often related to sensational issues or the identification of public figures as HIV infected, rather than examining the plight of the tens of thousands of persons living with HIV and AIDS or the crucial public health policies affecting care.[46]

The Role of People Living with AIDS

Perhaps the most important step toward the development of appropriate public health policies has been the self-empowerment of persons living with HIV and AIDS (PWAs) to act as advocates. PWAs have rejected the role of victim in favor both of an assertive, life-affirming, and active stance and of vigorous involvement in investigating, selecting, and implementing their treatments. In the face of a spreading epidemic and unresponsive scientific and medical institutions, PWAs have undertaken aggressive self-education that rejects the notion that they cannot be experts about their own health. In many places, PWAs have sought and achieved a vital role in the management of their illness.[47] Unfortunately, this type of self-empowerment is often not possible for PWAs who are geographically or culturally far removed from vital sources of information and peer support.

Grassroots advocacy groups such as the AIDS Coalition to Unleash Power (ACT UP) have often employed confrontational direct action tactics to capture the attention of unresponsive public and private institutions, and PWAs have also played a valuable role in collecting and disseminating information on medical and social issues.[48] Most notably, advocacy by PWAs has profoundly affected the development of and access to new treatments—institutional changes that will affect research on all major diseases in the future.

Public Policy Issues

Access to Health Care

The HIV/AIDS epidemic has provided telling evidence of the failure of the U.S. health care system to meet the needs of all Americans. Many persons with HIV have no means to pay for health care, and even those who participate in public or private health care plans are often unable to get the services or medications they need.

The crucial public policy issue is not the total cost of AIDS health care but how to finance the care of individuals. Despite concern over the cost of caring for persons with AIDS, it is estimated that the aggregate cost of care now and in the future will be no more than 2 percent of total U.S. health care expenditures.[49] However, the increase in the number of poor persons living with HIV and the growing refusal of private insurance carriers to cover persons with HIV/AIDS have led to what has been described as the "Medicaidization" of AIDS. Some 40 percent of persons with AIDS rely on Medicaid, the federal health insurance program for the poor and the disabled; only 29 percent have private insurance; and 29 percent are uninsured, which means they must rely entirely on public hospitals for health care.[50]

The Medicaid system often fails to provide meaningful access to care. Many persons cannot meet the Medicaid eligibility requirements, for which they must prove that they are disabled or impoverished. Eligibility based on disability is limited in many states to those with a clinical diagnosis of AIDS or the most severe HIV-related disease. Thus, coverage is not available at an earlier stage in the progression of the disease, when persons would benefit from treatments to maintain their health. Persons with private financial resources are forced to spend down to a poverty-level existence to be eligible for Medicaid and then cannot work without jeopardizing their health care coverage. Medicaid coverage also varies greatly from state to state and may not cover necessary treatments. Finally, it may be impossible in some areas for persons on Medicaid to obtain health care because of the shortage of private physicians willing to participate in the Medicaid program at current payment rates provided by the government.[51]

Even persons with private insurance may lose their coverage if it becomes known that they are HIV infected, or they may be denied coverage of expensive or experimental treatments.[52] Some PWAs have been forced to obscure the nature of their HIV-related illness or to pay for HIV-specific treatments themselves in order to avoid losing private health insurance.

For many persons with HIV, particularly the homeless and members of poor communities with inadequate community-based medical services, lack of access means an emergency room is a primary source of health care. Without continuity or coordination in their health care, they are effectively denied the benefits of new early-intervention strategies and life-prolonging treatments.

Research and the Approval of New Treatments

Biomedical research on HIV/AIDS and the development of new therapeutic tools have been fraught with controversy, including a long and public dispute between French and U.S. researchers over who would be credited with first identifying HIV as the causative agent of AIDS. Both the amount spent on research and its focus have frequently been the subject of debate. The research establishment has been particularly criticized for the fact that studies have largely ignored women, IV drug users, and persons of color.

The FDA drug approval process is long and thorough. Few treatments are available for HIV-related illness, and those that are in use are expensive and often toxic. New drugs are needed quickly, and early access to drugs—even before their final approval—is very important to persons with HIV and AIDS. The clinical trials conducted for AIDS drugs have been hotly debated, and new approaches have been developed to expand access to experimental drugs.

In addition to traditional clinical trials conducted through an AIDS Clinical Trial Group (ACTG), the National Institute of Allergy and Infectious Diseases (NIAID) conducts trials of AIDS drugs through a community-based program, the Community Programs for

Clinical Research on AIDS (CPCRA). Early access to experimental drugs still in trials is also available to some persons through a new parallel track program.[53]

Past clinical trials have been criticized for excluding women, persons of color, and poor persons; these groups have not been actively recruited and are often unable to obtain the medical monitoring necessary to participate. The National Commission on AIDS has called for better coordination between research agencies and agencies responsible for the financing and delivery of health care to broaden access to these trials.[54]

Prevention and Education

Public education to combat fear and discrimination against persons with HIV/AIDS and effective prevention campaigns to slow or halt the epidemic are cornerstones of appropriate public policy. However, effective education and prevention have been hampered by a host of problems.

We know how HIV is transmitted, and effective means of preventing its spread have been identified: (1) consistently and correctly using condoms and dental dams during sexual intercourse; (2) observing universal precautions in health care settings (measures involving cleanliness and the use of barrier protections to avoid exposure to bodily fluids); (3) testing the blood supply to reduce the risk of transmission through the use of blood and blood products; and (4) not sharing needles and disinfecting injection equipment with bleach.

There has been a failure to commit the necessary fiscal resources to prevention and education, in large part because those groups perceived to be at-risk are not at the center of U.S. society. Failing to approach this task as a public health challenge has made it an ideological struggle, accompanied by judgmental attitudes and objections to such measures as condom and clean-needle distribution on moral grounds. This has significantly impeded prevention efforts among youth and drug users. The availability of clean needles has been shown to slow the spread of HIV, yet possession of needles without a prescription is illegal in 11 states. The tragic result is that the HIV infection rate is now as high as 60 percent in some urban centers.[55]

The reluctance to talk candidly and explicitly about safer sex to persons of all ages has also impaired prevention. For example, the 1991 abandonment of a federally funded research project to determine patterns of adolescent sexual behavior means researchers will lack information needed to formulate prevention programs for teens, one of the groups at highest risk.[56]

Finally, prevention efforts have overlooked many persons and failed to reach others because the messages have not been culturally sensitive and effective. Women who have sex with women and gay men of color have been ignored.[57] Cultural attitudes toward women and gay and bisexual behaviors have not been taken into account in prevention efforts. Prevention education for heterosexual women has disregarded the realities that women often are not empowered to enforce the use of condoms and that the use of a contraceptive is not always desirable for women in their childbearing years. New protections must be developed that women can control, and men must be better educated on the risk to their female partners.[58]

Testing and Confidentiality

HIV testing raises many issues: (1) who has the authority to decide to test? (2) who controls dissemination of test results? and (3) what is the appropriate use of information that has been obtained? From the time a test for HIV became available in 1985, there have been concerns regarding the potential for widespread testing and the use of that information to discriminate against people with HIV and AIDS. Testing remains largely voluntary, although tests are required for induction and active duty in the U.S. military and certain other federal jobs, for immigration to the United States, and by many insurance companies that want to avoid insuring persons with HIV.[59]

Many states have enacted laws placing limits on the permissible disclosure of confidential HIV information and requiring informed consent based on accurate information regarding the meaning and implications of test results prior to testing. Most of these laws also require pre-test counseling and referral to any necessary services.[60] Nevertheless, abuse is common.

In some states, in fact, exceptions are made to allow testing of certain persons without their consent, such as persons who are incarcerated, persons who are indicted for or convicted of sexual crimes such as rape or prostitution, or patients who may have exposed a health care or emergency response worker to HIV.[61] Though they meet an emotional need, little scientific justification exists for testing in these situations, as there is a time lag between infection and development of antibodies (as well as a low risk of transmission from a single exposure).

Anonymous testing, using identification numbers or pseudo-nyms, is available in many states. All states require public health reporting of cases of CDC-defined AIDS, but states differ widely on reporting requirements regarding positive HIV-test results.[62] The rationale for reporting the names of persons with HIV infection is the importance of contact tracing and partner notification. However, because identification of the persons to be notified requires the cooperation of the HIV-positive person, most states have taken the position that it is more important to encourage testing by assuring confidentiality.

Risks are involved in taking the HIV test, despite legislative enactments and court decisions outlawing discrimination against persons with HIV. People with HIV and AIDS have faced substantial discrimination in housing, employment, and access to medical care and insurance, and they have faced hostility from neighbors, co-workers, and even family members. Though discrimination recently has become more subtle, reports show that it is still widespread.[63]

Systems of Care

All persons require the means necessary to meet basic human needs, including safe housing, adequate food, and access to primary health care. For persons whose immune systems are weakened by HIV, these essentials become a matter of life and death. HIV-related illness, chronic in nature, is typically characterized by alternating periods of good and bad health. From time to time, many persons with HIV or AIDS require income support, home care, mental health care and support, drug treatment, case management for the coordination of assistance, or other social supports.

Existing benefits for poor persons disabled by HIV comprise an arbitrary and inconsistent patchwork of federal disability benefits, state public relief programs, and private charity. Meanwhile, the epidemic is devastating poor urban communities where housing, social services, and health care systems are already inadequate and overburdened. Poverty among the HIV-ill is further exacerbated by federal and local requirements that persons spend down their assets to the poverty level if they are to qualify for financial assistance and medical care.

Increasingly, HIV-related illness is linked to homelessness. Hous-ing is lost due to discrimination or as fatigue, repeated illness, and periodic hospitalizations result in the loss of jobs and then of housing. The lack of HIV education and of the means to stop engaging in high-risk behaviors has also led to a tragic but predictable increase in HIV seropositivity among persons who were already homeless.[64]

The low level of Social Security disability benefits or local income maintenance (typically less than $500 per month) is insufficient to pay rent in many communities, much less to meet other needs. Little or no housing exists specifically for homeless persons with HIV/AIDS, and persons with HIV have been placed in competition with other needy persons for scarce housing and social support as local budget deficits have worsened in recent years. Moreover, access to even existing benefits and services is often frustrated by eligibility criteria that limit assistance to those who are in the end stages of HIV-illness or are able to meet the rigid CDC definition of AIDS.[65]

Access to appropriate care is also a problem for specific groups of people. The incidence of both HIV and tuberculosis is increasing at alarming rates in correctional facilities, yet these are typically overcrowded settings where health care is severely inadequate and HIV testing, counseling, and prevention often are simply unavailable. Officials' refusals to acknowledge the facts of drug use and sexual activity in prisons have meant that condoms and other preventive measures have been denied to incarcerated persons, despite these individuals' increased risk of transmission. Ironically, the health care and social service needs of prisoners with HIV have been cited in some cases as the justification for the involuntary segregation of such prisoners.[66]

Poor women constitute a growing group of persons living with HIV and a group largely disenfranchised by the economic, health care, and social service systems. These women, predominantly persons of color, often must cope not only with their own illness but also with the illness of a spouse or child who may or may not outlive them. Some are justifiably afraid that their children will be taken away from them permanently during hospitalization or drug treatment, and out of fear they may fail to seek care and preventive treatments. Women are much more likely to be infected than to transmit HIV as the result of sexual contact, and less than 1 percent of reported AIDS cases have been attributed to sexual transmission from a woman to a man.[67] Nevertheless, women have been viewed largely as vectors or carriers of HIV infection to men and newborns, and there has been a dearth of HIV/AIDS prevention and service programs targeted toward women.[68]

Women living with HIV have experienced great difficulty in exercising their reproductive rights. Most women with HIV are of childbearing age, and approximately two-thirds of children born to women with HIV and AIDS will be healthy and free of the virus, though this cannot be verified medically until a child is 18 months old. HIV-positive women may experience great pressure not to have children. Yet, in communities being decimated by AIDS, drug addiction, and violence, the right to bear children may be viewed as a matter of survival. In such a climate, and with a shortage of services, it is difficult for women to examine their reproductive options free from judgmentalism and biases and to receive the necessary support for their decisions regarding childbearing.[69]

Many homeless youth, who face a significant and growing risk of HIV infection, exist entirely outside of systems of care. The majority of homeless young people are throw-away youth who have been forced from their homes, often by physical or sexual abuse. They have a limited educational background and few skills and often engage in sex for survival. They are at-risk for violence, drug and alcohol addiction, and disease. Yet many never receive services of any kind. Moreover, the disproportionate number of street youth who are gay or lesbian have an even more difficult time accessing services because few institutions are prepared to acknowledge, much less affirm, their sexual orientation.[70]

Finally, although they are the majority of persons currently infected with HIV, active and former drug users have perhaps the most limited access to care, including little or no access to drug treatment. An ideological and political approach to drug use, rather than a public health approach, means that abstinence is perceived to be the only legitimate goal of interventions with active users, even though it is known that most chronic drug users have great difficulty achieving or sustaining abstinence. Further, many persons are not prepared to give up the drug use that ameliorates the pain engendered by their daily life situation.[71]

The nation's War on Drugs has been waged largely against drug users. Active drug users are specifically excluded from most public and private programs, including most federal and local housing programs and most AIDS supportive services.[72] Combined with the criminalization of drug use, this approach has prevented efforts to work with active users to minimize the harmful consequences of drug use. HIV infection, homelessness, hunger, and disease among drug users are not inevitable. Studies have shown that drug users will change behaviors to lessen risks and to improve their lives.[73]

Harm reduction must take priority over the insistence on abstinence if the nation is to make any progress in meeting the needs of chronic drug users. Needle exchange programs and education on safer drug-use methods have proven successful in reducing transmission of HIV and in engaging drug users in systems of care that provide the safety and self-respect necessary to end the harmful use of drugs.[74]

Conclusion

The HIV/AIDS epidemic presents health and social challenges that have tested and will continue to test not only the nation's scientific competence but also its humanity. Just as HIV renders the individual unusually vulnerable to disease, the virus has exposed a multitude of social, medical, and political ills in society that have been more easily ignored in other times. Most important, HIV and AIDS have altered the way people regard each other, presenting a stark choice—between prejudice and fear or acceptance and compassion.

Notes

1. Centers for Disease Control (CDC), *HIV-AIDS Surveillance Report* July 1992 (Atlanta: Centers for Disease Control), 13.

2. Ibid. See also National Commission on Acquired Immune Deficiency Syndrome (AIDS), *America Living with AIDS: Report of the National Commission on AIDS* (Washington, DC: National Commission on AIDS, 1991), 3.

3. World Health Organization, *Current and Future Dimensions of the HIV/AIDS Pandemic* (Washington, DC: World Health Organization, 1992), 4, 8.

4. The Global AIDS Policy Coalition, "AIDS in the World 1992: A Global Epidemic Out of Control?" (press release) (Boston: The Global AIDS Policy Coalition, 3 June 1992), 4.

5. CDC, *HIV/AIDS Surveillance Report Year-End Edition,* January 1992, 10.

6. For an overview of the HIV disease mechanism and related illnesses, see Alan R. Lifson, M.D., M.P.H., George W. Rutherford, M.D., and Harold W. Jaffe, M.D., "The Natural History of HIV Infection," *Journal of Infectious Diseases* 158 (1988): 1360; Jay A. Levy, M.D., "Human Immunodeficiency Viruses and the Pathogenesis of AIDS," *Journal of the American Medical Association (JAMA)* 261 (1989): 2997; Institute of Medicine, National Academy of Sciences, *Mobilizing against AIDS* (Washington, DC: National Academy Press, 1989); *The Science of AIDS: Readings from the Scientific American* (New York: W. H. Freeman & Co., 1989); AIDS Coalition to Unleash Power (ACT UP), *T&D Handbook: Treatment Decisions* (New York: ACT UP, n.d.).

7. Institute of Medicine, *Mobilizing against AIDS,* 114–130.

8. George F. Lemp, Dr.P.H., et al., "Projections of AIDS Morbidity and Mortality in San Francisco," *JAMA* 263 (1990): 1497.

9. James Curran, M.D., et al., "Epidemiology of HIV Infection and AIDS in the United States," *Science* 239 (1988): 610.

10. Lifson et al., "The Natural History of HIV Infection, 1363; Institute of Medicine," *Mobilizing against AIDS*, 65–80.

11. New Jersey Women and AIDS Network, *Me First: Medical Manifestations of HIV in Women* (New Brunswick, NJ: New Jersey Women and AIDS Network, 1990).

12. Institute of Medicine, *Mobilizing against AIDS*, 80–91.

13. Ibid., 65–80.

14. New York City Department of Health, "Tuberculosis, New York City, the 1990 Experience," *City Health Information* 10 (New York: New York City Department of Health, March 1991).

15. Karen Brudney, M.D., and Jay Dobkin, M.D., "Resurgent Tuberculosis in New York City: Human Immunodeficiency Virus, Homelessness, and the Decline of Tuberculosis Control Programs," *American Review of Respiratory Disease* 144 (1991) 745–749; Peter F. Barnes, M.D., et al., "Tuberculosis in Patients with Human Immunodeficiency Virus Infection," *JAMA* 324 (1991): 1644.

16. John M. McAdam, M.D., et al., "The Spectrum of Tuberculosis in a New York City Men's Shelter Clinic (1982–1988)," *Chest* (1990): 802.

17. Institute of Medicine, *Mobilizing against AIDS*, 65–80.

18. Ibid., 80–91.

19. CDC, "Revision of the CDC Surveillance Case Definition for Acquired Immunodeficiency Syndrome," *Morbidity and Mortality Weekly Report (MMWR)* (1987): 1S.

20. David Barr, "What Is AIDS? Think Again," *New York Times,* 1 December 1990, page A-25.

21. Mireya Navarro, "AIDS Definition Is Widened to Include Blood Cell Count," *New York Times,* 8 August 1991, page A-11. At the time of this writing (October 1992), no change in the CDC case definition has been implemented.

22. Institute of Medicine, *Mobilizing against AIDS*, 26–45.

23. CDC, "Public Health Service Statement on Management of Occupational Exposures to HIV, Including Considerations Regarding Zidovudine Post-Exposure Use," *MMWR* 36 (1990): RR1.

24. Alan R. Lifson, M.D., M.P.H., "Do Alternative Modes for Transmission of HIV Exist?" *JAMA* 259 (1989): 1355; Margaret A. Fischl, M.D., et al., "Evaluation of Heterosexual Partners, Children and Household Contacts of Adults with AIDS," *JAMA* 257 (1987): 642.

25. Lawrence K. Altman, M.D., "Rift Grows on Protecting Patients from Surgeons with AIDS Virus," *New York Times,* 22 January 1991, page C-3.

26. Benjamin Schatz, J.D., *May God and the Community Help Us All: Results of a Survey of HIV-Positive and High Risk Untested Health Care Workers* (San Francisco: American Association of Physicians for Human Rights, Medical Expertise Retention Program, 1991), 2.

27. CDC, "Recommendations for Preventing Transmission of Human Immunodeficiency Virus and Hepatitis B Virus to Patients during Exposure-Prone Invasive Procedures," *MMWR* 40 (1991): RR8.

28. Schatz, *May God and the Community Help Us All*, 4–5.

29. Institute of Medicine, *Mobilizing against AIDS*, 225–232.

30. Up-to-date information on treatments and treatment strategies is available from Project Inform, 1965 Market Street, #220, San Francisco, CA 94103, (800) 822-7422.

31. Milt Freudenheim, "FDA Approves a Second Drug, Still Being Tested, to Treat AIDS," *New York Times*, 10 October 1991, page B-2.

32. CDC, *Surveillance Report*, July 1922, 13.

33. Ibid., 10.

34. Ibid.

35. CDC *Surveillance Report*, January 1992, 11.

36. Ibid., 10.

37. National Coalition for the Homeless, *Fighting to Live: Homeless People with AIDS* (Washington, DC: National Coalition for the Homeless, 1990), 4.

38. Ramon A. Torres, M.D., et al., "Human Immunodeficiency Virus Infection among Homeless Men in a New York City Shelter," *Archives of Internal Medicine* 150 (October 1990): 2031.

39. Ernest Drucker, "Epidemic in the War Zone: AIDS and Community Survival in New York City," *International Journal of Health Services* 20 (1990): 601.

40. Ibid., 609.

41. National Commission on AIDS, *America Living with AIDS*, 11.

42. Harlon L. Dalton, "AIDS in Blackface," *Daedalus* 118 (1989): 205.

43. *Report of the Presidential Commission on the Human Immunodeficiency Virus Epidemic* (1988), 157–158; National Commission on AIDS, *America Living with AIDS*, 111–119, 149.

44. National Commission on AIDS, *America Living with AIDS*, 21.

45. Ibid., 118–119.

46. See Randy Shilts, *And the Band Played On: Politics, People, and the AIDS Epidemic* (New York: Penguin, 1988).

47. Katherine Bishop, "Underground Press Leads Way on AIDS Advice," *New York Times*, 16 December 1991, page A-16.

48. ACT UP, *A Capsule History of ACT UP* (New York: ACT UP, 1990).

49. National Commission on AIDS, *America Living with AIDS*, 68.

50. Ibid., 70–73.

51. Ibid.

52. Ibid., 71–72.

53. Thomas C. Merigan, M.D., "You Can Teach an Old Dog New Tricks: How AIDS Trials Are Pioneering New Strategies," *New England Journal of Medicine* 323 (1990): 1341.

54. National Commission on AIDS, *America Living with AIDS*, 93–106.

55. Robert A. Hahn, Ph.D., M.P.H., et al., "Prevalence of HIV Infection among Intravenous Drug Users in the United States," *JAMA* 261 (1989): 2680.

56. National Commission on AIDS, *America Living with AIDS*, 21.

57. Ibid., 26–27; Rebecca Cole and Sally Cooper, "Lesbian Exclusion from HIV/AIDS Education: Ten Years of Low-Risk Identity and High-Risk Behavior," *SIECUS Report* 19 (New York: Sex Information and Education Council of the U.S., Inc., 1990/1991): 18–21.

58. Helen Gasch et al., "Shaping AIDS Education and Prevention Programs for African Americans amidst Community Decline," *Journal of Negro Education* 60 (1991): 85–96; Zena A. Stein, M.A., M.B., B.Ch., "HIV Prevention: The Need for Methods Women Can Use," *American Journal of Public Health* 80 (1990): 460–462.

59. David A. Hansel, "HIV Antibody Testing: Public Health Issues," *AIDS Practice Manual: A Legal and Educational Guide* (San Francisco: National Lawyers Guild AIDS Network, 1991): 3.2.

60. Ibid., 3.4–3.6.

61. Ibid., 3.6–3.12.

62. Ibid., 3.12–3.13.

63. Nan Hunter, *Epidemic of Fear—A Survey of AIDS Discrimination in the 1980s and Policy Recommendations for the 1990s* (New York: American Civil Liberties Union AIDS Project, 1990).

64. National Coalition for the Homeless, *Fighting to Live*, 1–2.

65. Ibid., 1–13.

66. Bruce Lambert, "Prisons Criticized on AIDS Programs: Health and Legal Experts Say Inmates with Disease Face a Disastrous Situation," *New York Times*, 19 August 1990, page A-16.

67. Nancy S. Padian, Ph.D., et al., "Female-to-Male Transmission of Human Immunodeficiency Virus," *JAMA* 266 (1991): 1664–1666.

68. June E. Osborn, M.D., "Women and HIV/AIDS—The Silent Epidemic?" *SIECUS Report* 19 (New York: Sex Information and Education Council of the U.S., Inc., 1990/1991): 1–4; Kathryn Anastos, M.D., and Carola Marte, M.D., "Women—The Missing Persons in the AIDS Epidemic," *Health/PAC Bulletin* 19 (New York: Health/PAC, 1989): 6–13.

69. Margaret Hutchison, M.S.N., C.N.M., and Ann Kurth, M.P.H., M.S.N., C.N.M., "'I need to know that I have a choice...'—A Study of Women, HIV, and Reproductive Decision-Making," *AIDS Patient Care* (February 1991): 17–25.

70. National Commission on AIDS, *America Living with AIDS*, 13; National Coalition for the Homeless, *Fighting to Live*, 4–5; Larkin Youth Center, *HIV and Homeless Youth: Meeting the Challenge* (San Francisco: Larkin Street Youth Center, 1990), 1–7.

71. Ernest Drucker, *Drug Policy, Drug Treatment and Public Health* (New York: American Foundation for AIDS Research, 1991), 31–50.

72. National Coalition for the Homeless, *Fighting to Live*, 6.

73. Mireya Navarro, "Yale Study Reports Clean Needle Project Helps Check AIDS," *New York Times*, 1 August 1991, page A-1.

74. Drucker, *Drug Policy, Drug Treatment and Public Health*, 129–138.

2

Chronology

FOLLOWING IS A CHRONOLOGY of selected events in the development of the HIV/AIDS crisis in the United States. Events early in the first decade of the HIV epidemic in the U.S. reflect the scientific groundwork that was necessary for researchers to understand the challenge ahead of them when they first saw cases of mysterious diseases in the early 1980s. Later events demonstrate the significant social, economic, scientific, and political impact of the epidemic.

1970   H. M. Temin and S. Mitzutani, as well as D. Baltimore, discover reverse transcriptase. This enzyme is produced by retroviruses, which are a group of viruses containing the genetic material ribonucleic acid (RNA) and having the ability to copy RNA into deoxyribonucleic acid (DNA) inside an infected cell. The DNA that results from this process is then included in the genetic structure of the cell and passed to each infected cell's offspring cells.

1976   The T-cell growth factor, also called interleukin-2, is discovered by D. A. Morgan, F. W. Ruscetti, and Robert Gallo. T-cells are white blood cells used by the immune system to fight infection. Interleukin-2 is a substance important to immune response and results in expanded T-cell function.

1980–1981   The first human retrovirus is discovered by Robert Gallo, B. J. Poiesz, and others. It is called Human T-cell Leukemia Virus—Type I (HTLV-I).

1980–1981
cont.

By the end of 1980, the unknown virus was established in Africa, Europe, and North America. It would later be shown that, by the end of 1980, 80 young men had been diagnosed with at least one of the opportunistic infections that are the hallmark of AIDS.

1981

In February, Dr. C. Everett Koop, a prominent Philadelphia pediatric surgeon, is named assistant secretary of the U.S. Department of Health and Human Services; he subsequently is named U.S. surgeon general after a year-long confirmation battle. Koop's highly publicized position against abortion led supporters and critics of his nomination to conclude that they could predict his actions in office. He surprised observers by approaching critical issues as public health problems and not as ideological campaigns. His vigorous work to educate Americans about HIV/AIDS and his advocacy concerning the need for sex education in the public schools would eventually establish his reputation as an effective surgeon general.

The Centers for Disease Control (CDC) publishes its first report on the epidemic in the June 5 *Morbidity and Mortality Weekly Report*. The report is based on five Los Angeles cases of *Pneumocystis carinii* pneumonia (PCP) that have been diagnosed in recent months among homosexual men.

CDC also releases its first official report on Kaposi's sarcoma (KS) on July 4 in *Morbidity and Mortality Weekly Report*. New York City cases of KS and PCP among homosexual men are reported.

George Kenneth Horne, Jr., the first KS case reported to CDC, dies in San Francisco on November 30.

A December CDC report describes the case of an infant who developed the same immune deficiency disease previously reported in homosexual men. The infant had received blood transfusions.

The number of U.S. AIDS cases diagnosed in 1981 is 298.

1982

In early January, a new organization, the Gay Men's Health Crisis, forms in New York City to provide services to men with the new disease.

1982
cont.

As of March 19, the Centers for Disease Control reports 285 cases of the disease in 17 states. Half of the cases are in New York City. Outside the United States, 5 European nations have confirmed the presence of the disease.

Even while scientists cannot agree on a name for the illness, cases are increasing. Two weeks after the March report, CDC affirms cases in two additional states and two more European countries. U.S. cases now total 300: 242 in gay or bisexual men, 30 in heterosexual men, 10 in heterosexual women, and 18 in persons whose sexual preference was unknown.

In June, CDC reports that both Los Angeles and Orange County, California, have "clusters" of KS and PCP cases.

By late July, 471 cases of the newly named Acquired Immune Deficiency Syndrome (AIDS) disease are reported. Of those, 184 have died. Reported cases are in 24 states. Also in July, CDC reports on two other developments: (1) cases of PCP among hemophiliacs and (2) opportunistic infections and KS among Haitian immigrants living in the United States.

In August, CDC reports that nearly half of the AIDS cases are in New York City.

Guidelines for clinical and laboratory staff working with blood are released by CDC in November to address occupational health concerns.

The American Red Cross announces a review of its policies for choosing blood donors. The action is taken after a child develops AIDS. CDC reports a case of AIDS that is possibly linked to a blood transfusion.

In October, Congress appropriates the first federal funds for the epidemic. Under the leadership of Representative William Natcher (D-KY), $5.6 million goes to research.

The total number of U.S. AIDS cases diagnosed in 1982 is 1,120. Of the small number of cases identified in 1979, 85 percent are dead. Of cases in 1981, 60 percent are already dead; 1 in 4 of those reported in the first six months of that year have died. The 1982 rate of reported cases is triple what it had been the previous year.

1983

CDC's *Morbidity and Mortality Weekly Report* of January 7 names the two cases that identify yet another group to be hit with the epidemic: the female sexual partners of males with AIDS. The cases involve a 37-year-old woman with *Pneumocystis carinii* pneumonia (PCP) who lived with an intravenous drug user for 5 years and a 23-year-old Hispanic woman with lymphadenopathy who had lived with a bisexual with both Kaposi's sarcoma and PCP. CDC also has reports of 43 other women who have developed the opportunistic infections of AIDS. In most of these cases, the women previously had sexual relations with IV drug users. These cases give weight to the theory that the men are carrying an agent that could infect their partners while leaving the men themselves asymptomatic.

This issue of *Morbidity and Mortality Weekly Report* also addresses the growing number of cases of AIDS in prisons. Most of the reported cases are among prisoners who have been IV drug users.

When the Centers for Disease Control releases its report on February 2, the number of U.S. AIDS cases has surpassed 1,000. Almost half of the 1,025 cases are in New York State; at least 394 have died in the nation. Almost 25 percent of the cases have been reported in the two previous months, during which time 100 people have died.

In March, the American Red Cross announces that the following groups, believed to be at great risk for carrying the virus, would be advised not to donate blood: homosexual males, intravenous drug users, and Haitian immigrants in the United States.

In April, Health and Human Services (HHS) Secretary Margaret Heckler testifies before a House Appropriations Committee hearing, saying, "I really don't think there is another dollar that would make a difference, because the attempt is all out to find the answer."

In early May, more than 6,000 people march in San Francisco to focus attention on the growing wave of illness and death. Marchers with AIDS carry a banner that reflects the spreading outlook of those with the disease: "Fighting for Our Lives."

1983
cont.

Also in May, conservative political commentator Patrick Buchanan writes, "The poor homosexuals—they have declared war upon nature, and now nature is exacting an awful retribution."

The journal *Science* reports in May that both U.S. and French scientists have detected a retrovirus (referred to as HTLV-III/LAV) among people with AIDS or at-risk for AIDS. U.S. scientists subsequently release findings of a direct connection between the leukemia virus and the development of AIDS. Confusion remains about whether differences exist between the French and U.S. findings and about which country's scientists might have made the breakthrough discovery.

Also in May, the Conference of State and Territorial Epidemiologists recommends that AIDS be added to the list of notifiable diseases, meaning that it should be reported to CDC through local public health departments.

Assistant Secretary of Health and Human Services Edward Brandt announces that the Public Health Service has made research into HIV/AIDS its top priority.

In June, French researcher Dr. Luc Montagnier of the Pasteur Institute announces that French scientists have isolated an equine lentivirus (a virus that can remain dormant in the cells and then become active) that he calls Lymphadenopathy-Associated Virus, or LAV.

In September, CDC issues guidelines for health care workers and other health professionals who might be exposed to HIV. The government also announces that dentists, morticians, and medical examiners should take special precautions to avoid infection.

The total of U.S. AIDS cases diagnosed in 1983 is 3,005.

1984

In March, research into the virus causing AIDS takes an important step forward with the CDC isolation of French researchers' LAV from the blood of an asymptomatic Los Angeles nurse who had become infected from a blood transfusion. This demonstrated the virus's presence before the beginning of illness, plus it showed that the LAV in the blood donor's system could be transmitted to others.

1984
cont.

In early April, Dr. Mervyn Silverman, director of the San Francisco Department of Public Health, announces regulations to restrict high-risk sexual practices in the city's bathhouses. The enormously controversial move, coming after months of debate over the public health, political, economic, and social ramifications of the popular gay men's gathering places, only serves to anger both sides.

Also in April, HHS Secretary Margaret Heckler announces the U.S. discovery of HTLV-III, the agent causing AIDS. Heckler makes only passing mention of the work of French researchers in identifying LAV.

In May, the research group of Dr. Robert C. Gallo announces the Western blot technique for detecting antibodies to the HIV virus.

In June and the months after, the availability of the HIV antibody test makes it possible to see just how the virus is moving through the population. One study of IV drug users in a New York clinic shows an 87 percent rate of infection; studies of hemophiliacs who had used contaminated clotting factor show infection rates from 72 to 90 percent. Tests at a San Francisco VD clinic show a 65 percent infection rate, and an East Coast testing project finds a 35 percent positive result.

In August, Bobbi Campbell dies of cryptosporidiosis in San Francisco. Campbell, diagnosed with Kaposi's sarcoma (KS) when it was still regarded as "gay cancer," had publicly declared himself the "AIDS Poster Boy" two years earlier in an effort to focus attention and funding on those who were sick. He had appeared on the cover of *Newsweek* in 1983.

Also in August, scientists find that HTLV-III is present in the semen of both a man with AIDS and an asymptomatic man. This finding shows conclusively that one can be a carrier of the virus without showing symptoms. Further, the virus is also isolated in the vaginal fluid of a symptomatic woman, establishing the mother-to-infant mode of transmission.

In September, new studies are released showing high rates of infection among severe hemophiliacs who use Factor VIII, a clotting agent.

1984
cont.

In October, Dr. Mervyn Silverman of the San Francisco Department of Public Health orders the closing of the city's bathhouses.

In October, House-Senate budget negotiators agree on a $93 million figure for AIDS funding for the fiscal year. The final amount represents a 60 percent increase over Reagan administration requests. Part of the package is $8.35 million for expedited development of an HTLV-III antibody test. The Reagan administration announces that it will use less than half a million dollars for this; the rest of the funds will be returned to the treasury.

In December, University of California researchers announce that 10,000 human blood samples will be tested in 1985, using a new test to detect HIV in blood.

The total number of U.S. AIDS cases diagnosed in 1984 is 6,058.

1985

Interim Public Health Service guidelines for screening blood donations are announced by CDC in January. Blood will be examined for antibodies to HTLV-III/LAV. Total reported AIDS cases surpass 10,500 during this month.

Also in January, the Reagan administration announces its budget proposals for the coming fiscal year. The proposals call for a reduction in AIDS spending from $96 million to $85.5 million, with a 20 percent cut at CDC. Only about 5 percent of the budget is designated for prevention and education.

A new experimental drug is announced by the Pasteur Institute in February: HPA-23. Researcher Dr. Jean Claude Chermann states that the drug seems to inhibit reproduction of the virus.

Blood supply screening begins across the nation in March with an Abbott Laboratories test licensed by the federal government. The use of the test is heralded as an opportunity to virtually eliminate the chance of contracting HIV from a blood transfusion. Gay community leaders, however, remain concerned that the test could be used to discriminate against gay people.

1985
cont.

In April, the category of recent immigrants from Haiti is deleted by CDC from the list of those most at-risk for AIDS. Also in April, HHS Secretary Margaret Heckler tells the first International Conference on Acquired Immune Deficiency Syndrome in Atlanta, Georgia, that "AIDS will remain our number one public health priority until it has been conquered."

The *New England Journal of Medicine* reports in May that persons infected with HIV could be asymptomatic for four years or longer. Also in May, Martin Delaney starts Project Inform in San Francisco to bring together information on therapies for AIDS and to improve access to these therapies.

Drs. Robert C. Gallo, Mikulas Popovic, and M. G. Sarngadharan patent an antibody test for HTLV-III for the Department of Health and Human Services in June.

On July 25, it is officially confirmed that actor Rock Hudson is dying of AIDS in a Paris hospital.

Also in July, the pharmaceutical manufacturer Burroughs Wellcome begins testing the drug azidothymidine, or AZT, on more than 30 patients with HIV-illness. In an important scientific report, federal researchers announce their discovery that the virus attacks the T4 helper cells, a set of important blood cells whose role is to identify agents such as viruses and prompt the immune system to attack those agents.

In August, the Pentagon announces that all potential military recruits will be screened for HIV. Two polls by the Gallup Organization are released by CDC. They show that 95 percent of the U.S. population has heard of AIDS.

Also in August, Ryan White, a 13-year-old hemophiliac infected with HIV in a blood transfusion, is barred from public school in Kokomo, Indiana. Authorities fear he might infect other students. CDC guidelines issued the same month state that students with the virus should have their privacy protected by school administrators and should be allowed to attend school. Preschool students and handicapped children, however, are to be kept out of school under the guidelines, pending more information on how the virus is transmitted.

1985
cont.

CDC also recommends that the HIV antibody test be administered to children in adoption or foster care settings, either if their natural parents are in high-risk groups for the virus or if the natural parents' personal histories might not be known.

On one night in September, $1.3 million for HIV/AIDS research is raised by the gala Hollywood "Night of 1,000 Stars." The newly formed National AIDS Research Foundation names actress Elizabeth Taylor as its national chairperson. According to a *New York Times*/CBS News poll released in September, about half of all Americans believe casual contact is a possible transmission route for the virus, despite strong medical evidence to the contrary.

Also in September, the Food and Drug Administration (FDA) redefines the gay-related high-risk group for HIV/AIDS to include "any male who has had sex with another male since 1977." The experimental drug HPA-23 is approved by the FDA for U.S. use; the drug might inhibit the reproduction of the AIDS virus though it does not eliminate the immune system suppression that results.

Federal officials tell a House subcommittee that $70 million more is needed for HIV/AIDS research and treatment, an amount twice as high as the Reagan administration had requested.

In October, the Public Health Service announces its long-range plan for halting the spread of the virus. The plan focuses on curbing steady increases in the growth of the virus by 1990 and eliminating its spread by 2000. CDC announces that the risk of transmission from daily contact in ordinary household situations is nonexistent and that voluntary behavioral changes are being undertaken by gay and bisexual men in San Francisco, one of the epicenters of the disease. CDC also announces that Manhattan, San Francisco, and Los Angeles have been joined by Miami, Newark, and Houston as cities with large numbers of AIDS cases. At the same time, the Harvard School of Public Health announces that sexual transmission is responsible for the spread of the virus into the heterosexual population.

1985
cont.

Actor Rock Hudson dies of AIDS in October. His death is widely viewed as a turning point in the public perception of the epidemic. In response to the renowned actor's death, President Ronald Reagan makes his first public comment on AIDS.

The Pentagon announces plans to increase its screening procedures to include all 2.1 million military personnel, promising treatment, counseling, and honorable medical discharges for those who develop the disease. One rationale for the screening of all active duty personnel is that the military acts as its own blood bank in time of need.

The National Education Association (NEA) suggests that school officials decide on a case-by-case basis whether children with HIV should be permitted in the classroom. The NEA also endorses testing for students and teachers if there is reason to think they have contracted the virus.

In November, Indiana student Ryan White is granted leave to attend classes by school officials. The Public Health Service announces that food handlers and health care workers with HIV do not require special restrictions in the workplace, as there is no medical evidence that casual contact is a transmission route for the virus. Prostitutes, who had been targeted as a primary transmission source for heterosexual infection, are not found to present any particular risk for their customers, according to scientists, who state that female-to-male sexual transmission has been extremely rare.

The total of U.S. AIDS cases diagnosed in 1985 is 11,417.

1986

In April, John James publishes the first issue of *AIDS Treatment News,* which soon becomes the underground medical movement's chief source of information and communication. The first issue discusses AL 721, the egg lipid solution popular in the gay community and tested in Israel and France.

In June, the federal government's 85 top HIV/AIDS experts meet in Coolfont, West Virginia, to review Public Health Service plans on the epidemic. They project 270,000 cases and 179,000 deaths by 1991 in the United States.

1986
cont.

In October, the Institute of Medicine releases a massive report calling the federal response "woefully inadequate."

Also in October, Surgeon General C. Everett Koop releases the *Surgeon General's Report on the Acquired Immune Deficiency Syndrome*. The frank nature of the report, as well as its emphasis on the epidemic as a public health problem and not a political issue, takes both conservatives and liberals by surprise. It advises starting sex education for children at the earliest grade possible, using condoms, and abandoning as useless any ideas of quarantine or identification of HIV-infected people. Tens of thousands of copies are distributed.

In November, New York State's health commissioner announces that he will consider a small demonstration project to provide needle exchange services for IV drug users. The project's goal is to reduce the spread of HIV by cutting down on needle sharing by drug users.

The total of U.S. AIDS cases diagnosed in 1986 is 18,548.

1987

In January, the FDA's Anti-Infective Drugs Advisory Committee votes to release AZT as the only drug approved for use against HIV infection. The cost per person is estimated to be $10,000 annually.

In March, gay activist and writer Larry Kramer, speaking to a New York City audience, calls for the angry advocacy that led to the creation of ACT UP. Days later, hundreds block traffic on Wall Street to protest the cost of AZT.

In May, the Third International Conference on Acquired Immune Deficiency Syndrome convenes in Washington, D.C. At an awards dinner held in conjunction with the conference, President Ronald Reagan gives his first speech on HIV/AIDS. His major focus is on testing people for the virus. The following morning, Vice-President George Bush gives the opening address at the conference, defending the administration's testing proposals. More than 60 activists are arrested at the White House that day, protesting federal policy. Washington police don rubber gloves to make the arrests.

1987
cont.

In October, more than 1,000 members of ACT UP close down FDA headquarters in Washington's suburbs, as they protest FDA action on drugs for HIV/AIDS.

Also in October, the NAMES Project AIDS Memorial Quilt is displayed on the Mall in Washington, D.C. Each panel of the huge quilt—made by a friend or relative—commemorates a person who has died of HIV/AIDS.

The total of U.S. AIDS cases diagnosed in 1987 is 27,695.

1988

In January, New York State health officials announce that they have approved a plan to distribute clean syringes to IV drug users in an effort to curb the spread of HIV.

In March, young hemophiliac Ryan White testifies before the Watkins, or Presidential, Commission on AIDS, which subsequently releases a reporting identifying "complacency" as a major obstacle in ending the epidemic.

In August, New York City officials announce that they will adopt the proposed needle exchange plan, over the serious objections of law enforcement officials.

In November, New York City's Mayor Edward Koch announces that he has ruled out a needle exchange program at one city site, on the grounds that the site is located too close to a school. Another site is also found unacceptable. The city then begins a needle distribution program from an office in the city's health department in downtown Manhattan.

The total of U.S. AIDS cases diagnosed in 1988 is 33,862.

1989

In January, New York City officials admit that their needle exchange program has attracted few participants. Critics charge that the program's location in a city office building in downtown Manhattan does not encourage participation. Health officials say they will focus their efforts on drug treatment.

In April, the independent and star-studded American Foundation for AIDS Research (AmFAR) announces the award of $1.4 million to 16 community-based research centers to do further work on drug therapies.

1989
cont.

In June, ACT UP members take over the stage at the Fifth International Conference on AIDS in Montreal, to read aloud 12 principles on drugs and drug testing aimed at the FDA.

The activist AIDS Coalition to Unleash Power (ACT UP) brings 5,000 demonstrators to New York City's St. Patrick's Cathedral in December to protest the Roman Catholic Church's positions on homosexuality, safe sex, birth control, and abortion. The six people who are arrested for interrupting a church service become known as the "St. Patrick's Six."

Also in December, the National Commission on AIDS (NCOA) (formed that year by Congress) issues its first report: *Failure of U.S. Health Care System To Deal with HIV Epidemic.* The report finds "dangerous complacency" toward an epidemic that the public wants to believe is already over and laments the lack of a national plan to address that epidemic.

The total of U.S. AIDS cases diagnosed in 1989 is 38,742.

1990

In February, New York City Mayor David Dinkins, who had previously stated that he feared that needle exchange would encourage drug use, announces that he will drop the needle distribution program.

In March, President George Bush responds to the call by the National Commission on AIDS (NCOA) and issues a statement on the epidemic to a national meeting of business leaders.

In April, the National Commission on AIDS issues its second report, *Leadership, Legislation, and Regulation.* The report finds that a clear national plan with well-defined goals and responsibilities is essential to battling the epidemic.

Also in April, one of the earliest and most highly publicized cases involving HIV transmission by an accidental needlestick to a health care worker is settled in New York City. Dr. Veronica Prego, who had sued the city's Health and Hospitals Corporation and two other physicians for $175 million, accepts a settlement of $1.4 million for the needlestick, which occurred in 1983.

1990
cont.

Prego had sued her supervising intern for having left a needle in a patient's bed, and she sued another physician for revealing her HIV status to hospital personnel.

In June, the National Institutes of Health begin an investigation into the procedures surrounding Dr. Robert Gallo's discovery of the virus causing AIDS. Allegations persist that, in the highly competitive world of research, Gallo's virus might have actually been the French virus that was discovered before his.

In November, the federal Centers for Disease Control announce that HIV is now more prevalent in people over 50 than among children under age 13. Statistics show that although the majority of those affected are homosexual or bisexual, some 17 percent have acquired the virus from blood products used in surgery, which occurs more frequently among older people.

December 1 is the World Health Organization's third annual AIDS Awareness Day and also marks the second annual Day Without Art nationwide. The artists' observance, by 3,000 organizations throughout the nation, is intended to highlight the toll on the arts community of the epidemic and the artistic contributions that have been lost through the deaths of artists. In museums, paintings are covered or removed for the day. The lights of the Manhattan skyline, including the Empire State Building, Rockefeller Center, the World Trade Center, and the Chrysler Building, are dimmed for 15 minutes to commemorate all those who have died of AIDS. Cable TV stations go black, and Broadway theatres also dim their lights.

The activist organization ACT UP conducts a demonstration in December at New York City's St. Patrick's Cathedral to protest the Roman Catholic Church's role in influencing public policy on abortion, safe sex, birth control, and homosexuality. ACT UP had conducted a similar demonstration in December 1989. The organization also announces a lawsuit by advocates over the Roman Catholic Church's refusal to provide safe sex, birth control, and abortion information to HIV-positive clients who are in publicly financed, church-operated health care facilities.

1990
cont.

New York State officials had waived requirements for these services to ensure the church's participation in providing health facilities.

The total of U.S. AIDS cases diagnosed in 1990 is 40,022.

1991

In January, the American Dental Association (ADA), acting in response to the apparent infection of five patients by a Florida dentist, issues an interim policy urging dentists to refrain from invasive procedures or disclose their seropositive status. The ADA pledges to assist and support infected dentists who quit practicing, states that all HIV infected patients should disclose their status to their dentists, and urges dentists to develop confidentiality protocols for their practices.

In February, the New York City Board of Education narrowly votes to proceed with the plan of Chancellor Joseph Fernandez to offer access to condoms in the city's high schools. Under Fernandez's plan, students would become the first in the nation to have unrestricted access: no fees, no parental consent, no counseling requirements. The plan is vigorously opposed by religious and other groups, but a Gallup poll finds that 54 percent of public school parents support it.

As of March 31, 6,436 health care workers are known to be HIV infected in the United States, including 703 physicians, 47 surgeons, 1,358 nurses, and 171 dentists and dental hygienists. The nation's largest organization of bone and joint surgeons calls for HIV-infected surgeons to inform their patients and stop performing all procedures but emergency surgery.

In April, a San Francisco jury deadlocks when trying to reach a verdict in the case of two people arrested for distributing new syringes to addicts on the street. Jury foreman Spero Saridakis, swayed by the testimony he heard, subsequently joins the "Prevention Point" program and begins distributing syringes himself.

Also in April, a federal judge awards $3.8 million to Marine Martin Gaffney, 42, whose wife and one child have already died of AIDS. Gaffney's wife received a tainted blood transfusion in 1981 at a Navy hospital while giving birth.

1991
cont.

A subsequent child died of AIDS, and Gaffney had also tested positive for the virus. At the time of the court ruling, Gaffney is asymptomatic. (He died in November 1991, leaving one daughter, who was seronegative. He received his settlement just ten days before his death.) Gaffney's court battle lasted four years.

In May, National Institutes of Health (NIH) scientist Dr. Robert Gallo drops his claim of having co-discovered HIV, ending a seven-year dispute with French scientist Dr. Luc Montagnier.

NIH director Dr. Bernadine Healy says she thinks the National Cancer Institute (NCI) should be named co-inventor of the drug AZT. Such a move would end the often-criticized monopoly of pharmaceutical manufacturer Burroughs Wellcome.

Also in May, the tobacco company Philip Morris announces it will increase its charitable contributions to AIDS research. The activist group ACT UP had called for a boycott of the company in 1990 because of Philip Morris's support of conservative Republican Senator Jesse Helms of North Carolina.

Three people die of AIDS after receiving organ transplants from a man who died in 1985; two others who received transplants test positive for HIV. Although all but 3 of the 61 organs and tissues donated at the man's death had been used, some were processed in ways that would have killed the virus, whereas others were not.

In June, the Seventh International Conference on AIDS convenes in Florence, Italy. Demonstrators protest continuing U.S. immigration policy banning any HIV-positive person from entering the country. The policy poses a threat to the eighth international conference, planned originally for Boston in 1992 but held instead in Amsterdam, The Netherlands. Also in June, the American Medical Association votes in favor of voluntary testing of health care workers, and the American Nurses Association votes 577 to 13 to oppose compulsory HIV testing for its members and patients, paralleling the stand taken earlier by the American Medical Association.

1991
cont.

Also in June, CDC announces it is proposing to change the 1987 case definition for AIDS. A new definition, to be issued in final form in January 1992, would take effect in April 1992. Proposed definition changes, focusing on T4-cell counts, could raise the over 200,000 reported AIDS cases by 160,000 new cases.

In July, the U.S. Senate votes 81 to 18 in favor of a proposal by Senator Jesse Helms (R-NC) that would set a prison term of at least 10 years and a fine of $10,000 for any HIV-infected medical professional who performed an invasive procedure without disclosing serostatus. "I don't think 10 years is severe when you consider what these people are willing to do to innocent patients. Don't tell me this is too severe," says sponsor Helms. The provision is subsequently dropped in September in House-Senate budget negotiations.

In July, the Centers for Disease Control recommend that HIV-infected physicians and dentists stop performing certain procedures where there is a greater than normal chance of patients being exposed to the worker's blood during an accident. The CDC also recommends that anyone performing such procedures be tested for the virus. Although these recommendations are not legally binding, they are the basis for standards set by other medical bodies.

Also in July, the Food and Drug Administration (FDA) recommends that a new drug (didanosine or dideoxyinosine or ddI) be approved for marketing even though the drug has not yet been thoroughly tested in clinical trials. The drug would be used for adults and children who cannot use the more common drug azidothymidine (AZT) in advanced stages of AIDS because of side effects or because they are no longer responding to AZT. The FDA recommendation speeds the drug's release to the market at a time when AIDS activists, critical of the agency's procedures for drug approval, claim that with so few and such expensive drugs being the only choices open to persons with AIDS (PWAs), more drugs must be made available without lengthy testing procedures.

In August, the American Dental Association (ADA) amends its January 1991 interim policy on HIV to include a recommendation that dentists who believe they are at risk of HIV infection should seek testing.

1991
cont.

Also in August, former Surgeon General Dr. C. Everett Koop appeals for caution in public and legislative responses to the possible HIV infection of patients by health care providers. "Let me assure the American public that the chances of getting AIDS from a health care worker are essentially nil," Koop states. He condemns mandatory testing proposals for health care workers and state and federal efforts to regulate HIV-infected practitioners.

Just before school opens for the fall, Massachusetts state officials announce on August 28 their recommendation that high schools make condoms available to students. Although some local schools already distribute condoms, this is the first announced statewide policy in the nation.

On the same day, the statute of limitations expires on possible prosecution of arson charges for the torching of the Ray family home in Arcadia, Florida, in 1987. Florida authorities never found who started the fire, which burned out the three hemophiliac brothers, Ricky (15), Robert (13), and Randy (12), in DeSoto County after officials learned that the boys had acquired HIV from contaminated blood products. The family subsequently moved to Sarasota, Florida.

In September, 12,000 people take part in the fifth annual AIDSWALK in Washington, D.C., to raise funds for local services. The number of walkers is four times greater than the previous year; walkers raise $450,000.

Also in September, the federal Centers for Disease Control issue draft guidelines proposing that hospitals routinely offer and encourage HIV testing for patients, especially in areas with high rates of infection. CDC had previously estimated that only 12 percent of those infected had knowledge of their serostatus. The proposed guidelines represent CDC's first update of its advice to hospitals since 1987.

In October, Congress passes legislation requiring the states to adopt guidelines for physicians, dentists, and others performing invasive surgery. States are to adopt such guidelines within a year or risk losing federal public health funding. Congress acts in the wake of publicity from an alleged case of dentist-to-patient transmission in Florida, although CDC has found this case to be the only such instance in 11 years of the epidemic.

1991
cont.

Also in October, New York City Mayor David Dinkins announces that he will consider a new needle exchange program for IV drug users.

In November, Earvin "Magic" Johnson, well-known National Basketball Association star for the Los Angeles Lakers team, announces his immediate retirement from the game, after learning that he is HIV positive in a routine insurance physical. Johnson, who has recently married and whose wife is pregnant, says that his wife has tested negative. He states that he acquired the virus through heterosexual activity with another woman. Johnson, a role model for many young people, says he will devote himself to AIDS education, especially around the importance of safe sexual practices. Shortly thereafter, President Bush announces that Johnson will take the seat of the late Belinda Mason on the National Commission on AIDS.

Also in November, CDC publishes a draft of proposed revisions to the HIV/AIDS surveillance case definition. The proposed new definition is planned to take effect in April 1992.

Also in November, New York's Mayor David Dinkins, bowing to new research and political pressure, announces that he will support a new community-based needle distribution program. The new project will be funded privately but designed by city officials, who also will evaluate its operation.

A CDC report released in November estimates that up to 20 percent of homeless people in some areas are HIV infected. Rates among homeless teens are "alarmingly" high.

In December, Kimberly Bergalis dies. She was a Florida college student believed to have been one of five patients of an HIV-infected dentist to acquire the virus by doctor-patient transmission.

The total number of U.S. AIDS cases diagnosed in 1991 is 39,569.

1992

In March, researchers announce that they are making progress in finding ways to block the transmission of HIV from mother to unborn child.

1992
cont.

About 30 percent of children born to HIV-infected mothers prove to have the infection themselves.

In April, CDC does not implement the proposed new case surveillance definition as previously scheduled, but makes no announcement concerning its intentions.

Also in April, New York State announces that it will make Medicaid payments to people whose job will be to watch tuberculosis patients swallow their prescription medicine. Called "directly observed therapy," the $5.8 million program will involve up to 1,000 TB patients identified by physicians as being "recalcitrant" about taking their medications. Reimbursement will be at the rate of $32.82 per patient per week in a hospital or shelter, $95.90 if a worker visits a patient at home.

Also in April, a New York state judge upholds the New York City public high school system's access to condoms program, ruling that it does not violate the religious freedom of parents and does not require their consent. The ruling is the first legal challenge to the program and others like it in San Francisco, Philadelphia, Chicago, Seattle, and Los Angeles.

Also in April, scientific experts announce that the accelerated approval given to the drug ddI in July 1991 now seems justified. The drug had not been fully tested when it was released for limited use against HIV by people who cannot take the only other available drug, AZT, or have stopped responding to it.

Conditional approval by FDA was also given in April to a new drug, dideoxycytidine, or ddC, to be used in combination with AZT. The drug will be available under the "expanded access" program.

In May, New York City Mayor David Dinkins announces that he will drop his long-standing opposition to a needle exchange program for drug users and commence in June an ambitious effort to exchange 2.5 3 million clean syringes. Washington D.C.'s Mayor Sharon Pratt Kelly calls for condom distribution programs in public high schools, prisons, and jails, as well as a needle exchange effort.

1992
cont.

Robert Martinez, director of the federal Office of Drug Control Policy, denounces the mayors' programs as "wrong on moral grounds."

Also in May, a federal judge rules that the so-called "Helms rule" is unconstitutional. The 1987 CDC rule, adopted at the urging of Senator Jesse Helms (R-NC), forbids HIV/AIDS education materials from containing any material that could be deemed offensive to either the target audience or anyone else. Critics had argued that this restriction crippled their efforts to distribute materials that were sexually explicit and geared toward specific audiences.

Also in May, the *New England Journal of Medicine* reports that a study of the drug AZT showed that it prolonged the lives of patients with HIV. This seems to contradict the earlier findings of a Veterans Administration study that showed AZT had no effect on survival.

In June, scientists from the University of Washington and Northwestern University announce a breakthrough in HIV vaccine research. They discovered that an Asian monkey, the pigtail macaque, will become HIV-ill when infected by direct injection or exposure to infected blood. Previously, scientists had not been able to identify an animal whose immune system responded to the virus as does a human's, a factor considered necessary by scientists for possible vaccine testing.

Also in June, it is revealed that federal officials have shelved plans to loosen proposed restrictions on HIV-infected physicians, dentists, and others performing invasive procedures. This action leaves the states free to issue their own prohibitions and could mean that, where such HIV-infected persons continue to practice, they could be required to disclose their seropositive status to their patients.

In July, the Eighth International Conference convenes in Amsterdam. The conference was originally scheduled for Boston but was moved after the United States refused to lift travel restrictions on HIV-positive people.

In September, basketball star Earvin "Magic" Johnson resigns his professional appointment to the National

1992
cont.
Commission on AIDS, charging official inaction on HIV/AIDS policy. Johnson also announces that he will return to professional basketball in the coming season.

3

Biographical Sketches

RELATIVELY FEW PEOPLE have become well known because of the HIV/AIDS epidemic. Although numerous scientists and researchers have played crucial roles in the medical and scientific progress on the epidemic, having HIV/AIDS has been more a source of stigma than of fame. Those whose names have become known have most often been the cases that shocked the public—such as actor Rock Hudson, pianist Liberace, basketball player Earvin "Magic" Johnson, college student Kimberly Bergalis, newsman Max Robinson, designer Halston, actress Amanda Blake, tennis player Arthur Ashe, and hemophiliac Ryan White—and threatened the immunity to HIV that some took for granted.

However, the gay press has frequently highlighted the lives and contributions of the many gay men either who died before much attention was paid to the mounting casualties or whose lives were so ordinary that they were not candidates for extensive obituaries or coverage in the mainstream press. As the epidemic has spread to poor communities, no public notice has accompanied the deaths of the men, women, and children affected.

Some of these people are profiled in the following pages. Little will ever be known, however, of the thousands of people—men, women, and children—who either died uncounted in the epidemic or who have reached out to help those affected. Like most people, they are best known to their friends, co-workers, and family members.

Dr. Francoise Barre

Dr. Francoise Barre was a member of Dr. Luc Montagnier's research team at the Pasteur Institute in Paris. She first isolated the virus leading to AIDS.

Kimberly Bergalis

Kimberly Bergalis, age 23, became the most visible of the five patients believed to have been infected with HIV by Stuart, Florida, dentist Dr. David Acer. Bergalis particularly stirred public emotion and fear about contracting HIV. Bergalis developed symptoms in early 1989 while a college student. She wrote a blunt letter to Florida officials in 1991, when they were considering legislation to regulate testing for health care workers. In her letter, Bergalis stated, "I blame Dr. Acer and every single one of you bastards. Anyone who knew Dr. Acer was infected and had full-blown AIDS and stood by not doing a damn thing about it. You are all just as guilty as he was. You've ruined my life and my family's." Bergalis also traveled to Washington, D.C., in the final stages of her illness to testify for a few seconds before Congress on a mandatory HIV testing measure for health care workers. Bergalis died in December 1991.

Dr. Samuel Broder

Dr. Samuel Broder became chief of the National Cancer Institute, the largest of the National Institutes of Health; he had major responsibility for the controversial development of AZT with the pharmaceutical company Burroughs Wellcome.

Michael Callen

Michael Callen is a long-term survivor of HIV and a singer who founded the People with AIDS Coalition in New York City. He became a national spokesperson for the organization and has continued to perform and speak about his strategy for survival. He was diagnosed in early 1982.

Gaetan Dugas

Gaetan Dugas was an airline steward for Air Canada and one of the first North Americans diagnosed with AIDS; he is sometimes referred to as "Patient Zero." When the CDC reported on what became known as the "Orange County Connection" in June 1982, Dugas was at the center of an interconnected series of Kaposi's sarcoma and *Pneumo-cystis carinii* pneumonia cases that included him as a common sexual contact for a number of cases. He or his partners had sex with 40 of the first 248 gay men who had been diagnosed with the disease. This network of contacts involved people in 10 cities and created further generations of sexual contacts. This clustering of cases from a string of identifiable sexual contacts offered strong proof that a lone infectious agent was responsible for the transmission of the disease.

Dr. Robert Gallo

Dr. Robert Gallo, a leading retrovirologist with the National Cancer Institute, won international fame in 1984 when he co-discovered the virus causing AIDS and developed a test to check for its presence. The discovery was surrounded by controversy because of allegations that Gallo had, in fact, discovered the same virus earlier found by his co-discoverer, Dr. Luc Montagnier of Paris's Pasteur Institute. The conflict developed because of the exceptional similarity of strains of the two viruses and showed just how competitive the research environment had been.

Keith Haring

Keith Haring was an artist who died of AIDS in 1990 at the age of 29. He first gained notice for his subway drawings in white chalk on black paper pasted over old advertisements. His art was recognizable for its simple line quality and comic-book subject matter, such as barking dogs and spaceships, and became familiar on T-shirts.

George Kenneth Horne, Jr.

George Kenneth Horne, Jr., was the first Kaposi's sarcoma case reported to the CDC in 1981. He died in San Francisco in November 1981.

Rock Hudson

Rock Hudson was a U.S. movie star well known for his looks and his on-screen portrayal of conventionally masculine characters. In July 1985, it was officially confirmed that the actor was dying of AIDS in Paris; later Hudson's homosexuality also became public. When Hudson died in October 1985, his death drew such attention to AIDS that many viewed it as a turning point in thinking about the disease.

Earvin "Magic" Johnson

Earvin "Magic" Johnson, a famous National Basketball Association player for the Los Angeles Lakers, announced in November 1991 that he was infected with HIV and was retiring immediately from his basketball career to devote himself to AIDS education. President Bush named Johnson to the National Commission on AIDS; Johnson resigned in September 1992, charging official inaction. He subsequently announced his return to professional basketball for the 1992–1993 season.

Cleve Jones

Cleve Jones was a San Francisco gay activist and organizer of the Kaposi's Sarcoma Research and Education Foundation. He later founded the NAMES Project, which originated the huge memorial quilt that commemorates people who died in the epidemic.

Dr. C. Everett Koop

Dr. C. Everett Koop was one of the nation's leading pediatric surgeons when he was nominated by President Ronald Reagan to be the surgeon general of the U. S. Public Health Service. Koop's highly publicized position against abortion led supporters and critics of his nomination to conclude that they could predict his actions in office. He surprised critics and supporters alike, however, by approaching critical issues as public health problems and not as ideological campaigns. Koop issued blunt statements on the rights of handicapped children and the dangers of passive cigarette smoke, but it was his vigorous work to educate the United States about HIV/AIDS and the need for sex education in the schools that gave him a reputation as an effective surgeon general during his eight-year tenure.

Larry Kramer

Larry Kramer is a New York City novelist, playwright, columnist, and film producer who helped start Gay Men's Health Crisis in early 1982 and was controversial in the gay community for advising men to stop having sex to halt the epidemic. In 1987 he called for the angry advocacy that gave birth to ACT UP. Besides a column in the *Village Voice,* Kramer authored *Faggots, The Normal Heart,* and the screenplay for *Women in Love* based on D. H. Lawrence's book.

Dr. Mathilde Krim

Dr. Mathilde Krim is a socially prominent cancer researcher who had been working in the area of interferon research when the HIV/AIDS epidemic began. In 1983, she organized the AIDS Medical Foundation (AMF) to support AIDS research. AMF merged with a California group in 1985 to form the American Foundation for AIDS Research (AmFAR), the nation's largest private nonprofit devoted to education, clinical and laboratory research, and public policy.

Robert Mapplethorpe

Robert Mapplethorpe was a photographer whose work appeared in more than 200 exhibitions from 1973 to 1989. Later work of Mapplethorpe's aroused a storm of controversy from conservative politicians, especially Senator Jesse Helms (R-NC), for its depiction of homosexual activity and because Mapplethorpe's work had been financially supported by the National Endowment for the Arts. Mapplethorpe died of AIDS at the age of 42 in 1989.

Belinda Mason

Belinda Mason was the only original member of the National Commission on AIDS to have HIV/AIDS. She died of AIDS in September 1991, at the age of 33. A Kentucky journalist, Mason received a contaminated blood transfusion during the birth of her second child in 1987. She attributed her appointment to the commission to the facts that "I was Southern, I was white, I was articulate, and I got AIDS in a nice way." She wrote a highly publicized letter to President Bush in 1990 urging him to reject federal policies that would further stigmatize persons with AIDS (PWAs) by prohibiting the immigration of infected individuals and promoting mandatory screening of health care workers.

Dr. Luc Montagnier

Dr. Luc Montagnier was chief of the Pasteur Institute research team that in 1983 first isolated the AIDS virus, which he referred to as Lymphadenopathy-Associated Virus (LAV). Montagnier became embroiled in a dispute with U.S. scientist Dr. Robert Gallo over the original discovery of the virus; the two shared "co-discoverer" status until 1991, when Gallo conceded that the French had made the first discovery.

Dr. June Osborn

Dr. June Osborn is chair of the National Commission on AIDS (NCOA) and dean of the School of Public Health of the University of Michigan. NCOA was created by Congress in 1989 and has issued a series of provocative reports calling on the federal government to address the epidemic more effectively.

Dr. Grethe Rask

Dr. Grethe Rask was a Danish surgeon in Zaire and the first Westerner documented to have died of what became identified as AIDS. She died in December 1977 of *Pneumocystis carinii* pneumonia (PCP), the previously rare pneumonia that later became specifically identified as a primary opportunistic infection resulting from HIV.

Ryan White

Ryan White, a hemophiliac in Kokomo, Indiana, was 13 when he was diagnosed with HIV, which he received through a contaminated transfusion of Factor VIII (a clotting agent). He was subsequently denied the right to return to his school; he and his mother fought a lengthy public legal battle for Ryan's right to attend public school. Though he won in the courts, Ryan's family was the target of enormous hostility and ignorance in their hometown, and after a bullet was fired into their home, they relocated to Cicero, Indiana. There, Ryan met a welcoming community and found his battle had attracted the attention of numerous celebrities, such as Michael Jackson and Elton John. Ryan was memorialized on the NAMES Project AIDS Memorial Quilt as "Educator for Life" because of his efforts to speak out about HIV/AIDS and his numerous public appearances at fundraisers, before the Presidential Commission on AIDS, and in schools. Ryan White died on April 8, 1990, at age 18; his grave was repeatedly vandalized.

Phil Zwickler

Phil Zwickler died of AIDS in May 1991. He was an award-winning documentary director whose work included "Rights and Reactions: Lesbian and Gay Rights on Trial" (a documentary of the New York City Council hearings on gay rights legislation), and "Fear of Disclosure" (about dating problems faced by gay men). With Rosa Praunheim he made "SILENCE=DEATH" and "Positive," which showed the history of AIDS activism in New York City. For many years, Zwickler also edited the PWA Coalition newsletter.

4

Facts and Statistics

THIS CHAPTER PROVIDES important facts and statistics on HIV/AIDS in a way that will help the reader understand the impact of the disease on our society, our nation, and our world. Though the information provided here is as factual as possible, it is necessarily brief and intended to give the reader quick access to basic information about many aspects of HIV/AIDS. References in other chapters of this book provide sources for further research and information.

This chapter includes six sections. "Terminology for Understanding HIV/AIDS" explains the role language plays in understanding the epidemic and includes three mini-glossaries (the virus and its transmission, testing, and drug therapies and drug trials) of terms helpful for further reading. Also included is the most recent proposed CDC surveillance case definition.

"HIV/AIDS and the World" provides an overview of facts about the worldwide epidemic, which has been very different in nature from the U.S. epidemic. "HIV/AIDS and the Nation" is a compilation of facts and tables on federal funding and health care costs, plus an overview of the common diseases that accompany HIV-related illness. Also included are statistical pictures of those with HIV/AIDS and modes of transmission, plus a summary of U.S. deaths since the onset of the epidemic. "HIV/AIDS and the States" consists of facts on HIV/AIDS' impact on the states, plus a state-by-state summary of cases. Also, a summary is provided by subject area of state legislative measures over several years.

"HIV/AIDS and Specific Populations" includes tables and facts that provide a portrait of the epidemic in various subgroups of the

U.S. population, including children, racial minorities, youth, prisoners, members of the military, rural residents, and women. "HIV/AIDS and Public Opinion" provides information from polls and surveys that examine public awareness and understanding of HIV/AIDS.

Terminology for Understanding HIV/AIDS

The Importance of Language

When reading the material in this book, it is important to consider the evolution of the language used to refer to the HIV/AIDS epidemic and the accuracy of that language. Frequently we hear or read in the media about people "catching AIDS" or "testing for AIDS." These are very inaccurate statements. What is transmitted is HIV: the Human Immunodeficiency Virus. This is what one "catches" through unsafe sexual practices, sharing needles, and other risk behaviors. It is also what is tested for, because the test indicates whether antibodies to the virus are present. You cannot be tested for "AIDS," which actually is the end-stage of the suppression of the immune system through the presence of HIV.

Why is this distinction so important? Because the federal government estimates that *1 million* Americans have HIV at this time, many more than the almost 29,241 people who died of AIDS-related illnesses in 1991. Clearly, HIV is something to be concerned about, too.

Many people with HIV will remain free of symptoms for 5–10 years, possibly until superior treatments and cures are available for the virus and its illnesses. Stopping HIV's spread is at least as important as finding effective treatments for the myriad illnesses and infections that are AIDS.

AIDS as a term is defined by the federal government's medical and scientific experts: you must have the specific opportunistic infections (PC pneumonia, Kaposi's sarcoma, etc.) and other physical conditions that the government has decided constitute AIDS. Each person who dies of AIDS may have a different combination of these infections. There is not only one way to die of AIDS, though some people—especially women—do die of HIV-related illnesses that are not yet defined as AIDS. Problems and controversy surround the "case definition" of AIDS; many people feel the definition is much too restrictive and excludes people and illnesses. It is believed that an important result of this restrictiveness is that official HIV/AIDS numbers are lower than are the actual cases.

You cannot advance directly to having AIDS in any way; you must have HIV first, and possibly for years. Therefore, you cannot "catch AIDS." People are presently alive and well who were diagnosed with HIV five to ten years ago, so clearly there are circumstances where life is prolonged through education, health care, and preventive behavior.

Former Surgeon General C. Everett Koop has stated, "In addition to illness, disability, and death, AIDS has brought fear to the hearts of most Americans—fear of disease and fear of the unknown." Knowledge can help address fear, and that knowledge can be expressed in accurate and factual language (an important contribution to any discussion), as well as in the straightforward discussion of topics that make many people uncomfortable: human sexual behavior, homosexuality, prostitution, and drug use. Each accurate use of relevant language, and each refusal to use popular but inaccurate terms, establishes another opportunity to dispel ignorance and educate others, and thus to shorten the epidemic.

Here are some of the terms most frequently used in discussing HIV and AIDS:

Inaccurate	More Accurate
AIDS virus	HIV (Human Immunodeficiency Virus)
HIV virus	HIV
Infected with AIDS	HIV infection
AIDS test	HIV antibody test
AIDS transmission	HIV transmission
AIDS victim	PWA (person with AIDS)
High-risk groups	High-risk behaviors

Terms To Understand: Three Mini-Glossaries

The following three mini-glossaries define terms that are basic to any discussion of the science and medicine of the virus (HIV) and its transmission; HIV testing; and drug therapies being used against the progression of AIDS, as well as drugs being tested for future use against HIV/AIDS. Additional terms and their definitions can be found in the Glossary at the back of this book.

I: HIV/AIDS and Its Transmission

Acquired Immune Deficiency Syndrome (AIDS)   The final stage of a series of specific health conditions and problems as well as opportunistic infections (OI) caused by a virus, HIV. HIV can be passed from person to person chiefly by sexual contact, through the sharing of syringes used for intravenous drug injection, or through transmission from an infected mother to her unborn child. In a person who has developed AIDS, the body's natural immune system is suppressed and allows for the active presence of microorganisms that otherwise would be fought off by the immune system. The acronym *AIDS* was first used by the Centers for Disease Control (CDC) in late 1982 to name cases of illness that were first reported in 1981.

AIDS (Acquired Immune Deficiency Syndrome)   Infection with the Human Immunodeficiency Virus (HIV) is manifested by a depressed immune system that is overtaken by one or more of the diseases defined by the Centers for Disease Control (CDC).

AIDS virus   A popular and widely used but inaccurate term for the Human Immunodeficiency Virus (HIV), the virus that leads to AIDS.

antibody   The body's immune system develops this special protein in the blood when a foreign substance is present; an antibody is the body's defense against illness. Specific antibodies are developed by the body to fight various infections.

antigen   This substance, when introduced into the body, provokes the production of an antibody that will specifically react to the antigen.

ARC (AIDS-Related Complex)   This term has not been defined or recognized by CDC but is used frequently in the subject literature to describe symptoms found in some persons with HIV. It is also used to describe symptomatic HIV infection. Some of the symptoms are recurring fever, weight loss, fungal infection in the mouth and throat, and swollen lymph nodes.

asymptomatic   Having no symptoms. Persons infected with HIV may not have symptoms for years.

body fluids   A euphemism that refers to semen, blood, saliva, urine, and other fluids found in the body and central to the discussion of HIV transmission.

case definition   The official Centers for Disease Control (CDC) definition of AIDS.

casual contact   Ordinary daily activity. For instance, HIV cannot be transmitted by shaking hands with someone who has it, by using a telephone touched by a person who has HIV, or by sitting in a classroom with a child who has HIV.

CD4 Also known as T4, CD4 is a protein in T-lymphocyte helper cells. HIV first infects cells by becoming attached to CD4 molecules. HIV destroys T4-cells, and a T4-cell count is one laboratory means of assessing the status of the immune system.

CD8 Also known as T8, CD8 is a protein in T-lymphocyte suppressor cells. The ratio between CD4 and CD8 cells is one important means of judging the viability of a person's immune system.

Centers for Disease Control (CDC) A federal government agency responsible for infectious disease control. The agency is located in Atlanta, Georgia, and operates under the U.S. Public Health Services, a part of the U.S. Department of Health and Human Services.

clean needles Usually refers to syringes used for injection of drugs. Clean needles reduce the chance of passing HIV via blood that accumulates in the syringe. A clean needle can also be one that has been sterilized with bleach after being previously used.

condom A shield placed over the penis during sexual intercourse. Condoms may be made of latex or sheep's intestine, though only latex condoms help prevent the spread of HIV. The condom acts like a bag to collect semen, thus also acting as a birth control device and to prevent transmission of other sexual diseases. Condoms are also known as "gloves," "French letters," and "rubbers."

dental dam A latex square that can protect against the transmission of HIV when placed over the vagina, clitoris, or anus during sexual activity.

Factor VIII A component of the blood system that causes it to clot. The shortage of this element is the source of hemophilia. Some hemophiliacs have contracted HIV from transfusions of contaminated Factor VIII.

full-blown AIDS A case of HIV infection that meets the requirements of CDC's case definition.

helper T-cells Also known as T4 and CD4, these are a set of T-cells (helper, killer, or suppressor cells) that prompt antibody response and other immune functions.

hemophilia A disorder of the blood system found in some males in which they do not have a sufficient amount of the clotting factor in their blood.

high-risk behaviors The preferred term for referring to actions that place one in danger of being exposed to HIV. In the early years of the epidemic, "high-risk groups" were described as being gay men, IV drug users, their sexual partners, and others, but the evolution of language to discuss the virus has placed the emphasis on behaviors that can be changed or influenced, rather than on groups of people whose sexuality or drug use makes them targets of other discrimination. High-risk behaviors include unprotected sexual intercourse and sharing of needles in IV drug use.

HIV or HIV-1   Human Immunodeficiency Virus, the retrovirus that causes AIDS.

HTLV-III   Human T-Lymphotropic Virus—Type III. U.S. scientists first used this term to refer to the virus that causes AIDS.

HTLV-III/LAV   Human T-Lymphotropic Virus—Type III/lymphadenopathy-associated virus. Two very similar viruses that are considered a primary cause of AIDS. Despite the confusion it causes, the virus that causes AIDS is referred to by several different names in the medical and scientific literature.

immunodeficient   An immune system that is not functioning or is suppressed in some way, making the person vulnerable to infection and disease.

interferon   A protein made by the lymphocyte that prevents a virus from spreading to other cells.

intravenous drugs   Chemical substances used in the body by means of inserting a syringe or needle into a vein.

IVDU   Intravenous drug user.

Kaposi's sarcoma (KS)   A rare form of cancer usually found in older men, until the arrival of the HIV epidemic. The cancer is most widely recognized by purple spots on the skin, resulting from tumors in the walls of blood vessels. However, the lesions can occur inside the body as well.

KS-OI (Kaposi's sarcoma [KS] and opportunistic infections [OI])   This early name was used by CDC officials for what was eventually called AIDS.

LAS (Lymphadenopathy Syndrome)   Chronically enlarged lymph nodes often found in HIV infection.

LAV (Lymphadenopathy-Associated Virus)   A retrovirus in a person with enlarged lymph nodes who may have engaged in high-risk behavior. LAV is believed to be the same virus as HTLV-III.

LAV-HTLV-III   Another of the names used for the virus that causes AIDS.

needle exchange   The practice of providing clean syringes to intravenous drug users in an effort to reduce the incidence of transmission of HIV.

opportunistic infections   A general term for the variety of diseases and infections that can surface and become problematic when a person's immune system is depressed as the result of HIV infection. The infections would not have an effect in a healthy person.

perinatal   Any event that takes places at or around the time of birth.

PGL (Persistent Generalized Lymphadenopathy)   Chronic noncancerous lymph node enlargement.

Pneumocystis carinii **pneumonia (PCP)** A parasitic, fungal pneumonia common in persons with AIDS. It is the most life-threatening of the opportunistic infections.

retrovirus HIV is a retrovirus. This group of viruses contains the genetic material ribonucleic acid (RNA) and copies it into deoxyribonucleic acid (DNA) inside an infected cell. The DNA that results from this process is then included in the genetic structure of the cell as a provirus. Proviruses are passed to each infected cell's offspring cells. In the case of HIV, the problem that this presents is that, in order to kill the virus, the cell must also be killed.

reverse transcriptase An enzyme in retroviruses that can copy RNA into DNA. This copying process is necessary to the life cycle of HIV.

risk factors Generally refers to behaviors or practices that place a person at-risk for HIV transmission. The most common risk factors are IV drug use and unprotected sexual intercourse. Previously, use of blood or blood products was also a risk factor.

safe sex A general term to describe sexual practices and attitudes that protect a person from transmitting or receiving HIV. Also describes any sexual activity that does not involve the exchange of bodily fluids.

seroconversion When a person's antibody status (seronegative) changes to positive.

sharing needles Using a syringe to inject drugs after it has been used by someone else or passing a syringe to another person after using it yourself. A small amount of blood accumulates in a syringe when it is used and, if it is infected, this blood can transmit HIV to another user.

SIDA The acronym for AIDS in Spanish and French.

STD (sexually transmitted disease) More than 25 different infections are now classified as STDs, including gonorrhea, syphilis, and herpes simplex. Most STDs can be treated.

suppressor T-cells A type of T-cell that stops antibody production and some other immune responses.

T4 See CD4.

T-cells or T-lymphocytes The immune system uses these white blood cells to fight infection. There are three types of cells: helper, killer, and suppressor. They are mainly found in the blood and lymph system and are targeted by HIV. Many clinics stop monitoring T-cell counts after they fall to 200 from the normal level of 1,000 or more. Recent reports show that many AIDS-linked infections and deaths occur at T-cell levels below 50.

T-lymphocytes See T-cells.

tuberculosis (TB) Acute or chronic infection that is being seen more frequently in HIV-positive people and poor people. It is caused by an airborne pathogen passed through inhalation, thus contributing to its spread in crowded physical situations, such as overcrowded housing, prisons, and shelters. Though TB was once believed to be all but wiped out in this country, case numbers have been rising in recent years.

unprotected sex Sexual activity without a condom or dental dam.

virus This organism causes infectious disease and needs living cells (a host) to reproduce. A virus may take over the cell's normal functioning and cause it to behave in ways determined by the virus.

wasting Involuntary weight loss that is a common symptom of HIV infection. Weight loss indicates progression of HIV disease and can occur at any stage of the infection. It can result from malabsorption of nutrients and is thus associated with malnutrition, which can contribute to immune suppression.

II: HIV/AIDS Testing Terms

antibody-positive This term refers to the result of a blood test that shows that a person has been exposed to a particular infection at some time and developed antibodies to it.

ELISA (enzyme-linked immunosorbent assay) A simple blood test that can measure antibodies to HIV. Because this test can produce some false-positive results, the test is repeated when positive and confirmed with a more sophisticated test, the Western blot test.

false negative The result of a blood test where the blood sample contains too few antibodies or antigens to show a positive result. A person with this test result could be thought not to be carrying the virus, even though the virus actually is present.

HIV antibody screening test Refers to the two tests for the HIV antibody—ELISA and the Western blot. This term is infrequently used compared to the grossly inaccurate term *AIDS test*.

HIV negative A test result that does not show the presence of antibodies to HIV. This result does not mean that a person does not have HIV, however, as it may take as long as six months for the body to produce antibodies. During this period, the person can still transmit the virus to others and not show any symptoms.

HIV positive A test result that shows the presence of antibodies to HIV. This result does not mean that the person has AIDS or will develop AIDS.

mandatory testing Refers to required HIV antibody testing.

p-24 antigen test   Used to monitor the immune status of an infected person.

serologic test   A class of laboratory tests performed on the serum portion of the blood, which is the clear, liquid portion of blood.

seronegative   This test result reflects a negative result for the HIV antibody test.

seropositive   This test result reflects a positive result for the HIV antibody test.

seroprevalence   A number that would express the frequency or absolute number of people in a given group (city, state, clinic) with positive results for the HIV antibody test.

Western blot   This laboratory procedure detects antibodies to HIV. The Western blot test is more difficult than the ELISA test and is used as a back-up for ELISA results that show positive.

III: Drug Therapies and Drug Trials

Acyclovir   An antiviral agent approved to treat herpes simplex and varicella-zoster infections. It is also under investigation for use against cyclomega-lovirus (CMV), a pathogen.

aerosolized pentamidine   This drug, administered by inhalation of a fine mist, is approved for use against one of the primary fatal infections of AIDS, *Pneumocystis carinii* pneumonia. Injectable pentamidine is also used.

AIDS Clinical Trial Group (ACTG)   Medical centers that are taking part in the evaluation of treatments for HIV-related infections. These sites, of which there were 46 in 1991, are sponsored by the National Institute of Allergy and Infectious Diseases.

AL-721 (Active Lipid)   This antiviral drug is used to treat conditions related to AIDS. The drug was developed from an egg-based compound and affects membrane fluidity without being toxic. It was tested in France and Israel and was popular as a self-administered therapy in the mid-1980s, but it did not meet with institutional success once AZT became available.

Amphotericin-B   An antifungal medication used to treat cryptococcal meningitis.

Ampligen   A drug still in trials that may be an immunomodulator and an antiviral.

antibiotic   A type of drug used to fight bacterial infection.

antiviral drug   A medication that will halt the work of a virus before the virus multiplies or damages other cells.

antivirals   These agents may be effective in treating AIDS; they are being studied in experiments to see whether they halt the work of the virus or kill it entirely.

AZT (Azidothymidine)   An antiviral and the first prescription drug approved (in 1987) by the Food and Drug Administration (FDA) for use in prolonging life. The drug was approved for use before testing was completed; testing was done only on male subjects. AZT has a high cost and has shown extreme toxicity, as well as a loss of effectiveness over time. Research released in early 1992 showed that the drug did not prolong the life of users.

Bactrim   This antibiotic has been effective in treating *Pneumocystis carinii* pneumonia (PCP). The drug has notable side effects.

chemotherapy   Treatment of the body with drugs that fight cancer.

clinical trial   A research study in which new therapies are tested in humans. Therapies are tested in humans after those therapies have been tried in animals and laboratory studies.

compassionate use   A means of using an investigational new drug before there is much established data on its capacity to produce results. These drugs must generally be given free of charge to patients by the companies manufacturing them. The FDA gives specific approval for each drug used this way.

Compound Q   A highly purified protein made from root tubers that is being investigated in drug trials to inhibit HIV replication in both acute and chronic infections.

ddC (dideoxycytidine)   A potent HIV inhibitor drug being tested in vitro in drug investigations.

ddI (dideoxyinosine)   An HIV inhibitor approved for use in 1991. ddI was the second drug approved by FDA to fight HIV, and it can be administered only for patients who cannot take the first approved drug (AZT) or who did not improve while taking AZT. As part of the process to speed development of new drugs, ddI was approved before all the research studies were completed. Studies were completed in early 1992.

dextran sulfate   An antiviral that has inhibited HIV in test-tube studies. It will be studied further but is in use in the drug "underground."

double blind   A component of a drug trial in which neither the subjects nor the researchers know which subjects are receiving a test drug and which are receiving placebos or other substances. The structure is based on a belief that this method promotes faster and more objective results, because neither party has specific expectations about the outcome.

Erythropoietin A drug approved for treatment of severe anemia that can accompany AZT use. The drug is based on a naturally occurring compound and stimulates red blood cell production.

expanded access Provisions in drug development regulation for distribution of unlicensed but potentialy life-saving drugs to seriously ill individuals.

Fluconazole A drug approved for use against candidiasis and cryptococcal meningitis.

Food and Drug Administration (FDA) The federal agency charged with approving new drug treatments for use by the public.

Foscavir An antiviral agent approved for use against cytomegalovirus (CMV) retinitis, CMV colitis, and strains of herpes simplex and zoster.

Ganciclovir An antiviral drug approved for treatment of cytomegalovirus (CMV) retinitis.

immune boosters or immune modulators Substances that enhance the body's natural defenses against infection and disease. A course of immune boosters has been found helpful to some HIV-positive individuals who are trying to prolong the period of time before the onset of full-blown AIDS.

institutional review board A group composed of physicians, scientists, and people with HIV/AIDS who ensure that a clinical drug trial or research program is safe and that the rights of participants are protected.

parallel track An expanded access strategy to facilitate use of experimental therapies by people who do not qualify for inclusion in clinical protocols, conducted in partnership with traditional clinical trials.

passive immunotherapy A process where the filtered blood of asymptomatic HIV-positive persons is used for persons with AIDS (PWAs) in an effort to boost immune functions with a transfusion of HIV antibodies.

placebo A substance administered in a drug investigation to measure the efficiency of a specific drug. A placebo is an inactive substance but can cause a change called the "placebo effect" in a patient, due to the expectations of the recipient.

protocol A set of rules for a clinical trial. The protocol describes what types of patients will participate, the schedule of tests and procedures, drugs and dosages, and the length of time the study will be conducted.

recombinant human alpha interferon A drug approved for use against Kaposi's sarcoma.

side effects Unwanted or unexpected actions or responses caused by a drug. Experimental drugs are studied for both short-term and long-term side effects.

sulfonamides A type of antibiotic drug.

toxicity The extent to which a substance is harmful or poisonous to the body.

treatment IND (investigational new drug) This program offers experimental treatment to patients without satisfactory alternative treatments.

underground A general term to refer to self-help activities by PWAs and HIV-positive people that either bring untested or unapproved drugs into the country from other sources or manufacture such drugs outside official laboratory environments.

CDC Surveillance Case Definition

The surveillance case definition is the official Centers for Disease Control (CDC) definition of AIDS; many aspects of an individual's treatment and access to benefits revolve around whether a clinical diagnosis of "CDC AIDS" is present. The last existing definition was adopted in 1987; it has been criticized for shortcomings that include its rigidity and the omission of many manifestations seen in HIV-ill women.

In late 1991, the CDC proposed a revised classification system for HIV infection and an expanded AIDS surveillance case definition for adolescents and adults. The new definition was proposed for adoption in April 1992, but it was not adopted as scheduled. The CDC made no announcement at the time concerning its intentions. However, some modified version of the proposal was expected to be adopted sometime during 1992.

Because of its value as a primary document that defines whether or not an individual has AIDS, an edited version of the proposed case definition is reprinted here. The sources cited in its notes are scientific references on HIV/AIDS. A current version of the operating definition can be obtained from the National AIDS Information Clearinghouse, (800) 458-5231.

The CD4+, or T-helper, lymphocyte is the primary target cell for HIV infection, and a decrease in the number of these cells correlates with the risk and severity of HIV-related illnesses. CDC is revising the classification system for HIV infection to emphasize the clinical importance of the CD4+ lymphocyte count in the categorization of HIV-related clinical conditions. This revised system replaces the classification published in 1986. Consistent with this revision, CDC is also expanding the AIDS surveillance case definition to include all HIV-infected persons with less than 200 CD4+ lymphocytes/mm³. This expansion includes the clinical conditions in the AIDS surveillance case definition published in 1987.

BACKGROUND

The etiologic agent of acquired immunodeficiency syndrome (AIDS) is a retrovirus designated human immunodeficiency virus (HIV). The CD4+ lymphocyte is the primary target for HIV infection because of the affinity of the virus for the CD4 surface marker.[1] The CD4+ lymphocyte coordinates a number of important immunologic functions, and a loss of these functions results in a progressive impairment of the immune response. Studies of the natural history of HIV infection have documented a wide spectrum of disease manifestations, ranging from asymptomatic infection to life-threatening conditions characterized by severe immunodeficiency, serious opportunistic infections, and cancers.[2-11] Studies have shown a strong association between the development of life-threatening opportunistic illnesses and the absolute number or percentage of CD4+ lymphocytes.[12-19] As the number of CD4+ lymphocytes decreases, the risk and severity of opportunistic illnesses increases.

Measures of CD4+ lymphocytes are currently used to guide clinical and/or therapeutic actions for HIV-infected persons.[20] Antimicrobial prophylaxis and antiretroviral therapies have been shown to be most effective within certain levels of immune dysfunction.[21-23] As a result, antiretroviral therapy is recommended for all persons with a CD4+ lymphocyte count of less than 500/mm³, and prophylaxis against *Pneumocystis carinii* pneumonia, the most common serious opportunistic infection diagnosed in AIDS patients, is recommended for all persons with CD4+ lymphocyte counts of less than 200/mm³. These recommendations have resulted in CD4+ lymphocyte determinations becoming an integral part of medical management of HIV-infected persons.

The revised classification system for HIV infection and the expanded AIDS surveillance case definition include the CD4+ lymphocyte count as a marker for HIV-related immunosuppression. The objectives of these changes are to simplify the classification and reporting process, to be consistent with standards of medical care for HIV-infected persons, to better categorize HIV-related morbidity, and to more accurately record the number of persons with severe HIV-related immunosuppression who are most affected by clinical conditions.

REVISED HIV CLASSIFICATION SYSTEM FOR ADOLESCENTS AND ADULTS

The revised CDC classification system for HIV-infected adolescents and adults* emphasizes the importance of CD4+ lymphocyte testing in the clinical management of HIV-infected persons. This classification system categorizes the clinical conditions associated with HIV infection on the basis of the CD4+ lymphocyte count. The system, outlined in Table 1, is based on three ranges of laboratory categories (CD4+ lymphocyte counts) and three clinical categories, represented by a matrix of nine mutually exclusive categories. This system replaces the classification system published in 1986 which included only clinical disease criteria and which was developed before the widespread use of CD4+ cell testing.[24]

Laboratory Categories

The three designated laboratory categories, _Category 1_- ≥ 500 cells; _Category 2_- 200-499 cells; and _Category 3_- < 200 cells, correspond to CD4+ lymphocyte counts per mm^3 of blood that guide clinical and/or therapeutic actions in the management of HIV-infected adolescents and adults.[20-23]

Criteria for HIV Infection: Persons aged 13 years or older with repeatedly reactive screening tests for HIV-1 antibody (e.g., enzyme immunoassay) who also have specific antibody identified by the use of supplemental tests (e.g., Western blot, immunofluorescence assay) are considered to be infected. Other specific methods for the diagnosis of HIV-1 include direct identification of virus in host tissues by virus isolation, antigen detection, and detection of HIV genetic material (DNA or RNA) by polymerase chain reaction (PCR).

Clinical Categories

The clinical categories are defined as follows:

Category A- One or more of the conditions listed below occurring in an adolescent or adult with documented HIV infection. Cdnditions listed in categories B and C must not have occurred.

- Asymptomatic HIV infection
- Persistent generalized lymphadenopathy (PGL)
- Acute (primary) HIV infection with accompanying illness[25,26] or history of acute HIV infection

Category B- Symptomatic conditions occurring in an HIV-infected adolescent or adult which are not included among conditions listed in clinical category C and which meet at least one of the following criteria: (a) the conditions are attributed to HIV infection and/or are indicative of a defect in cell-mediated immunity; or (b) the conditions are considered by physicians to have a clinical course or management that is complicated by HIV infection. Examples of conditions in clinical category B include, **but are not limited to:**

- Bacterial endocarditis, meningitis, pneumonia, or sepsis
- Candidiasis, vulvovaginal; persistent (>1 month duration), or poorly responsive to therapy
- Candidiasis, oropharyngeal (thrush)
- Cervical dysplasia, severe; or carcinoma[27,28]
- Constitutional symptoms, such as fever ($\geq$38.5°C) or diarrhea lasting >1 month
- Hairy leukoplakia, oral
- Herpes zoster (shingles), involving at least two distinct episodes or more than one dermatome
- Idiopathic thrombocytopenic purpura
- Listeriosis
- *Mycobacterium tuberculosis*, pulmonary
- Nocardiosis
- Pelvic inflammatory disease
- Peripheral neuropathy

Category C- Any condition listed in the 1987 surveillance case definition for AIDS and affecting an adolescent or adult (appendix I).[29] The conditions in clinical category C are strongly associated with severe immunodeficiency, occur frequently in HIV-infected individuals, and cause serious morbidity or mortality.

HIV-infected persons should be classified based on both the lowest accurate (but not necessarily the most recent) CD4$^+$ lymphocyte determination and the most severe clinical condition diagnosed regardless of the patient's current clinical condition (e.g., someone previously treated for oral or persistent vaginal candidiasis but who is now asymptomatic should be classified in clinical category B). The classification system is based on the absolute number of CD4$^+$ cells but allows for the use of the CD4$^+$ percent when the counts cannot be obtained or are outdated in view of the patient's current clinical condition (appendix II).[20]

EXPANSION OF THE CDC SURVEILLANCE CASE DEFINITION FOR AIDS

The 1992 expansion of the AIDS surveillance case definition includes all adolescents and adults with HIV infection who have laboratory evidence of severe immunosuppression. Severe immunosuppression is defined as an absolute CD4$^+$ lymphocyte count of less than 200/mm^3, or a CD4$^+$ percent of total lymphocytes less than 14 if the absolute count is not available. The expanded AIDS surveillance case definition also includes persons with clinical conditions listed in the 1987 case definition (appendix I).[29] This expanded definition for reporting of AIDS cases is effective April 1, 1992.

The expanded AIDS surveillance case definition is consistent with the revised HIV classification system. Specifically, subcategories A3, B3, C1, C2, and C3 will be defined as cases of AIDS for surveillance purposes (Table 1).

COMMENTARY

The revised classification system for HIV infection is based on the recommended clinical standard of obtaining CD4$^+$ lymphocyte counts, since this parameter consistently correlates with HIV-related immune dysfunction and disease progression and this information is needed to guide medical management of persons infected with HIV.[12-16,20-23] Measures of CD4$^+$ lymphocyte counts should be conducted in experienced laboratories using established quality assurance procedures.[20,30] Other markers of immune status, such as serum neopterin, beta-2 microglobulin, HIV p24 antigen, soluble interleukin-2 receptors, immunoglobulin A, and delayed type hypersensitivity (DTH) skin-test reactions, may be useful in the evaluation of individual patients, but are not as strongly predictive of disease progression or as specific for HIV-related immunosuppression as measures of CD4$^+$ lymphocytes.[12-19,31] DTH skin-test reactions are often used in conjunction with the Mantoux tuberculin skin test to evaluate HIV-infected patients for tuberculosis infection and anergy.[31-33]

Other systems have been used to classify and stage HIV infection.[24,31,34-39] In 1990, the World Health Organization (WHO) published an interim proposal for a staging system for HIV infection and diseases that was based primarily on clinical criteria and included the use of CD4$^+$ lymphocyte determinations.[34]   WHO incorporated provisions, such as the use of a performance scale and total lymphocyte counts (in lieu of CD4$^+$ lymphocyte determinations), both to allow and encourage the use of the system in countries where CD4$^+$ lymphocyte determinations are not available.   The HIV classification system described in this document relies on the use of CD4$^+$ lymphocyte counts, but allows for use of the CD4$^+$ percent when the counts cannot be obtained (appendix II).

The revised HIV classification system should be used by state and territorial health departments conducting HIV infection surveillance.   Because the expanded AIDS surveillance data will continue to represent only a portion of the total morbidity caused by HIV infection, HIV infection reporting may provide more accurate information regarding the total impact of HIV on health care systems.[40]

The expanded AIDS surveillance case definition will both reflect the current standard of medical practice in the United States and provide more accurate data to assess resource needs for prevention programs and health care delivery systems.   The proposed expansion of the AIDS surveillance case definition has been supported by both the Council of State and Territorial Epidemiologists and the Association of State and Territorial Health Officers.

The AIDS surveillance case definition was last revised in 1987 before the widespread use of prophylaxis against *Pneumocystis carinii* pneumonia and antiretroviral therapy in persons infected with HIV.[20-23,29]   These therapies delay the onset of illnesses that are included in the 1987 AIDS surveillance case definition and may change the spectrum of illnesses found in HIV-infected persons.   For example, among AIDS cases reported to CDC in men who have sex with other men, the proportion with *Pneumocystis carinii* pneumonia as their initial diagnosis decreased from 62 percent in 1988 to 46 percent in 1990.[41]   This trend is expected to continue.   The number of persons developing conditions meeting the current AIDS surveillance case definition annually is projected to remain relatively stable through 1995.   In contrast, the prevalence of HIV-infected persons with CD4$^+$ lymphocyte counts of less than 200/mm^3 who do not have an AIDS-defining clinical condition, however, is projected to increase by 40 percent through 1995.[42]   Thus, the utility of the current AIDS surveillance case definition in accurately identifying the number of persons with late-stage HIV disease is expected to decrease over the next few years.

The expanded AIDS surveillance case definition can be used to more accurately determine the morbidity and health care needs of all individuals with severe HIV-related immunosuppression.   Numerous infectious diseases and other conditions not included in the current AIDS surveillance case definition are diagnosed in HIV-infected persons.   These infections are also diagnosed in persons with normal immune function with or without HIV infection, but tend to increase in frequency among persons with immunosuppression.   As an example, the percentage of persons in a CDC study with recorded CD4+ lymphocytes and who were diagnosed with pneumonia (not in the 1987 case definition) or sepsis increased from 3 percent in HIV-infected persons with CD4+ lymphocyte counts of 500/mm³ or more to 11 percent in HIV-infected persons with less than 200/mm³.[43;unpublished data] In this study, 69 percent of persons with pneumonia and sepsis had CD4+ lymphocyte counts of less than 200/mm³. The addition of an immunologic marker to the AIDS surveillance case definition allows for all persons with severe HIV-related immunosuppression to be defined as having AIDS.

The ability to report HIV-infected persons on the basis of their CD4+ lymphocyte counts would simplify the AIDS case reporting process. A simplified AIDS case definition may be particularly important for outpatient clinics in which the availability of staff to conduct surveillance is limited and from which an increasing proportion of AIDS cases is reported. From pre-1985 to 1988, the proportion of AIDS cases reported from outpatient sites in the State of Washington increased from 6 percent (9/155) to 25 percent (55/219).[44] A similar increase was seen in Oregon (25 percent [44/171] before 1987 to 38 percent [40/105] in the first half of 1989).[45]

The expanded AIDS surveillance case definition is expected to have a substantial impact on the number of reported AIDS cases. Of the estimated 1 million persons infected with HIV, 160,000 individuals without an AIDS-defining illness are estimated to have CD4+ counts less than 200.[42,46] However, not all of these persons are aware of their HIV infection, and of those who know they are infected, not all have had a CD4+ count taken. Approximately half of persons diagnosed with HIV infection and with CD4+ counts less than 200/mm³ do not meet the 1987 AIDS surveillance case definition (Greenberg AE, New York City Department of Health, unpublished data; CDC, unpublished data).

Although the AIDS surveillance case definition could be changed by adding other clinical conditions, at least two important factors weigh against this approach. First, adding numerous conditions would increase the complexity of the AIDS surveillance case definition at a time when CDC and the state health departments have sought ways to simplify reporting. Second, a specific and objective measurement of the severity of immunodeficiency is preferable to the addition of more clinical conditions, which are generally less specific and less objective measures of HIV disease. Conditions such as bacterial pneumonia, sepsis, endocarditis, and pulmonary tuberculosis are likely to be associated not only with HIV disease, but also with other factors such as drug injection, malnutrition, and poverty.

A number of gynecologic conditions have been reported in HIV-infected women, and have been proposed for inclusion in the AIDS surveillance case definition.[27,28,47,48] However, these conditions are also commonly diagnosed in women without HIV infection and are neither specific for nor highly predictive of severe HIV-related immunosuppression. The proposed expansion of the AIDS surveillance case definition will comprehensively represent HIV-infected women with severe immunodeficiency. In a study in New York City which included 282 HIV-infected women seen as outpatients in 1989, the number of women meeting the AIDS surveillance case definition after the expansion would increase from 115 to 168, representing a 46 percent increase.[49;unpublished data] Among 626 HIV-infected women receiving clinical care for HIV infection in nine U.S. cities through March 1991, those meeting the AIDS surveillance case definition after the expansion would increase by 57 percent.[43;unpublished data] Of the 626 women in this study, 494 did not meet the 1987 AIDS surveillance case definition; 75 (15 percent) had a CD4$^+$ lymphocyte count less than 200/mm^3, but only 14 (3 percent) had selected gynecologic conditions (recurrent vaginal candidiasis, cervical cancer, or pelvic inflammatory disease) reported in the medical record at settings where they were receiving care for their HIV infection. The frequency of gynecologic conditions in the 494 women are likely underascertained, possibly due to the separation of gynecologic and HIV clinical services or limitations in access to these services. However, these data suggest that the use of CD4$^+$ lymphocyte counts rather than gynecologic conditions will allow more women to be reported with AIDS from these sites.

The reporting and analysis of CD4$^+$ lymphocyte counts in conjunction with HIV-related clinical conditions should facilitate efforts to evaluate health care and referral needs for persons with HIV infection and to project future needs for these services. CD4$^+$ lymphocyte test results should be included in HIV infection and AIDS case reports. By incorporating CD4$^+$ lymphocyte counts, the revised HIV classification system and expanded AIDS surveillance case definition will reflect current knowledge, promote optimal medical care, and provide uniform and simple criteria for categorizing conditions in adolescents and adults with HIV infection.

REFERENCES

1. McDougal JS, Kennedy MS, Sligh JM, et al. Binding of the HTLV-III/LAV to T4+ T cells by a complex of the 110K molecule and the T4 molecule. Science 1985;231:382-385.
2. Moss AR, Bacchetti P. Natural history of HIV infection. AIDS 1989;3:55-61.
3. Rutherford GW, Lifson AR, Hessol NA, et al. Course of HIV-1 in a cohort of homosexual and bisexual men: an 11 year follow-up study. Br Med J 1990;301:1183-1188.
4. Muñoz A, Wang MC, Bass S, et al. Acquired immunodeficiency syndrome (AIDS)-free time after human immunodeficiency virus type 1 (HIV-1) seroconversion in homosexual men. Am J Epidemiol 1989;130:530-539.
5. Rezza G, Lazzarin A, Angarano G, et al. The natural history of HIV infection in intravenous drug users: risk of disease progression in a cohort of seroconverters. AIDS 1989;3:87-90.
6. Selwyn PA, Hartel D, Schoenbaum EE, et al. Rates and predictors of progression to HIV disease and AIDS in a cohort of intravenous drug users (IVDUs), 1985-1990. VI International Conference on AIDS, San Francisco, CA. 22 June 1990;2:117 (Abstract F.C.111).
7. Medley GF, Anderson RM, Cox DR, Billard L. Incubation period of AIDS in patients infected via blood transfusion. Nature 1987;328:719-721.
8. Ward JW, Bush TJ, Perkins HA, et al. The natural history of transfusion -associated infection with human immunodeficiency virus. N Engl J Med 1989;321:947-952.
9. Goedert JJ, Kessler CM, Aledort LM, et al. A prospective study of human immunodeficiency virus type 1 infection and the development of AIDS in subjects with hemophilia. N Engl J Med 1989;321:1141-1148.
10. Auger I, Thomas P, De Gruttola V, et al. Incubation periods for paediatric AIDS patients. Nature 1988;336:575-577.
11. Krasinski K, Borkowsky W, Holzman RS. Prognosis of human immunodeficiency virus in children and adolescents. Pediatr Infect Dis J 1989;8:216-220.
12. Goedert JJ, Biggar RJ, Melbye M, et al. Effect of T4 count and cofactors on the incidence of AIDS in homosexual men infected with human immunodeficiency virus. JAMA 1987;257:331-334.
13. Nicholson JKA, Spira TJ, Aloisio CH, et al. Serial determinations of HIV-1 titers in HIV-infected homosexual men: association of rising titers with CD4 T cell depletion and progression to AIDS. AIDS Res Hum Retroviruses 1989;5:205-215.
14. Lang W, Perkins H, Anderson RE, Royce R, Jewell N, Winkelstein W. Patterns of T lymphocyte changes with human immunodeficiency virus infection: from seroconversion to the development of AIDS. J Acquir Immune Defic Syndr 1989;2:63-69.

15. Lange MA, de Wolf F, Goudsmit J. Markers for progression of HIV infection. AIDS 1989;3(suppl.1):S153-160.
16. Taylor JM, Fahey JL, Detels R, Giorgi J. CD4 percentage, CD4 numbers, and CD4:CD8 ratio in HIV infection: which to choose and how to use. J Acquir Immune Defic Syndr 1989;2:114-124.
17. Masur H, Ognibene FP, Yarchoan R, et al. CD4 counts as predictors of opportunistic pneumonias in human immunodeficiency virus (HIV) infection. Ann Intern Med 1989;111:223-231.
18. Fahey JL, Taylor JMG, Detels R, et al. The prognostic value of cellular and serologic markers in infection with human immunodeficiency virus type 1. N Engl J Med 1990;322:166-172.
19. Fernandez-Cruz E, Desco M, Garcia Montes M, Longo N, Gonzalez B, Zabay JM. Immunological and serological markers predictive of progression to AIDS in a cohort of HIV-infected drug users. AIDS 1990;4:987-994.
20. NIH. State-of-the-art conference on azidothymidine therapy for early HIV infection. Am J Med 1990;89:335-344.
21. CDC. Guidelines for prophylaxis against *Pneumocystis carinii* pneumonia for persons infected with human immunodeficiency virus. MMWR 1989;38(no. S-5):1-9.
22. Fischl MA, Richman DD, Hansen, et al. The safety and efficacy of zidovudine (AZT) in the treatment of subjects with mildly symptomatic human immunodeficiency virus type 1 (HIV) infection: a double blind, placebo controlled trial. Ann Intern Med 1990;112:727-737.
23. Volberding PA, Lagakos SW, Koch MA, et al. Zidovudine in asymptomatic human immunodeficiency virus infection: a controlled trial in persons with fewer than 500 CD4-positive cells per cubic millimeter. N Engl J Med 1990;322:941.
24. CDC. Classification system for human T-lymphotropic virus type III/lymphadenopathy-associated virus infections. MMWR 1986;35:334-339.
25. Ho DD, Sarngadharan MG, Resnick L, et al. Primary human T-lymphotropic virus type III infection. Ann Intern Med 1985;103:880-883.
26. Tindall B, Cooper DA. Primary HIV infection: host responses and intervention strategies. AIDS 1991;5:1-14.
27. CDC. Risk for cervical disease in HIV-infected women- New York City. MMWR 1990;39:846-849.
28. Schäfer A, Friedman W, Mielke M, Schwartländer B, Koch M. The increased frequency of cervical dysplasia-neoplasia in women infected with the human immunodeficiency virus is related to the degree of immunosuppression. Am J Obstet Gynecol 1991;164:593-599.
29. CDC. Revision of the CDC surveillance case definition for acquired immunodeficiency syndrome. MMWR 1987;36:1-15S.
30. Valdiserri RO, Gross GD, Gerber AR, Schwartz RE, Hearn TL. Capacity of US labs to provide TLI in support of early HIV-1 intervention. Am J Public Health 1991;81:491-494.

31. Redfield RR, Wright DC, Tramont EC. The Walter Reed Staging Classification for HTLV-III/LAV infection. N Engl J Med 1986;314:131-132.
32. CDC. Guidelines for preventing the transmission of tuberculosis in health-care settings, with special focus on HIV-related issues. MMWR 1990;39(no. RR-17):1-29.
33. CDC. Purified protein derivative (PPD)-tuberculin anergy and HIV infection. MMWR 1991;40(RR-15):37-43.
34. WHO. Interim proposal for a WHO staging system for HIV infection and diseases. Weekly Epidemiol Record 1990;65:221-224.
35. Chaisson RE, Volberding PA. Clinical manifestations of HIV infection. In: Mandell GL, Douglas RG, Bennett JE, eds. Principles and practice of infectious diseases. New York, NY: Churchill Livingston, 1990:1061.
36. Haverkos HW, Gottlieb MS, Killen JY, Edelman R. Classification of HTLV-III/LAV-related diseases. J Infect Dis 1985;152:1905.
37. Zolla-Pazner S, DesJarlais DC, Friedman SR, et al. Nonrandom development of immunologic abnormalities after infection with human immunodeficiency virus: implications for immunologic classification of the disease. Proc Natl Acad Sci USA 1987;84:5404-5408.
38. Royce RA, Luckmann RS, Fusaro RE, Winkelstein W Jr. The natural history of HIV-1 infection: staging classifications of disease. AIDS 1991;5:355-364.
39. Justice AC, Feinstein AR, Wells CK. A new prognostic staging system for the acquired immunodeficiency syndrome. N Engl J Med 1989;320:1388-1393.
40. CDC. Surveillance for HIV infection-United States. MMWR 1990;39:853,859-861.
41. Ciesielski CA, Fleming PL, Berkelman RL. Changing trends in AIDS-indicator diseases in the U.S.-- Role of therapy and prophylaxis? 31st Interscience Conference on Antimicrobial Agents and Chemotherapy, Chicago, Illinois. 1991:141(Abstract 254).
42. Brookmeyer R. Reconstruction and future trends of the AIDS epidemic in the United States. Science 1991;253:37-42
43. Farizo K, Buehler J, Chamberland M, et al. CD4 lymphocytes and the spectrum of disease in HIV infection. VII International Conference on AIDS, Florence, Italy. 1991;1:296(Abstract M.B.2457).
44. Hopkins S, Lafferty W, Honey J, Hurlich M. Trends in the outpatient diagnosis of AIDS: implications for epidemiologic analysis and surveillance. V International Conference on AIDS, Montreal, Canada. 1989:111(Abstract T.A.P.72).
45. Modesitt S, Espenlaub C, Klockner R, Fleming D. AIDS cases diagnosed as outpatients. VI International Conference on AIDS, San Francisco, California. 1990;1:309(Abstract Th.C.736).
46. CDC. HIV prevalence estimates and AIDS case projection for the United States: report based upon a workshop. MMWR 1990;39(No. RR-16).

47.   Rhoads JL, Wright C, Redfield RR, Burke DS. Chronic vaginal candidiasis in women with human immunodeficiency virus infection. JAMA 1987;257:3105-3107.

48.   Mayer KH, Carpenter CCJ, Stein M, et al. The clinical spectrum of illness among HIV infected New England women. 31st Interscience Conference on Antimicrobial Agents and Chemotherapy, Chicago, Illinois. 1991:141(Abstract 253).

49.   Greenberg AE, Thomas PA, Landesman SH, et al. The spectrum of HIV-related disease among outpatients in New York City. VII International Conference on AIDS, Florence, Italy. 1991;1:296(Abstract M.B.2456).

50.   Kessler HA, Landay A, Pottage JC, Benson CA. Absolute number versus percentage of T-helper lymphocytes in human immunodeficiency virus infection. J Infect Dis 1990;161:356-357.

Table 1. 1992 Revised Classification System for HIV Infection and Expanded AIDS
Surveillance Case Definition for Adolescents and Adults*

	CLINICAL CATEGORIES		
CD4+ CELL CATEGORIES	(A) Asymptomatic, or PGL**	(B) Symptomatic, not (A) or (C) conditions	(C) AIDS-indicator conditions***
(1) ≥500/mm³	A1	B1	C1
(2) 200-499/mm³	A2	B2	C2
(3) <200/mm³ AIDS-indicator cell count	A3	B3	C3

* The shaded cells illustrate the expansion of the AIDS surveillance case definition. Persons
with AIDS-indicator conditions (Category C) are currently reportable to the health department in
every state and U.S. territory. In addition to persons with clinical category C conditions
(categories C1, C2, and C3), persons with CD4+ lymphocyte counts of less than 200/mm³
(categories A3 or B3) will also be reportable as AIDS cases in the United States and Territories,
effective April 1, 1992.

** PGL = persistent generalized lymphadenopathy. Clinical category A includes acute
(primary) HIV infection.

*** See appendix I.

APPENDIX I

List of conditions in the 1987 AIDS surveillance case definition:[29]

- Candidiasis of bronchi, trachea, or lungs
- Candidiasis, esophageal
- Coccidioidomycosis, disseminated or extrapulmonary
- Cryptococcosis, extrapulmonary
- Cryptosporidiosis, chronic intestinal (> 1 month duration)
- Cytomegalovirus disease (other than liver, spleen, or nodes)
- Cytomegalovirus retinitis (with loss of vision)
- HIV encephalopathy
- Herpes simplex: chronic ulcer(s) (> 1 month duration); or bronchitis, pneumonitis, or esophagitis
- Histoplasmosis, disseminated or extrapulmonary
- Isosporiasis, chronic intestinal (> 1 month duration)
- Kaposi's sarcoma
- Lymphoma, Burkitt's (or equivalent term)
- Lymphoma, immunoblastic (or equivalent term)
- Lymphoma, primary in brain
- *Mycobacterium avium complex* or *M. kansasii*, disseminated or extrapulmonary
- *Mycobacterium tuberculosis*, disseminated or extrapulmonary
- *Mycobacterium*, other species or unidentified species, disseminated or extrapulmonary
- *Pneumocystis carinii* pneumonia
- Progressive multifocal leukoencephalopathy
- Salmonella septicemia, recurrent
- Toxoplasmosis of brain
- Wasting syndrome due to HIV

APPENDIX II

Equivalences for CD4$^+$ Lymphocyte Count and Percent of Total Lymphocytes

Compared with the absolute CD4$^+$ lymphocyte count, the CD4$^+$ percent of total lymphocytes is less subject to variation on repeated measurements.[16,50] However, data correlating natural history of HIV infection with the CD4$^+$ percent of total lymphocytes have not been as consistently available as data on absolute CD4$^+$ lymphocyte counts.[12-14,16-17,19,31] Therefore, the revised classification system is based on CD4$^+$ lymphocyte counts. When the count is not obtainable, the CD4$^+$ percent of total lymphocytes may be used.

The equivalences in the following table were derived from analyses of more than 15,500 lymphocyte subset determinations from seven different sources: one multicenter study of diseases in HIV-infected adolescents and adults, and six laboratories (2 commercial, 1 research, and 3 university-based). The six laboratories are involved in proficiency testing programs for lymphocyte subset determinations. In the analyses, concordance was defined as the proportion of patients classified as having a CD4$^+$ lymphocyte count in a particular range among patients with a given CD4$^+$ percent of total lymphocytes. A threshold value of the CD4$^+$ percent of total lymphocytes was calculated to obtain optimal concordance with each stratifying value of the CD4$^+$ lymphocyte counts (i.e., <200/mm^3 and ≥ 500/mm^3). The thresholds for the CD4$^+$ percent of total lymphocytes that best correlated with a CD4$^+$ lymphocyte count of <200/mm^3 varied minimally among the seven data sources (range 13%-14%, median 13%, mean 13.4%). The average concordance for a CD4$^+$ percent of <14% and a CD4$^+$ lymphocyte count of <200/mm^3 was 90.2%. The threshold for the CD4$^+$ percent of total lymphocytes most concordant with CD4$^+$ lymphocyte counts of ≥ 500/mm^3 varied more widely among the seven data sources (range 22.5%-35%, median 29%, mean 29.1%). This wide range of percentages optimally concordant with ≥ 500/mm^3 CD4$^+$ lymphocytes makes the concordance at this stratifying value less certain. The average concordance for a CD4$^+$ percent of ≥ 29 percent and a CD4$^+$ lymphocyte count of ≥ 500/mm^3 was 85 percent (CDC, unpublished data). Clinicians and other practitioners must recognize that these suggested equivalences may not always correspond with values observed in individual patients.

Laboratory category	CD4$^+$ cells/mm^3	CD4$^+$ percent of total lymphocytes
(1)	$\geq$ 500	$\geq$ 29
(2)	200 - 499	14 - 28
(3)	< 200	< 14

HIV/AIDS and the World

The following are statistics from the World Health Organization (WHO)[1] concerning the spread of AIDS/HIV on a global scale.

As of January 1992, 10–12 million people—including 1 million children—were infected with HIV, the virus that causes AIDS.

WHO predicts that AIDS will shortly be the leading cause of premature death in many Western cities; up to 10 million African children will be orphaned by AIDS by the end of the 1990s.

About 90 percent of new infections are the result of heterosexual transmission.

By the year 2000, the total number of cases may rise to 40 million. Of these, 90 percent will be in developing countries in sub-Saharan Africa, South and Southeast Asia, Latin America, and the Caribbean.

On a worldwide basis, 70 percent of those infected are female.

WHO estimates that 2 million cases of AIDS have occurred since the beginning of the epidemic.

Another report views these global numbers as being too conservative. A mid-1992 report of the Global AIDS Policy Coalition[2] found that:

Since 1981, the AIDS pandemic has increased more than 100-fold. In early 1992, at least 12.9 million people in the world—including 7.1 million men, 4.7 million women, and 1.1 million children—had HIV infection, compared to about 100,000 people in 1981.

About 2.6 million of the currently infected have developed AIDS, and nearly 2.5 million have died.

The spread of HIV has not been halted in any nation or community and continues to increase. There will be an estimated 40,000–80,000 new infections in the United States during 1992, and more than 75,000 new infections in Europe. The number of infected Africans has tripled in five years.

The worldwide pandemic will have a growing impact. An estimated 3.8 million people will be infected from 1992 to 1995, more than the total number of people who developed the disease in the preceding decade. By the year 2000, the number infected may be ten times the 1992 figures.

Financial resources to fight AIDS are slowing. Less than $50 million went to the World Health Organization in 1991, a 40 percent drop in funds from 1990 and the first decline since the epidemic began.

There is increasing polarization in finances, treatment, prevention, and policy between developed countries and less developed countries. About 6 percent of the total funds expended worldwide in 1990–1991 went to areas of the world accounting for 80 percent of HIV infections.

In North America, about $2.70 per person was spent on prevention in 1991; about $1.18 was spent in Europe. In sub-Saharan Africa, 7 cents per person was spent on prevention; a mere 3 cents was spent in Latin America.

Travel and immigration restrictions exist in over 50 countries, including the United States.

Access to health care remains a privilege in many poor countries, and unscreened blood is often the norm.

Epidemiologists have identified three global patterns for the spread of HIV:

1. Pattern I countries (United States, some western European countries, some Central American countries, Canada, New Zealand, and some countries in southern Africa): cases are disproportionately male, and perinatal transmission is low.
2. Pattern II countries (central, eastern, and some southern African countries; most of the Caribbean): male and female cases are approximately equal, and transmission rates from male to female and female to male are about even.
3. Pattern III countries (eastern Europe, northern Africa, most of Asia, and the Middle East): relatively few cases to date.

The primary modes of transmission on a global basis are:

- Blood transfusion: 3–5 percent.
- Perinatal: 5–10 percent.
- Sexual intercourse: 70–80 percent. Of these cases, vaginal transmission accounts for 60–70 percent and anal transmission is responsible for 5–10 percent.
- IV drug use: 5–10 percent.
- Health care needlesticks, etc.: less than 0.01 percent.

Table 4-1 presents estimates for worldwide cases of HIV/AIDS, broken down by region.

TABLE 4-1
Estimated Cases of HIV/AIDS Worldwide

	HIV		AIDS	
	1992	1995	1992	1995
North America	1,167,000	1,495,000	257,500	534,000
Western Europe	718,000	1,186,000	99,000	279,500
Australia/Oceania	28,000	40,000	4,500	1,500
Latin America	995,000	1,407,000	173,000	417,500
Sub-Saharan Africa	7,803,000	11,449,000	1,367,000	3,277,500
Caribbean	310,000	474,000	43,000	121,000
Eastern Europe	27,000	44,000	2,500	9,500
Southeastern Mediterranean	35,000	59,000	3,500	12,000
Northeast Asia	41,000	80,000	3,500	12,000
Southeast Asia	675,000	1,220,000	65,000	240,500
Total	11,799,000	17,454,000	2,018,500	4,918,000

Source: Lawrence K. Altman, "Researchers Report Much Grimmer AIDS Outlook," *New York Times*, 4 June 1992, page A-I.

HIV/AIDS and the Nation

Every day, more than 100 people in the United States die of AIDS, or 1 every 15 minutes.[3]

CDC estimates that 111,000–122,000 people are living with AIDS in the United States; CDC's projection for 1993 is 151,000–225,000.[4] CDC also estimates that 1 adult male out of every 100 in the United States is HIV infected and that 1 adult female out of every 600 is.[5]

From June 1981 (when the first U.S. AIDS cases were reported) through December 1987, 50,000 U.S. cases were reported to CDC. Less than 2 years later—in August 1989—the total reported cases had risen to 100,000. The second 100,000 cases were reported for the period September 1989–November 1991. The first 100,000 cases occurred over a period of slightly more than 8 years, and the second 100,000 cases came in slightly over 2 years.[6]

By June 30, 1992, the total number of diagnosed cases since the beginning of the U.S. epidemic was 230,179. Reported deaths totaled 152,153.

Funding

Federal Funding in the Early Years[7]

In fiscal year 1981 (FY 81), the National Institutes of Health (NIH) spent about $3,225 per death on AIDS, and $8,991 in FY 82. In FY 82, the National Heart, Lung, and Blood Institute spent a total of $5,000 on AIDS.

Legionnaire's disease is a form of pneumonia that killed 29 people at an American Legion meeting in Philadelphia in 1976. It was later proven to have been caused by an organism that had been present for years. Spending by NIH on Legionnaire's disease in FY 82 was $34,841 per death.

Toxic shock syndrome was solved by FY 82, but NIH spent $36,100 per death on it that year.

Recent Funding Facts

The Ryan White Comprehensive AIDS Resources Emergency (CARE) Act of 1990 made funding available to cities hit hardest by the epidemic. Cities that had reported 2,000 or more AIDS cases to CDC or that had a cumulative incidence of at least 25 cases per 100,000 cases are eligible for funding to expand social services for HIV-infected people.

Cities receiving the most in funding were New York City, $17.6 million; San Francisco, $6.3 million; Los Angeles, $3.9 million; and Newark, New Jersey, $2.1 million.

Cities receiving $1–2 million were Houston; Chicago; Washington, D.C.; Boston; Miami; and Philadelphia.

Cities receiving less than $1 million were Atlanta; Fort Lauderdale, Florida; Jersey City, New Jersey; San Diego; San Juan, Puerto Rico; and Dallas.

Tables 4.2 and 4.3 tabulate HIV/AIDS funding by the National Institutes of Health (NIH) and the Centers for Disease Control (CDC), respectively.

TABLE 4-2
National Institutes of Health (NIH)* HIV/AIDS Funding,**
FY 82–91

FY 82: $3.4 million	FY 87: $260.9 million
FY 83: $21.7 million	FY 88: $473.3 million
FY 84: $44.1 million	FY 89: $602.3 million
FY 85: $63.7 million	FY 90: $740.5 million
FY 86: $134.7 million	FY 91: $804.6 million (est.)

* NIH is one of several federal agencies expending funds on HIV/AIDS.

** Spending is for research grants, research training, research and development, intramural research, research management and support, and miscellaneous spending (National Library of Medicine, NIH director's office, etc.).

Source: *NIH AIDS Program Data Book* (Washington, DC: Institute of Medicine, 1991).

TABLE 4-3
Centers for Disease Control (CDC)* HIV/AIDS Funding, FY 81–91

FY 81: $200,000	FY 87: $136 million
FY 82: $2 million	FY 88: $304.9 million
FY 83: $6.2 million	FY 89: $377.6 million
FY 84: $13.7 million	FY 90: $442.8 million
FY 85: $33.3 million	FY 91: $508.8 million
FY 86: $62.1 million	

* CDC is one of several federal agencies expending funds on HIV/AIDS.

Source: *CDC HIV/AIDS Prevention Fact Book 1990* (Atlanta: Centers for Disease Control, 1990).

Federal Spending in 1991

According to the *CDC HIV/AIDS Prevention Fact Book 1990* (Atlanta: Centers for Disease Control, 1990), the federal government spent about $1.6 billion in FY 90 on all HIV/AIDS-related activities in the Public Health Service. This figure includes:

- National Institutes of Health (NIH): $743.5 million, or 46.9 percent
- Centers for Disease Control (CDC): $442.8 million, or 28 percent
- Alcohol, Drug Abuse, and Mental Health Administration (ADAMHA): $214.6 million, or 13.5 percent
- Health Resources and Services Administration (HRSA): $112.5 million, or 7.1 percent
- Food and Drug Administration (FDA): $56.2 million, or 3.5 percent
- Occupational Safety and Health Administration (OSHA): $16.2 million, or 1 percent

State Spending on HIV/AIDS

Table 4-4 shows the ten highest-ranking states according to cumulative HIV/AIDS caseload as of June 1991. Table 4-5 lists the top ten states by total state fund spending for fiscal year 1991; Table 4-6 ranks the top ten states by per capita state spending for the same time period.

TABLE 4-4
States Ranked by Cumulative HIV/AIDS Caseload, June 1991

1. New York	6. Illinois
2. California	7. Pennsylvania
3. Florida	8. Georgia
4. Texas	9. Massachusetts
5. New Jersey	10. Maryland

Source: "National Survey of State-Only HIV/AIDS Funds," Intergovernmental AIDS Reports (Washington, DC: AIDS Policy Project, Intergovernmental Health Policy Project, November 1991), 12.

TABLE 4-5
States Ranked by Total Spending of Solely State Funds, FY 91

1. New York	$90,492,958
2. California	42,738,000
3. Florida	20,993,691
4. Massachusetts	18,241,650
5. Michigan	16,220,630
6. Texas	14,685,276
7. New Jersey	14,446,000
8. Illinois	12,623,195
9. Louisiana	12,256,986
10. Maryland	9,099,006

Source: "National Survey of State-Only HIV/AIDS Funds," Intergovernmental AIDS Reports (Washington, DC: AIDS Policy Project, Intergovernmental Health Policy Project, November 1991), 9.

TABLE 4-6
States Ranked by Per Capita Spending of Solely State Funds, FY 91

1. District of Columbia	$10.92
2. New York	5.03
3. Hawaii	4.16
4. Massachusetts	3.03
5. Louisiana	2.90
6. Connecticut	2.48
7. Maryland	1.90
8. New Jersey	1.84
9. Washington	1.82
10. Michigan	1.75

Source: "National Survey of State-Only HIV/AIDS Funds," Intergovernmental AIDS Reports (Washington, DC: AIDS Policy Project, Intergovernmental Health Policy Project, November 1991), 9.

Health Care Costs and Concerns

The annual direct medical cost for an individual with AIDS was estimated to be $32,000 in 1990. Indirect costs of the HIV epidemic include efforts at prevention and education, blood supply screening, and necessary HIV/AIDS training and education for health care professionals.[8]

Early intervention for an HIV-infected person was estimated in 1990 to cost about $6,000.[9] Much of the cost for this and

AIDS care in general—possibly as much as 90 percent of the cost—is due to high drug costs.[10]

About 29 percent of people with AIDS are covered by private health insurance; about 40 percent are covered by Medicaid, including 90 percent of pediatric cases. Just 2 percent are covered by Medicare. The balance—29 percent—have no insurance.[11]

Costs for HIV care in the future are estimated to amount to about 2 percent of total U.S. health care expenditures.[12]

Who Gets HIV/AIDS, and How Do They Get It?

Tables 4-7 and 4-8 show the percentages of people with case-definition AIDS in the United States who fall into different categories by race/ethnicity and method of transmission of HIV. For instance, according to the third column in Table 4-7, 76 percent of all cases among white people are transmitted by male to male sexual contact, whereas this mode accounts for 58 percent of total cases (far left column, Table 4-7). The numbers reflect the diagnosed AIDS cases reported to the Centers for Disease Control through June 1992; the numbers do not reflect all the persons with HIV.

Facts on HIV Testing

More than 1.3 million people were given the HIV antibody test at public testing programs in 1990, according to the Centers for Disease Control. Test sites included prisons, drug treatment centers, and health clinics. Overall, about 3.7 percent of the tests were positive. This figure represents a drop from 1988 positive test results, because of the increased number of low-risk persons who have been tested. Heterosexuals who reported a risk factor accounted for more than 40 percent of the tests.

The highest rate of infection was in prisons, where 5.8 percent of the tests were positive. The figures do not represent tests administered in private doctors' offices, hospitals, blood centers, military installations, or other sites.

In 1990, the Centers for Disease Control reported infection rates of 0.7 percent at large urban hospitals, 0.1 percent in military tests, and 0.008 percent at American Red Cross blood centers.

TABLE 4-7
Race/Ethnicity of Reported Adult/Adolescent AIDS Cases

Mode*	All Cases	White, Not Hispanic	Black, Not Hispanic	Hispanic	Asian/ Pacific Islander	Am. Indian/ Alaskan Native
1	58%	76%	35%	40%	74%	54%
2	23%	9%	39%	40%	4%	19%
3	6%	7%	6%	6%	2%	14%
4	1%	1%	0%	0%	1%	2%
5	6%	2%	13%	7%	4%	3%
6	2%	3%	1%	1%	7%	2%
7	4%	3%	6%	5%	7%	6%

* Modes of transmission are:
1. Male to male sexual contact
2. Intravenous (IV) drug use
3. Male to male sexual contact plus IV drug use
4. Hemophilia/coagulation disorder
5. Heterosexual contact
   a. Sex with IV drug user
   b. Sex with bisexual male
   c. Sex with person with hemophilia
   d. Born in country where transmission is mainly heterosexual
   e. Sex with person from country where transmission is mainly heterosexual
   f. Sex with transfusion recipient with HIV infection
   g. Sex with HIV-infected person, risk not specified
6. Recipient of blood transfusion, blood components, or tissue
7. Other/undetermined

Source: Centers for Disease Control. *HIV/AIDS Surveillance Report Year-End Edition*, January 1992: 9.

TABLE 4-8
Race/Ethnicity of Reported Pediatric[a] AIDS Cases

Mode[b]	All Cases	White, Not Hispanic	Black, Not Hispanic	Hispanic	Asian/ Pacific Islander	Am. Indian/ Alaskan Native
1	5%	15%	1%	3%	16%	
2	85%	64%	93%	87%	47%	100%
3	8%	19%	3%	7%	37%	
4	3%	2%	3%	2%		

[a] "Pediatric" refers to children under 13 years of age
[b] Modes of transmission are:
1. Hemophilia/coagulation disorder
2. Mother with/at-risk for HIV infection
   a. IV drug use
   b. Sex with IV drug user
   c. Sex with bisexual male
   d. Sex with person with hemophilia
   e. Born in country where transmission is mainly heterosexual
   f. Sex with person born in country where transmission is mainly heterosexual
   g. Sex with transfusion recipient
   h. Sex with HIV-infected person, risk not specified
   i. Receipt of blood transfusion, blood components, or tissue
   j. Has HIV infection, risk not specified
3. Receipt of blood transfusion, blood components, or tissue
4. Undetermined

Source: Centers for Disease Control, *HIV/AIDS Surveillance Report* , July 1992: 9.

Nationally, the CDC estimates that about 1 million people are HIV infected but it is believed that only about 12 percent of those 1 million know of their infection.

What Diseases Strike People with AIDS?

Table 4-9 shows some of the different diseases most commonly found in adults and children with AIDS in 1991 and reported to the Centers for Disease Control (CDC). These diseases are frequently referred to as opportunistic infections. The specific diseases and conditions listed are indicative of severe immune suppression related to infection with HIV. Some patients have more than one of the diseases listed.

HIV/AIDS and Tuberculosis

Tuberculosis (TB) is listed in Table 4-9 as one of the diseases that strikes people with HIV/AIDS. For many years, tuberculosis was thought to be a disease of the past; U.S. cases were declining an average of 5 percent per year until 1985.[13] But recent evidence from CDC shows that tuberculosis is rising at alarming rates. Further, cases of Drug-Resistant TB (DR-TB) and Multi–Drug Resistant TB (MDR-TB) are increasing at alarming rates and pose dangers for both those infected and those working with them—whether health care workers, shelter workers, corrections officials, or others in close proximity. These forms of TB have appeared in 17 states since 1989; they are fatal 50–80 percent of the time. They are sometimes the result of a patient abandoning medication before completing a full and effective course of treatment, which usually takes 6 months or more. In 13 states with MDR-TB cases in early 1991, 90 percent involved people with HIV or AIDS.[14]

Since 1988, TB cases have been rising. In 1990, 25,701 cases were reported, an increase of 9.4 percent over 1989 and the largest annual increase since 1953. The largest increase was in the 25–44 age group; CDC attributes this increase to the increase in HIV/AIDS cases. The 1989 total was 23,495 cases, an increase of 4.7 percent.[15]

Thirty-one states reported increases in 1990; the largest increases were in New York, California, and Texas. Cities with the largest increases were New York City, Los Angeles, and Oakland, California.[16]

States reporting the highest numbers of AIDS cases to CDC have shown the highest increases in TB cases among males 25–44 years old, the group that also accounted for 68.4 percent of all AIDS cases in 1990.[17]

TABLE 4-9
Diseases Common in Persons with AIDS (PWAs)

Indicator Disease	Adults/Adolescents	Children under 13
Bacterial infections, multiple or recurrent	N/A[a]	18%
Candiasis of bronchi, trachan, lungs	2%	5%
Candidiasis of esophagus	15%	14%
Coccidioidomycosis	0%	0%
Cryptococcosis	5%	0%
Cryptosporidiosis	2%	3%
Cytomegalovirus disease	4%	5%
Cytomegalovirus retinitis	4%	0%
HIV encephalopathy (dementia)	6%	14%
Herpes simplex	4%	2%
Histoplasmosis	1%	0%
Isosporiasis	0%	0%
Kaposi's sarcoma	10%	0%
Lymphoid interstitial pneumonia	N/A[a]	21%
Lymphoma, Burkitt's	1%	1%
Lymphoma, immunoblastic	2%	0%
Lymphoma, primary in brain	1%	0%
Mycobacterium avium	6%	3%
M. tuberculosis	3%	1%
Mycobacterial disease	2%	0%
Pneumocystis carinii pneumonia (PCP)	46%	33%
Progressive multifocal leukoencephalopathy	1%	0%
Salmonella septicemia	0%	N/A[b]
Toxoplasmosis of brain	5%	1%
HIV wasting syndrome	19%	12%

[a] Not an indicator of AIDS in adults/adolescents
[b] Included in "Bacterial infections"

Source: Centers for Disease Control, *HIV/AIDS Surveillance Report Year-End Edition*, January 1992: 16.

In July 1991, CDC reported outbreaks of Multi–Drug Resistant TB (MDR-TB) in four hospitals in Florida and New York City.[18] Other outbreaks of TB were reported in 1991 in the New York State prison system and the shelter system, both of which provide the optimum environment for TB to flourish: crowded and often unsanitary conditions, poor ventilation, little or no health care, poor residents with little health care history, and numbers of people at significant risk for HIV/AIDS.

How Many People Are Dying from AIDS Each Year?

Table 4-10 shows the numbers of adult and pediatric AIDS deaths reported to the Centers for Disease Control during each year since the recorded beginning of the disease in the United States.

TABLE 4-10
Number of AIDS Deaths Each Year

Year	Adults/Adolescents	Children Under Age 13
1991	28,953	199
1990	27,757	364
1989	26,271	347
1988	19,920	303
1987	15,483	282
1986	11,611	156
1985	6,686	114
1984	3,354	49
1983	1,454	29
1982	441	13
1981	126	9
Pre-1981	30	1
Total*	150,114	2,039

* Death totals include 193 adults/adolescents and 4 children known to have died but whose dates of death are unknown.

Source: Centers for Disease Control, *HIV/AIDS Surveillance Report,* July 1992: 13.

HIV/AIDS and the States

How States Are Affected by AIDS

Following are some figures reflecting AIDS cases in the states. These figures do not give any indication of how many people have HIV infection or conditions short of CDC-defined AIDS.

Highest annual number of adult/adolescent AIDS cases reported in 1991: New York State (8,164).[19]

Lowest number of adult/adolescent AIDS cases reported in 1991: South Dakota (3).[20]

Highest annual rate of AIDS cases per 100,000 population in 1991: District of Columbia (120.4); in 1990: District of Columbia (121.9).[21]

Lowest annual rate of AIDS cases per 100,000 population in 1991: South Dakota (0.4); in 1990: North Dakota (0.3).[22]

Highest number of pediatric AIDS cases reported in 1991: New York State (953); in 1990: New York State (201).[23]

States with no pediatric AIDS cases reported in 1990: Alaska, Delaware, Hawaii, Idaho, Kansas, North Dakota, South Dakota, Wyoming; in 1991: North Dakota, Wyoming.[24]

How Many People Have AIDS in Each State?

Table 4-11 shows the number of AIDS cases each state or other jurisdiction reported to the Centers for Disease Control in 1990 and 1991; it also shows the rate of cases in each state per 100,000 people.

HIV/AIDS and State Law, Selected Years

Table 4-12 shows the number of states passing laws on a specific topic during the legislative year indicated. Table 4-13 lists yearly totals for HIV/AIDS laws proposed and passed between 1983 and 1991.

Needle Exchange Programs in the States

Needle exchange programs offer drug users a chance to cut down on the spread of HIV by trading in used syringes for clean ones. Critics argue, however, that distributing drug-use equipment in this way assists people in acting illegally and immorally. Possession of needles is illegal without a prescription in 11 states. Needle exchange programs have been tried in a number of communities, however; only some are legally sanctioned through the suspension of laws making possession illegal. The following list of such exchange programs is based on Mireya Navarro's "New York City Resurrects Plan on Needle Swap," *New York Times,* 5 May 1992: page A-1).

Marin County, CA (not legal)

Oakland, CA (not legal)

Sacramento, CA (not legal)

San Francisco, CA (not legal)

San Mateo, CA (not legal)

Santa Clara, CA (not legal)

Santa Cruz, CA (not legal)

Boulder, CO (legal)

New Haven, CT (legal)

Honolulu, HI (legal)

Chicago, IL (not legal)

Boston, MA (not legal)

Baltimore, MD (not legal)

New York, NY (proposed legal program)

Portland, OR (legal)

Philadelphia, PA (not legal)

Seattle, WA (legal)

Spokane, WA (legal)

Tacoma, WA (legal)

Vancouver, WA (legal)

HIV/AIDS and Specific Populations

Women and HIV/AIDS

The number of AIDS cases reported in U.S. women was 24,323 as of June 1992, or 10.7 percent of the total.[25] This figure represents a steady increase in cases in women, as shown by the following figures:

1989: 9 percent

1983: 6.8 percent

1981: 3 percent

TABLE 4-7
AIDS Cases by State

State	1991 Cases	1991 Rate	1990 Cases	1990 Rate
Alabama	374	9.2	238	5.9
Alaska	19	3.4	24	4.4
Arizona	283	7.5	311	8.5
Arkansas	196	8.3	209	8.9
California	7,709	25.4	7,342	24.7
Colorado	435	13.0	360	10.9
Connecticut	564	17.1	423	12.9
Delaware	88	13.1	93	14.0
District of Columbia	727	120.4	740	121.9
Florida	5,551	41.9	4,021	31.1
Georgia	1,434	21.8	1,227	18.9
Hawaii	200	17.8	156	14.1
Idaho	32	3.2	28	2.8
Illinois	1,591	13.9	1,276	11.2
Indiana	315	5.7	292	5.3
Iowa	82	3.0	68	2.4
Kansas	101	4.1	137	5.5
Kentucky	166	4.5	190	5.2
Louisiana	757	17.9	704	16.7
Maine	49	4.0	66	5.4
Maryland	977	20.2	994	20.8
Massachusetts	970	16.0	842	14.0
Michigan	584	6.3	577	6.2
Minnesota	216	4.9	203	4.6
Mississippi	199	7.7	275	10.7
Missouri	655	12.8	582	11.4
Montana	30	3.7	17	2.1
Nebraska	63	4.0	584	3.73
Nevada	264	21.3	190	15.8
New Hampshire	51	4.5	65	5.9
New Jersey	2,305	29.7	2,462	31.8
New Mexico	111	7.2	109	7.2
New York	8,164	45.3	8,390	46.6
North Carolina	590	8.8	565	8.5
North Dakota	4	0.6	2	0.3
Ohio	600	5.5	665	6.1
Oklahoma	192	6.1	203	6.5
Oregon	257	9.0	336	11.8
Pennsylvania	1,222	10.3	1,197	10.0
Rhode Island	93	9.2	88	8.8
South Carolina	331	9.4	353	10.1
South Dakota	3	0.4	9	1.3
Tennessee	350	7.1	340	7.0
Texas	3,087	17.9	3,342	19.7
Utah	135	7.7	98	5.7
Vermont	17	3.0	22	3.9
Virginia	680	10.8	743	12.0
Washington	556	11.3	710	14.6
West Virginia	62	3.5	64	3.6
Wisconsin	214	4.4	209	4.3
Wyoming	17	3.8	5	1.1
States Total	**43,672**	**17.2**	**41,616**	**16.7**
Guam	3	2.2	2	1.5
Pacific Islands	0	0	1	0.4
Puerto Rico	1,810	50.9	1,722	48.9
Virgin Islands	21	20.5	11	10.8
Grand Total	**45,506**	**17.8**	**43,352**	**17.2**

TABLE 4-8
HIV/AIDS and State Law

Topic	Law(s) Passed during		
	1989	1990	1991
Discrimination	25	11	3
Education/Prevention	25	7	9
Notification of school officials	3	1	2
School attendance	4	1	0
Insurance: Practices and coverage	28	22	8
Alternative care facilities	8	9	5
Worker exposure and notification	24	9	5
Public health laws	18	4	3
HIV reporting	15	4	5
Studies	29	21	17
Confidentiality/Testing disclosure	30	22	15
Contact/partner reports	11	6	4
Counseling information	11	1	3
Premarital tests	3	1	0
Prisoner testing	9	6	
Prostitute/sex crime tests	11	9	9
Willful exposure	10	2	2
Informed consent	20	10	10

Sources: "A Summary of AIDS Laws from the 1989 Legislative Session" (Washington, DC: AIDS Policy Project, Intergovernmental Health Policy Project, April 1990); "A Summary of HIV/AIDS Laws from the 1990 State Legislative Sessions" (Washington, DC: AIDS Policy Project, Intergovernmental Health Policy Project, January 1991); "A Summary of HIV/AIDS Laws from the 1991 State Legislative Session" (Washington, DC: AIDS Policy Project, Intergovernmental Health Policy Project, January 1992).

TABLE 4-9
State HIV/AIDS Laws Introduced and Passed 1983–1990

Year(s)	Introduced	Passed
1983–1985	115	21
1986	220	49
1987	585	116
1988	662	136
1989	571	149
1990	292	61
1991	577	105

Sources: "AIDS Bills Introduced and Passed," Intergovernmental AIDS Reports (Washington, DC: AIDS Policy Project, Intergovernmental Health Policy Project, July 1990); "A Summary of HIV/AIDS Laws from the 1991 State Legislative Session" (Washington, DC: AIDS Policy Project, January 1992).

New York State, California, Florida, and New Jersey have the highest numbers of cases for both women and men.

Heterosexual transmission is rapidly rising for women. As of June 1992, it represented 8,524 cases, or 35 percent of the women's total.[26] This is a steady increase over time, as shown by the following:

1989: 31 percent

1986: 26 percent

1984: 17 percent

1982: 14 percent

About 25 percent of the U.S. population is made up of racial and ethnic minorities, yet 75 percent of women with AIDS are from minority groups: African-American, 53 percent; Hispanic, 21 percent; Asian, 0.5 percent; and Native American, 0.2 percent. White women account for only 25 percent of the cases.

Within the penal system, most female prisoners are mothers (80 percent), and most are single mothers (70 percent).[27] Most are young, between 20 and 34 years of age. According to the Bureau of Justice Statistics, 25 percent of women in the corrections system are pregnant or have recently given birth. Thus, not only are women at-risk from a lack of general health care in prisons, but also they are especially at-risk if they are HIV infected, as are their children on the outside. Just as with unincarcerated HIV-infected women, the children of these women may become orphans and/or HIV/AIDS statistics themselves.

Pediatric HIV/AIDS

In December 1982, CDC reported the first cases of children with HIV/AIDS. In its first report, 2 of the children were hemophiliacs and 1 had received a blood transfusion. In a second report just a few weeks later, CDC reported on 4 infants with opportunistic infections and immune system deficiencies. A short while later, CDC adopted a reporting category of "pediatric AIDS"; this category extends to age 13.

About 85 percent of all pediatric AIDS cases are related to the exposure to HIV of the mother. This can occur through either IV drug use or sex with an IV drug user or other person who is infected with HIV.

A diagnosis of pediatric AIDS requires documentation of an opportunistic infection (such as PCP) or an AIDS-related malignancy (such as Kaposi's sarcoma). Congenital disorders and other infections must be ruled out. In addition, a diagnosis is made if either lymphocytic interstitial pneumonia or one of the indicator diseases used for adults is present.

Higher numbers of pediatric HIV/AIDS cases have been re-ported among black and Hispanic children, who represent a dispro-portionate percentage of the cases. Many cases are transmitted perinatally; a few cases have been reported where transmission occurred through sexual abuse by infected males.

Some differences in pediatric AIDS were noticed almost as soon as an official category was established for it. The presence of a mother's antibodies in her infant's system postponed conclusive diagnosis of serostatus to age 15–18 months. Some opportunistic infections, such as Kaposi's sarcoma (KS), were not seen very often. Others, such as lymphocytic interstitial pneumonia, were most com-monly seen in children. There was a more rapid onset of symptoms among children, and developmental difficulties were seen in chil-dren who tested positive for HIV.

In addition, with maternal seropositivity or full-blown AIDS present, and with drug use often a factor, there was a rapid increase in the number of "boarder babies" living in hospitals because they had no homes to go to. Foster homes for HIV-positive children were hard to find. However, public sympathy toward infected infants was demonstrably higher than for adults, who were regarded as having caused their own illness through their sexual behavior or drug use.

New York City estimates that 20,000 children will be orphaned as a result of the epidemic over the next few years, meaning that these children—who may themselves be infected—must be cared for by relatives or placed in foster homes.[28]

Racial/Ethnic Minority Groups and HIV/AIDS

With the spread of HIV to intravenous drug users and their sexual partners and to heterosexuals, black and Hispanic people have come to represent an increasing percentage of the total caseload. Table 4-14 shows what percentage of the total U.S. population is represented by each of the major racial/ethnic groups and what percentage of all reported AIDS cases are in that group.

HIV/AIDS and Adolescents

At what age does the possibility of HIV transmission present itself in the life of an adolescent or other young person? According to a 1990 report by the Alan Guttmacher Institute in New York City and the Urban Institute in Washington, D.C., both young men and young women are more likely to be sexually experienced at a younger age than were their peers of even the early 1980s. According to the report,half of the young women had their first sexual experience by age 17, and half of the young men first had sex by age 16. Of 19-year-olds, 3 out of 4 unmarried women and 5 out of 6 unmarried men had already had sex.[29]

TABLE 4-14
AIDS Cases by Ethnic Group

Category	White	Black	Hispanic	Asian/ Pacific Islander	American Indian/ Alaskan Native
U.S. population	80%	12%	6%	2%	1%
All AIDS cases	59%	27%	13%	1%	<1%
Adult AIDS cases					
Male	62%	24%	13%	1%	<1%
Female	29%	54%	16%	1%	<1%
Pediatric cases	25%	55%	20%	<1%	<1%

Source: Centers for Disease Control, *AIDS and Human Immunodeficiency Virus Infection in the United States: 1988 Update,* May 12, 1989, Vol. 38: 18.

Among inner-city youth in detention, the average age for a first experience of sexual intercourse is 12 years. Early intercourse and multiple sexual partners increase the likelihood of transmission of sexual diseases and the risk of HIV exposure, but symptoms may not become apparent until an individual has aged beyond the teenage years.

According to the National Network of Runaway and Youth Services, 20 percent of all reported AIDS cases are among people 20–29 years old, meaning that they were probably infected as teens. For teens, the rate of heterosexual transmission is twice as high as for adults. Nationally, high rates of teenage pregnancy and sexually transmitted diseases (STDs) demonstrate that teens frequently have unprotected sexual intercourse, increasing their risk of HIV infection. In addition, around 20 percent of homeless and runaway youth use alcohol or drugs, increasing the likelihood that they will not practice safe sex or will trade sex for alcohol or drugs. In some shelters for youth, 7–15 percent of those tested are seropositive.

According to Dr. Robert Johnson of Adolescent Medicine at the University of Medicine and Dentistry in New Jersey, the relationship between adolescent sexual behavior and substance use is strong. In testimony before the National Commission on AIDS in 1991, Dr.

Johnson reported that all of his recent patients who had heterosexual transmission of HIV also had admitted sexual behavior that was accompanied by alcohol use. Further, although these adolescents used condoms in other situations, they did not do so in situations involving alcohol.[30]

On any given day, 50,000 adolescents are in custody in the United States; 600,000 are held during the course of one year. A 1990 survey by the Bureau of Justice Statistics found that 63 percent of these youth were regular drug users.

Table 4-15 shows the percentage of youth who engage in various risk behaviors.

TABLE 4-15
Percentage of 9th- to 12th-Grade Students
Engaging in Risk Behaviors

IV drug use: 2.7%

Sexual intercourse: 58.5%

Four or more sex partners: 21.3%

Source: Data from selected schools in selected states, 1989 National School-Based Survey, *CDC HIV/AIDS Prevention Fact Book 1990* (Atlanta: Centers for Disease Control, 1990).

HIV in the Job Corps

The Job Corps is a federal training program for disadvantaged and out-of-school youth, age 16–21. Like the military, the program has a mandatory HIV test for participants.

Screening of over 137,000 Job Corps participants during the years 1987–1990 revealed very high HIV-infection rates. A rate of 3.6 per 1,000 people was found; this rate is almost 10 times higher than for military applicants of the same age group.

The overall rate was 3.7 per 1,000 for males and 3.2 per 1,000 for females, but among the 16- and 17-year-olds, the HIV-positive rate was 1.5 per 1,000 for males and 2.3 per 1,000 for females.

HIV/AIDS in Adolescents and Young Adults: How Are They Exposed?

Table 4-16 shows the percentages of each of the major sources of exposure to HIV for persons with AIDS in two age groups. These cases were reported during a period of two years to the Centers for Disease Control.

TABLE 4-16
Sources of Exposure to HIV for Two Age Groups

Mode of Exposure	13–19 Years Old		20–24 Years Old	
	1991	1990	1991	1990
Male to male sexual contact	20%	16%	45%	51%
IV drug use	16%	12%	20%	19%
Male to male sexual contact plus IV drug use	3%	3%	7%	9%
Hemophilia/coagulation disorder	30%	32%	3%	2%
Heterosexual contact*	13%	22%	14%	13%
Recipient of blood transfusion, blood components, or tissue	5%	5%	1%	1%
Undetermined	13%	10%	10%	6%
Total number of cases reported	160	170	1,485	1,626

* Types of heterosexual exposure are:
a. Sex with IV drug user
b. Sex with bisexual male
c. Sex with person with hemophilia
d. Born in country where transmission is mainly heterosexual
e. Sex with person from country where transmission is mainly heterosexual
f. Sex with transfusion recipient with HIV infection
g. Sex with HIV-infected person, risk not specified

Source: Centers for Disease Control, *HIV/AIDS Surveillance Report Year-End Edition*, January 1992: 12.

HIV/AIDS and IV Drug Use[31]

An estimated 500,000–1.5 million people use IV drugs in the United States, which places them at-risk for HIV infection.

About 32 percent of all adults and adolescent AIDS cases are tied to IV drug use.

Some 70 percent of all perinatal-transmission pediatric AIDS cases are related to women being exposed to HIV through IV drug use or through sex with an IV drug user.

Some 26 percent of male AIDS cases are tied to IV drug use, as a single factor or in combination with male to male sexual contact.

In 1991 the White House issued a strategy on drug control that proposed that $100 million be added to the federal budget for drug treatment expansion to allow 11,000 additional treatment slots to be created. In early 1991, the National Institute of Medicine estimated that 66,000 people were on waiting lists for various treatment programs. The National Institute of Drug Abuse has issued even higher estimates, indicating that as many as 107,000 people are on waiting lists at any one time.[32]

HIV/AIDS in Correctional Facilities

As HIV/AIDS has grown first to become an epidemic of IV drug users and then more generally an epidemic disproportionately affecting poor people and racial minorities, it has become crucial to focus on the environments in which there is overrepresentation of these hard-hit groups. One of these environments is the corrections system at large, represented at the municipal, county, state, and federal levels. Following are a number of facts that give a picture of both the corrections system and its role as a factor in the prevention of HIV/AIDS, in the education of those at-risk, and in the spread of HIV during the first decade of the epidemic. Material in this section is drawn from the March 1991 National Commission on AIDS report *HIV Disease in Correctional Facilities.*

Growth in Numbers of People Incarcerated

Eighteen states, the District of Columbia, and the federal prisons have doubled their prison populations since 1980, resulting in about 1 million Americans being incarcerated. Four states tripled their prison populations during this period. In 1988, there was a demand for 800 new prison beds per week. Such growth is only expected to continue, as mandatory drug sentencing laws put more people in jails.

The women's federal prison population tripled from 1980 to 1989, growing from 13,000 to almost 41,000. In 1989, the population grew by 25 percent, whereas the male population grew by only 13 percent.

About 60 percent of the federal female inmates are serving time for drug-related offenses, according to the Federal Bureau of Prisons. In 1979, the General Accounting Office estimated that 50–60 percent of these inmates had alcohol or drug problems, but that estimate has risen to 70–80 percent.

Among those being incarcerated under mandatory sentencing policies are drug users who are at-risk of HIV infection or may already be HIV infected. IV drug use accounts for 28 percent of all AIDS cases reported from 1981 to 1989 in the United States, and the percentage of drug offenders in federal custody is expected to rise from 47 percent to 70 percent by 1995.

Seventy percent of all persons arrested in Washington, D.C., San Diego, New York, and Philadelphia tested positive for at least one drug, according to a study by the National Institute of Justice.

Seroprevalence in Prisons

According to a survey by the National Institute of Justice that included the Federal Bureau of Prisons, state prison systems, and a sample of 27 to 38 county and city jails, there were 5,411 confirmed cases of AIDS as of October 1989. This figure reflects a minimum level of reporting, as it does not indicate those prisoners in the early stages of HIV infection. In November 1985, the figure was 766 cases, representing a 606 percent increase in 4 years.

In 1989, 45 of 50 state corrections systems reported at least 1 inmate with AIDS. Seven of the systems reported 79 percent of all the cases, with New York, New Jersey, Florida, Texas, and California reporting the most.

Surveys by CDC, the National Institute of Justice, and Johns Hopkins University found that male seroprevalence for incoming prison inmates was 2.1 percent to 5.9 percent, and for women it was 3.2 percent to 7.8 percent. In jails, the rates for males were 2.3 percent to 7.6 percent and 2.5 percent to 14.7 percent for women.

Prison Conditions and Access to Care

With about 1 million people confined in jails and prisons in the United States, aggressive health policies are necessary to contain and treat all health problems. Yet, as of 1990, 37 states, Washington, D.C., Puerto Rico, and the U.S. Virgin Islands all operate prison systems under court order, due to findings of poor conditions, overcrowding, or lack of medical care—the very conditions that can exacerbate HIV-illness.

According to a study by the Correctional Association of New York, prisoners with AIDS and a history of IV drug use lived 159 days after diagnosis, compared to 318 days for nonprisoners with drug-use history. These are median values in the study, meaning that half the subjects were either above or below this figure.

A 1988 study of New York State prisons found that 25 percent of prisoners with AIDS were not diagnosed until the time of their autopsy.

Some institutions choose to segregate inmates in order to manage them better, to prevent the spread of infection (despite little evidence to support the public health merit of this action), or to provide access to specialized care. According to a 1990 study, 16 state systems segregate all prisoners with AIDS. Five segregate those with AIDS-Related Complex (ARC), and four segregate all those who test positive for HIV. Some 36 percent of all city and county jails segregate those with AIDS. This often limits the inmates' access to religious services, visiting rooms, educational programs, work programs, Alcoholics Anonymous and Narcotics Anonymous programs, and other opportunities to enhance their physical and mental health.

The Parallel TB Epidemic

Just as it is outside prisons, tuberculosis is frequently seen among prison inmates with HIV-illness. In 1989, all of the 70 HIV cases reported in the New York State system had active TB.

Increasing numbers of Drug-Resistant TB cases are being seen both inside and outside prisons. Drug-resistant cases are classified as those that do not respond to 1 or more of the 13 antibiotics commonly used for TB.

Prevention and Education

Access to condoms in correctional facilities is limited. Vermont was the first state to provide such a service; Mississippi, New York City, and Philadelphia make condoms available in prison infirmaries, according to a 1990 study.

In 1988, a Federal Bureau of Prisons survey found that HIV-infected inmates caused almost 40 percent of prison staff to be "bothered a great deal"; 14 percent considered leaving their jobs because of this concern.

HIV Infection and the Military[33]

All military personnel must be tested for HIV at least biennially. All potential recruits must also be tested; anyone who tests positive cannot enlist in the military. According to the General Accounting

Office (GAO), from October 1985 to August 1989 more than 6,000 members of the nation's 2.3 million active duty service members tested positive.

The Walter Reed Army Institute of Research in Washington, D.C., which manages the Department of Defense HIV screening and testing program, estimates that its tests cost only about $3 each and return results in 24 hours, compared to private tests that can cost up to $150 and take as long as 2 weeks.

Military personnel who test positive are issued orders commanding them both to inform prospective sexual partners of their serostatus and to practice safe sex. Disobeying such an order is grounds for court-martial or for action under the Uniform Code of Military Justice.

The GAO predicts 1,500 to 1,700 new infections annually in the military from now until the year 2000. The projected lifetime cost for caring for an HIV-infected person in the military was estimated in 1989 to be $200,000.

HIV/AIDS in Rural Areas

According to the National Commission on AIDS (NCOA), the number of new AIDS cases diagnosed in rural areas has been growing at an alarming rate. "Although the epidemic continues to be most severe in urban areas, there has been a 37 percent increase in diagnosed AIDS cases in rural areas compared to a 5 percent increase in metropolitan areas with populations of over 500,000 in just a one-year period."

The commission also found that:

> In rural America, there is an epidemic of fear and bigotry, fanned by the absence of education and knowledge, surrounding HIV infection and AIDS.... The fear of being "found out" is almost as great as the fear of the disease itself. NCOA member Belinda Mason of Kentucky, who died of AIDS in September 1991, noted, "I have seen rural America at its warm, supportive best and at its close-minded, bigoted worst."[34]

According to NCOA, AIDS education is virtually nonexistent in rural areas, and the singular lack of access to primary health care services in the rural United States was shocking and heartrending to commission members.

HIV/AIDS and Public Opinion

What Do Americans Understand about HIV/AIDS?

Table 4-17 shows breakdowns by various groups of the answer to the question, "Have you heard or read about a disease called AIDS?" The results are from a Gallup poll done for the New York City Department of Health in June 1985. The poll questioned two groups of respondents: one in New York City and one outside the city. The results in Table 4-17 reflect the non–New York City respondents.

TABLE 4-17
Have You Heard or Read about a Disease Called AIDS?

Respondents' Characteristics	Yes Response
Age	
18–34 years	96%
35–49 years	96%
over 50 years	92%
Sex	
Male	94%
Female	95%
Race	
White	95%
Black	93%
Education	
Non–high school graduate	85%
High school graduate	96%
College graduate	99%
Total number of respondents	1,545

Source: Reported in *Morbidity and Mortality Weekly Report,* 34 (August 23, 1985): 514.

Tables 4-18 and 4-19 provide the results of another group of questions asked in the same Gallup poll. Table 4-18 contains the answers by adults, and Table 4-19 contains the answers given by teens. Again, the results are for the group of non–New York City respondents. Although this poll was intended to test knowledge and beliefs about "AIDS," it does not distinguish between HIV and AIDS in the questions. In addition, the poll assumed that sexual contact is heterosexual and that drug users are male and engage in at least some heterosexual contact.

TABLE 4-18
Whom Do Adults Think Is Most Likely To Have AIDS?

Statement	Response		
	True	False	Unknown
True Statements			
Some people get AIDS when they receive blood transfusions.	92%	3%	5%
Drug users who share needles have a higher risk of getting AIDS.	84%	8%	8%
Most people with AIDS are homosexual men.	80%	12%	7%
Some wives and girlfriends of drug users have gotten AIDS.	67%	15%	18%
False Statements			
You can get AIDS by shaking hands with someone who has it.	9%	81%	9%
You can get AIDS by being in a crowded place with someone who has it.	9%	81%	9%
Women cannot get AIDS.	6%	88%	6%

Source: Reported in *Morbidity and Mortality Weekly Report,* 34 (August 23, 1985): 514.

TABLE 4-19
Whom Do Teens Think Is Most Likely To Have HIV/AIDS?

Statement	Response		
	True	False	Unknown
True Statements			
Some people get AIDS when they receive blood transfusions.	86%	11%	3%
Drug users who share needles have a higher risk of getting AIDS.	79%	18%	3%
Most people with AIDS are homosexual men.	75%	23%	2%
Some wives and girlfriends of drug users have gotten AIDS.	61%	34%	5%
False Statements			
You can get AIDS by shaking hands with someone who has it.	12%	86%	2%
You can get AIDS by being in a crowded place with someone who has it.	14%	84%	2%
Women cannot get AIDS.	8%	90%	2%

Source: Reported in *Morbidity and Mortality Weekly Report,* 34 August 23, 1985: 514.

Facts on HIV/AIDS Education and Prevention Issues

A New York Times/CBS poll in 1985 showed that 34 percent of those surveyed believed it was unsafe to associate with a person who had "AIDS" even if there was no direct physical contact with the person. "AIDS" could be transmitted on toilet seats, according to 28 percent of those polled, and 47 percent of those in the survey believed "AIDS" could be passed by sharing a drinking glass with an infected person.

Since its opening in October 1987, the National AIDS Information Clearinghouse (NAIC) has distributed more than 45 million educational items. The most widely distributed are *What You Should Know about AIDS, Understanding AIDS,* and *The Surgeon General's Report on Acquired Immune Deficiency Syndrome (AIDS).*[35]

A Roper Organization survey released in June 1991 found that 8 out of 10 people interviewed believed that AIDS is a major problem in the United States and that it should be one of the nation's highest health priorities. Three out of 10 people interviewed said they personally knew someone who had tested positive for HIV; 1 out of 5 knew someone who had died.

The same poll found that 25 percent of those polled believe they know "a great deal" about AIDS and 57 percent believe they know "a fair amount."

Some 78 percent said they wanted more information on prevention issues to talk with children about. Sixteen percent felt it was appropriate for children age 6 or younger to learn about AIDS in school, and another 21 percent felt that children ages 7 to 9 should receive such instruction.

Parents should discuss anal intercourse with children as young as age 12, according to 58 percent of those questioned; 84 percent felt that children in that age group should be taught about sexually transmitted diseases.

Children age 12 and younger should be told about the use of condoms, according to 67 percent of those interviewed, and 64 percent of those polled felt that sexually active high school students should have access to condoms in their schools. Forty-seven percent felt condoms should be available in junior high schools. Only 1 out of 7 people polled believed that sexual abstinence is a realistic solution to the AIDS crisis.

In August 1991, Massachusetts state officials recommended that high schools make condoms available, making it the first such state-wide policy in the nation.

Is HIV/AIDS a Problem?

In 1991, 45 percent of those questioned identified AIDS as the nation's most urgent health problem, ahead of cancer, access to health care, and drug abuse. In 1987, 68 percent thought it was the most critical problem.

In 1987, 51 percent of Americans polled believed it was a person's own fault if he or she contracted HIV. In 1991, 1 in 3 respondents believed this.

According to 59 percent of the people in 1991, the government has not taken enough action in response to the epidemic; in 1987, 60 percent of those polled agreed with this statement.

Testing

Most Americans favor testing of physicians and dentists (87 percent) as well as nurses (84 percent).

Testing for patients entering the hospital was supported by 79 percent of those polled.

All Americans should be tested for the presence of HIV, according to 46 percent of those polled in 1991; in 1987, 52 percent of those asked agreed with this statement.

Even higher numbers of people support the testing of other groups. The following numbers show the percentages in agreement in 1991 and 1987, respectively:

Inmates of federal prisons: 78 percent/88 percent

Immigrants applying for permanent resident status: 81 percent/90 percent

Members of the armed forces: 67 percent/83 percent (Note: mandatory testing is in place in the armed forces.)

Visitors from foreign countries: 62 percent/66 percent

Couples seeking marriage licenses: 82 percent/80 percent

Treatment of People with HIV/AIDS[36]

In 1991, 91 percent of those questioned felt that people with AIDS should be treated with compassion; 78 percent felt this way in 1987.

An employee with AIDS should be liable for dismissal by an employer, according to 21 percent of those polled in 1991. In 1987, 33 percent of those asked agreed with this statement.

A tenant with AIDS should be liable for eviction by the landlord, said 10 percent of those asked in 1991; 17 percent of those questioned said this in 1987.

Sixteen percent of those questioned in 1991 said they would refuse to work alongside someone who has AIDS; in 1987, 25 percent of those asked agreed with this position.

Fifty-nine percent of those asked felt that anyone who tests positive for HIV antibodies should have to carry an identification card; in 1987, 60 percent of the respondents agreed with this.

Ten percent of those polled in 1991 felt that a person with AIDS should be isolated from the rest of society, but 21 percent felt this way in 1987.

Notes

1. "U.N. Sees H.I.V. Cases Nearing 12 Million," *New York Times,* 13 January 1992, A-17. This news article reported on the World Health Organization document *Current and Future Dimensions of the HIV-AIDS Pandemic.*

2. The Global AIDS Policy Coalition, "AIDS in the World 1992: A Global Epidemic Out of Control?" (press release) (Boston: The Global AIDS Policy Coalition, 3 June 1992).

3. National Commission on AIDS (NCOA), *America Living with AIDS* (Washington, DC: National Commission on AIDS, 1991), 11.

4. Ibid., 69.

5. Ibid., 12–13.

6. CDC, "The Second 100,000 Cases of Acquired Immune Deficiency Syndrome— United States, June 1981–December 1991," *MMWR,* no. 2-28 (1992): 41.

7. Randy Shilts, *And the Band Played On: Politics, People, and the AIDS Epidemic* (New York: St. Martin's Press, 1987), 80, 186.

8. NCOA, *America Living with AIDS,* 70.

9. Ibid.

10. Ibid., 75.

11. Ibid., 70.

12. Ibid., 68.

13. John A. Jereb et al., "Tuberculosis Morbidity in the United States: Final Data, 1990," CDC Surveillance Summaries, January 1991, *MMWR* 40, no. SS-3 (1991): 23.

14. Geoffrey Cowley, "Tuberculosis: A Deadly Return," *Newsweek*, 16 March 1992, 53, 55, 56.

15. Jereb et al., 23.

16. Ibid., 24.

17. Ibid., 25.

18. CDC, "Nosocomial Transmission of Multidrug-Resistant Tuberculosis among HIV-Infected Persons—Florida and New York, 1988–1991," *MMWR* 40, no. 34 (1991): 586–592.

19. CDC, *HIV/AIDS Surveillance Report Year-End Edition,* January 1992 (Atlanta: Centers for Disease Control, 1992), 6.

20. Ibid.

21. Ibid.

22. Ibid.

23. CDC, *HIV/AIDS Surveillance Report Year-End Edition,* January 1991 (Atlanta: Centers for Disease Control, 1991), 4.

24. CDC, *HIV/AIDS Surveillance Report Year-End Edition,* January 1992, 6.

25. CDC, *HIV/AIDS Surveillance Report,* July 1992, 10.

26. Ibid.

27. NCOA, *HIV Disease in Correctional Facilities* (Washington, DC: National Commission on AIDS, 1990), 25–26.

28. NCOA, *America Living with AIDS,* 12.

29. *USA Today*, "Fewer Kids Save Sex for Adulthood," 5 March 1991, 1D, 1E.

30. NCOA, *The Twin Epidemics of Substance Use and HIV* (Washington, DC: National Commission on AIDS, July 1991), 6.

31. Ibid., 4.

32. Ibid., 8.

33. U.S. General Accounting Office (GAO), *Defense Health Care: Effects of AIDS in the Military* (Washington, DC: GAO, 1990).

34. NCOA, *Research, the Workforce, and HIV Epidemic in Rural America* (Washington, DC: National Commission on AIDS, 1990).

35. *National AIDS Information Clearinghouse User Guide,* 9.

36. "Large Majorities Continue to Back AIDS Testing," by George Gallup, Jr., and Dr. Frank Newport, in *The Gallup Poll Monthly,* May 1991: 25–28.

5

Documents and Reports

THIS CHAPTER OFFERS A DOCUMENTARY portrait of HIV/AIDS in the United States in two sections. Such a portrait is necessarily complex, but this one has been organized with accessibility and immediacy as the primary goals. The first section gives a detailed look at the development of HIV/AIDS during its first visible years in the United States. Utilizing the most clinical of documents—the Centers for Disease Control's (CDC) *Morbidity and Mortality Weekly Report (MMWR)*—as a source, excerpts from the key public health developments are woven together with historical narrative that offers a setting for understanding the building epidemic. These are followed by excerpts from former Surgeon General C. Everett Koop's 1986 report on HIV/AIDS.

"Perspectives on the Epidemic," the second section, provides a voice for many of the people affected by HIV/AIDS through statements and testimony coming directly from people with HIV/AIDS.

The Onset of the Epidemic in the United States

> By the time America paid attention to the disease, it was too late to do anything about it. The virus was already pandemic in the nation, having spread to every corner of the North American continent. The tide of death that would later sweep America could, perhaps, be slowed, but it could not be stopped...

> But from 1980, when the first isolated gay men began falling ill from strange and exotic ailments, nearly five years passed before all these institutions—medicine, public health, the federal and private scientific research establishments, the mass media, and the gay community's leaders—mobilized the way they should in a time of threat. The story of these first five years of AIDS in America is a drama of national failure, played out against a background of needless death.[1]

The arrival of AIDS as a recognizable disease in the United States is generally traced to 1981, when epidemiologists first began studying cases of unusual infections and deaths among gay men. Since that time, it has been recognized that other cases were present in this country early in the 1970s. The first published reports of 1981, however, are those that marked the arrival of a new and mysterious malady, unidentified at first as medical experts grappled with clusters of otherwise rare infections and malignancies, some of which had only been seen previously in animals or very select groups of humans.

The following material has been chosen to illustrate the growth of the epidemic, as chronicled in official public health documents. When reading the following selections, it is important to bear in mind the evolution of the language used to refer to the epidemic and the accuracy of that language. It is helpful to read the comments on language that are included in Chapter 4.

The following edited excerpts from published reports of the Centers for Disease Control (CDC) in *Morbidity and Mortality Weekly Report* (*MMWR*) convey just what was known about the early cases and also give a clear indication of why the early manifestations of AIDS were quickly labeled for the public as a gay disease. The relative frequency of the reports also shows just how rapidly the disease was spreading.

The Opportunistic Infections

Pneumocystis Pneumonia—Los Angeles

In the period October 1980–May 1981, 5 young men, all active homosexuals, were treated for biopsy-confirmed *Pneumocystis carinii* pneumonia at 3 different hospitals in Los Angeles, California. Two of the patients died. All 5 patients had laboratory-confirmed previous or current cytomegalovirus (CMV) infection and candidal mucosal infection...

The patients did not know each other and had no known common contacts or knowledge of sexual partners who had similar illnesses. The 5 did not have comparable histories of sexually transmitted diseases... Two of the 5 reported having frequent homosexual contacts with various partners. All 5 reported using inhalant drugs, and 1 reported parenteral drug abuse...

Editorial note: *Pneumocystis* pneumonia in the United States is almost exclusively limited to severely immunosuppressed patients. The occurrence of *pneumocystosis* in these 5 previously healthy individuals without a clinically apparent underlying immunodeficiency is unusual. The fact that these patients were all homosexuals suggests an association between some aspect of a homosexual lifestyle or disease acquired through sexual contact and *Pneumocystis* pneumonia in this population...

All of the above observations suggest the possibility of a cellular-immune dysfunction related to a common exposure that predisposes individuals to opportunistic infections such as *pneumocystosis* and candidiasis.

Source: *MMWR* 30 (5 June 1981): 250–252.

Just one month later, CDC reported on the occurrence of another uncommonly reported ailment that had been found among gay men over two years before. Some patients had already died. CDC points out that the additional cases mean that the previous report did not describe an isolated circumstance and also that it could not be certain of a link to the gay community in these cases.

Kaposi's Sarcoma and *Pneumocystis* Pneumonia among Homosexual Men—New York City and California

During the past 30 months, Kaposi's sarcoma (KS), an uncommonly reported malignancy in the United States, has been diagnosed in 26 homosexual men (20 in New York City [NYC], 6 in California). The 26 patients range in age from 26–51 years (mean 39 years). Eight of these patients died (7 in NYC, 1 in California)—all 8 within 24 months after KS was diagnosed...

A review of the New York University Coordinated Cancer Registry for KS in men under age 50 revealed no cases from 1970–1979 at Bellevue Hospital and 3 cases in this age group at the New York University Hospital from 1961–1979...

Since the previous report of 5 cases of *Pneumocystis* pneumonia in homosexual men from Los Angeles, 10 additional cases (4 in Los Angeles and 6 in the San Francisco Bay area) of biopsy-confirmed PC pneumonia have been identified in homosexual men in the state. Two of the 10 patients also have KS. This brings the total number of *Pneumocystis* cases among homosexual men in California to 15 since September 1979. Patients range in age from 25 to 46 years...

Editorial note: ... [KS] affects primarily elderly men...

The occurrence of this number of KS cases during a 30-month period among young, homosexual men is considered highly unusual. No previous association between KS and sexual preference has been reported...

That 10 new cases of *Pneumocystis* pneumonia have been identified in homosexual men suggests that the 5 previously reported cases were not an isolated phenomenon...

Although it is not certain that the increase in KS and PC pneumonia is restricted to homosexual men, the vast majority of recent cases have been reported from this group. Physicians should be alert for Kaposi's sarcoma, PC pneumonia, and other opportunistic infections associated with immunosuppression in homosexual men.

Source: *MMWR* 30 (4 July 1981): 305–308.

Just eight weeks later, CDC reported that it had word of more than twice as many new cases of PCP and KS, the majority of them among gay white men.

Follow-Up on Kaposi's Sarcoma and *Pneumocystis* Pneumonia

Twenty-six cases of Kaposi's sarcoma (KS) and 15 cases of *Pneumocystis carinii* pneumonia (PCP) among previously healthy homosexual men were recently reported. Since July 3, 1981, CDC received reports of an additional 70 cases of these 2 conditions in persons without known underlying disease...

The majority of the reported cases of KS and/or PCP have occurred in white men. Patients ranged in age from 15–52 years; over 95% were men 25–49 years of age. Ninety-four percent (95/101) of the men for whom sexual preference was known were homosexual or bisexual. Forty percent of the cases were fatal.

Source: *MMWR* 30 (28 August 1981): 409–410.

As researchers worked to identify the still unnamed disease, they focused their efforts on possible links to the sexual preference of those affected. Sexual practices, the frequency and number of sexual partners, and drug use were examined.

Persistent, Generalized Lymphadenopathy among Homosexual Males

Since October 1981, cases of persistent, generalized lymphadenopathy—not attributable to previously identified cases—among homosexual males have been reported to CDC by physicians in several major metropolitan areas in the United States. These reports were prompted by an awareness generated by ongoing CDC and state investigations of other emerging health problems among homosexual males...

Recorded medical histories for the 57 patients suggested that the use of drugs such as nitrite inhalants, marijuana, hallucinogens, and cocaine was common. Many of these patients have a history of sexually transmitted infections.

Source: *MMWR* 31 (21 May 1982): 249–252.

The following CDC report, published less than a month later, shows that what CDC refers to here as an "epidemic" is more diversified than previously thought in several ways: by sexual orientation of those affected, by race, and by geography. According to this report, similar opportunistic infections have been reported in twenty states.

Update on Kaposi's Sarcoma and Opportunistic Infections in Previously Healthy Persons—United States

Between June 1, 1981, and May 28, 1982, CDC received reports of 355 cases of Kaposi's sarcoma (KS) and/or serious opportunistic infections (OI), especially *Pneumocystis carinii* pneumonia (PCP), occurring in previously healthy persons between 15 and 60 years of age. Of the 355, 281 (79%) were homosexual or bisexual men, 41 (12%) were heterosexual men, 20 (6%) were men of unknown sexual orientation, and 13 (4%) were heterosexual women. This proportion of heterosexuals (16%) is higher than previously described.

Five states—California, Florida, New Jersey, New York, and Texas—accounted for 86% of the reported cases. The rest were reported by 15 other states...

Both male and female heterosexual PCP patients were more likely than homosexual patients to be black or Hispanic...

Editorial note: Sexual orientation information was obtained from patients by their physicians, and the accuracy of reporting cannot be determined; therefore, comparisons between KSOI cases made on the basis of sexual orientation must be interpreted cautiously. Similarities between homosexual and heterosexual cases in diagnoses and geographic and temporal distribution suggest that all are part of the same epidemic... However, differences in race, proportion of PCP cases, and intravenous drug use suggest that risk factors may be different for these groups.

Source: *MMWR* 31 (11 June 1982): 294–301.

One week later, CDC reported on what became known as the "Orange County Connection," an interconnected series of KS and PCP cases that included the same non-Californian as a sexual contact in an improbable fashion. Air Canada steward Gaetan Dugas, sometimes referred to as "Patient Zero," was one of the first North Americans diagnosed with AIDS, though his case was not followed clinically in the United States because of his nationality. Dugas had a KS lesion removed from his face in the spring of 1980.

According to CDC researcher William Darrow, as of April 12, 1982, Dugas or one of his partners had had sex with 40 of the first 248 gay men who were diagnosed with the disease. This network of contacts involved people in 10 cities and created further generations of sexual contacts. This clustering of cases from a string of identifiable sexual contacts offered strong proof that a lone infectious agent was responsible for the transmission of the disease.[2]

In addition, Darrow found that all of the early New York City cases among gay men could be traced to a similar string of common sexual contacts during the summer of 1976. However, it was not until 1978 and 1979 that these men first became ill, lending credence to a theory that the causative agent of the disease could maintain a prolonged latency period.[3]

A Cluster of Kaposi's Sarcoma and *Pneumocystis Carinii* Pneumonia among Homosexual Male Residents of Los Angeles and Orange Counties, California

In the period June 1, 1981–April 12, 1982, CDC received reports of 19 cases of biopsy-confirmed Kaposi's sarcoma (KS) and/or *Pneumocystis carinii* pneumonia (PCP) among previously healthy homosexual male residents of Los Angeles and Orange counties, California. Following an unconfirmed report of possible associations among cases in southern California, interviews were conducted with all 8 of the patients still living and with the close friends of 7 of the other 11 patients who had died...

Within 5 years of the onset of symptoms, 9 patients (6 with KS and 3 with PCP) had sexual contact with other patients with KS or PCP. Seven patients from Los Angeles County had sexual contact with other patients from Los Angeles County, and 2 from Orange County had sexual contact with 1 patient who was not a resident of California. Four of the 9 patients had been exposed to more than 1 patient who had KS or PCP...

The other 4 patients in the group of 13 had no known sexual contact with reported cases. However, 1 patient with KS had an apparently healthy sexual partner in common with 2 persons with PCP; 1 patient with KS reported having had sexual contact with 2 friends of the non-Californian with KS; and 2 patients with PCP had most of their anonymous contacts (80%) with persons in bathhouses attended frequently by other persons in Los Angeles with KS or PCP.

The 9 patients from Los Angeles and Orange counties directly linked to other patients are part of an interconnected series of cases that may include 15 additional patients (11 with KS and 4 with PCP) from 8 other cities. The non-Californian with KS mentioned earlier is part of this series...

Editorial note: ... The probability that 7 of 11 patients with KS or PCP would have sexual contact with any one of the other 16 reported patients in Los Angeles County would seem to be remote. The probability that 2 patients with KS living in different parts of Orange County would have sexual contact with the same non-Californian with KS would appear to be even lower.

Source: *MMWR* 31 (18 June 1982): 305–307.

Naming the Disease

In September 1982, CDC reported on the rapid growth of the disease now christened Acquired Immune Deficiency Syndrome, or AIDS. Just a few months before, scientists had finally come to agreement on a name for what was killing people, discarding GRID (Gay Related Immune Deficiency), CAIDS (Community Acquired Immune Deficiency Syndrome), and ACIS (Acquired Community Immune Syndrome). Kaposi's sarcoma alone had frequently been referred to as gay cancer. CDC at this time also published its first definition of the disease.

Update on Acquired Immune Deficiency Syndrome (AIDS)— United States

Between June 1, 1981, and September 15, 1982, CDC received reports of 593 cases of acquired immune deficiency syndrome (AIDS). Death occurred in 243 cases (41%)...

The incidence of AIDS by date of diagnosis (assuming an almost constant population at risk) has roughly doubled every half-year since the second half of 1979. An average of one to two cases are now diagnosed every day. Although the overall case-mortality rate for the current total of 593 is 41%, the rate exceeds 60% for cases diagnosed over a year ago...

Editorial note: CDC defines a case of AIDS as a disease, at least moderately predictive of a defect in cell-mediated immunity, occurring in a person with no known cause for diminished resistance to that disease. Such diseases include KS, PCP, and serious OI [opportunistic infection]. These infections include pneumonia, meningitis, or encephalitis due to one or more of the following: aspergillosis, candidiasis, cryptococcosis, cytomegalovirus, nocardiosis, strongyloidosis, toxoplasmosis, zygomycosis, or atypical mycobacteriosis (species other than tuberculosis or lepra); esophagitis due to candidiasis, cytomegalovirus, or herpes simplex virus; progressive multifocal leukoencephalopathy, chronic enterocolitis (more than 4 weeks) due to cryptosporidiosis, or unusually extensive mucocutaneous herpes simplex of more than 5 weeks duration. Diagnoses are considered to fit the case definition only if based on sufficiently reliable methods (generally histology or culture). However, this case definition does not include the spectrum of AIDS manifestations, which may range from absence of symptoms (despite laboratory evidence of immune deficiency) to non-specific symptoms (e.g., fever, weight loss, generalized, persistent lymphadenopathy) to specific diseases that are sufficiently predictive of cellular immunodeficiency to be included in incidence monitoring (e.g., tuberculosis, oral candidiasis, herpes zoster) to malignant neoplasms that cause, as well as result from, immunodeficiency. Conversely, some patients who are considered AIDS cases on the basis of diseases only moderately predictive of cellular immunodeficiency may not actually be immunodeficient and may not be part of the current epidemic. Absence of a reliable, inexpensive, widely available test for AIDS, however, may make the working case definition the best currently available for incidence monitoring.

Two points in this update deserve emphasis. First, the eventual case-mortality rate of AIDS, a few years after diagnosis, may be far greater that the 41% overall case-mortality rate noted above. Second, the reported incidence of AIDS has continued to increase rapidly. Only a small percentage of cases have none of the identified risk factors (male homosexuality, intravenous drug abuse, Haitian origin, and perhaps Hemophilia A). To avoid a reporting bias, physicians should report cases regardless of the absence of these factors.

Source: MMWR 31 (24 September 1982): 507–514.

Blood and Blood Products

In July 1982, CDC released information on the first cases of opportunistic infection among hemophiliacs. Hemophilia A is an inherited disorder, linked to gender, and characterized by a deficiency in Factor VIII, a clotting component of the blood. Approximately 20,000 people in the United States have this form of hemophilia; about 60 percent of them have cases classified as "severe." They are treated intravenously with Factor VIII products, often made with a concentrate made from the blood donations of over 1,000 people. These blood products, produced commercially and from donations, are regulated by the federal Food and Drug Administration (FDA).

Pneumocystis Carinii Pneumonia (PCP) among Persons with Hemophilia A

CDC recently received reports of three cases of *Pneumocystis carinii* pneumonia among patients with hemophilia A and without other underlying diseases. Two have died, one remains critically ill. All three were heterosexual males; none had a history of intravenous (IV) drug abuse...

For each patient, records of the administration of Factor VIII concentrate were reviewed to determine manufacturer and lot numbers. No two of the patients are known to have received concentrate from the same lots.

Source: *MMWR* 31 (16 July 1982): 365–367.

Just four months after its first report on opportunistic infections among hemophiliacs, CDC updated its report with the news that the first three patients had died, and four others had been reported.

Update on Acquired Immune Deficiency Syndrome (AIDS) among Patients with Hemophilia A

In most cases, these patients have been the first AIDS cases in their cities, states, or regions. They have had no common medications, occupations, habits, types of pets, or any uniform antecedent history of personal or family illnesses with immunological relevance...

Two of the patients described here are 10 years of age or less, and children with hemophilia must now be considered at risk for the disease. In addition, the number of cases continues to increase, and the illness may pose a significant risk for patients with hemophilia.

The National Hemophilia Foundation and CDC are now conducting a national survey of hemophilia treatment centers to estimate the prevalence of AIDS-associated diseases during the past 5 years and to provide active surveillance of AIDS among patients with hemophilia.

Source: *MMWR* 31 (10 December 1982): 644–652.

As early as mid-1981, CDC epidemiologist Dr. Mary Guinan had thought that, if this disease spread like hepatitis B, through contact with the blood of intravenous drug users, then hemophiliacs and blood transfusion recipients—frequently affected by hepatitis B— were another likely group to show signs of the new disease.[4] Yet the advent of the first hemophilia cases described above did not prompt action by the voluntary blood banks, the for-profit blood products manufacturers, or the government. Instead, even though each use of Factor VIII exposed a recipient hemophiliac to many individual donors, Assistant Secretary for Health and Human Services (HHS) Dr. Edward N. Brandt, Jr., did not stray from the Food and Drug Administration's (FDA) official policy on the nation's blood supply, stating at an August 1982 conference, "We can't be sure there is a connection between blood products used by these patients and AIDS."[5]

However, in the same December issue of *MMWR*, CDC reported on a case identified in August by prominent pediatric immunologist Dr. Art Ammann in San Francisco: a transfusion-related case of AIDS in an infant. Even this report was not enough evidence to persuade blood industry officials to take any action.[6]

Possible Transfusion-Associated Acquired Immune Deficiency Syndrome (AIDS)—California

CDC has received a report of a 20-month old infant from the San Francisco area who developed unexplained cellular immunodeficiency and opportunistic infection. This occurred after multiple transfusions, including a transfusion of platelets from the blood of a male subsequently found to have the Acquired Immune Deficiency Syndrome (AIDS)...

The parents and brother of the infant are in good health. The parents are heterosexual non-Haitians and do not have a history of intravenous drug abuse. The infant had no known personal contact with an AIDS patient...

Editorial note: ... This report and continuing reports of AIDS among persons with hemophilia A raise serious questions about the possible transmission of AIDS through blood and blood products. The Assistant Secretary for Health is convening an advisory committee to address these questions.

Source: *MMWR* 31 (10 December 1982): 652–654.

The advisory group convened in January 1983 and included representatives from the National Institutes of Health (NIH) and FDA, the National Gay Task Force, the American Red Cross, the American Association of Blood Banks, and representatives of the Pharmaceutical Manufacturers Association, which represents commercial blood products makers. They discussed the relatively small number of cases that had appeared so far, the possible future impact given the apparent latency of the disease for long periods, the cost burden of testing blood for hepatitis B antibodies, the discouraging effect on the donor base among urban gay men of screening questionnaires, and other issues. The participants could not reach agreement on any plan of action.[7]

Perinatal Transmission

Just one week later, CDC published another important report supporting the theory that a new infectious agent was behind the epidemic.

CDC has received reports of four infants (under 2 years of age) with unexplained cellular immunodeficiency and opportunistic infections...

   None of the four infants described in the case reports was known to have received blood or blood products before onset of illness...

Editorial note: ... Although the etiology of AIDS remains unknown, a series of epidemiological observations suggests it is caused by an infectious agent. If the infants described in the four case reports had AIDS, exposure to the putative "AIDS Agent" must have occurred very early... Transmission of an "AIDS Agent" from mother to child, either in utero or shortly after birth, could account for the early onset of immunodeficiency in these infants.

Source: *MMWR* 31 (17 December 1982): 665–667.

Transmission among Heterosexuals and Prison Inmates

The first CDC report of 1983 gave news of the further spread of the epidemic into two areas: heterosexual contacts and prison inmates. With the addition of heterosexual contacts to a list that only recently included blood transfusion recipients, virtually anyone was at risk for AIDS.

Immunodeficiency among Female Sexual Partners of Males with Acquired Immune Deficiency Syndrome (AIDS)—New York

CDC has received reports of two females with cellular immunodeficiency who have been steady sexual partners of males with the Acquired Immune Deficiency Syndrome (AIDS)...

Editorial note: ... Epidemiological observations increasingly suggest that AIDS is caused by an infectious agent. The description of a cluster of sexually related AIDS patients among homosexual males in southern California suggested such an agent could be transmitted sexually or through other intimate contact... The present report suggests the infectious agent hypothesis and the possibility that transmission of the putative "AIDS agent" may occur among both heterosexual and male homosexual couples.

Source: *MMWR* 31 (7 January 1983): 697–698.

Acquired Immune Deficiency Syndrome (AIDS) in Prison Inmates—New York, New Jersey

CDC has received reports from New York and New Jersey of 16 prison inmates with the Acquired Immune Deficiency Syndrome (AIDS).

New York: Between November 1981 and October 1982, ten AIDS cases...were reported among inmates of New York State correctional facilities. The patients had been imprisoned from 3 to 36 months before developing symptoms...

All ten patients reported that they were heterosexual before imprisonment, one is known to have had homosexual contacts since confinement. However, the nine patients were regular users of intravenous drugs...before imprisonment... The ten patients were housed in seven different prisons when they first developed PCP or KS...

New Jersey: Of the 48 AIDS cases reported from New Jersey since June 1981, six have involved inmates of New Jersey State correctional facilities... They were imprisoned from 1 to 36 months before onset of symptoms...

All six patients have histories of chronic IV drug abuse... Four were heterosexual, and one was homosexual. The two living patients have denied both IV drug use and homosexual activity since imprisonment. No two of the six patients had been confined in the same facility at the same time.

Source: *MMWR* 31 (7 January 1983): 700–701.

Risk Reduction

CDC published its first guidelines on risk reduction in March 1983. These guidelines were the federal government's only effort to date to stop the spread of the disease.

Prevention of Acquired Immune Deficiency Syndrome (AIDS): Report of Inter-Agency Recommendations

No AIDS cases have been documented among health care or laboratory personnel caring for AIDS patients or processing laboratory specimens. To date, no person-to-person transmission has been identified other than through intimate contact or blood transfusion.

Several factors indicate that individuals at risk for transmitting AIDS may be difficult to identify... The pool of persons potentially capable of transmitting an AIDS agent may be considerably larger than the presently known number of AIDS cases. Furthermore, the California cluster investigation and other epidemiologic findings suggest a "latent period" of several months to 2 years between exposure and recognizable clinical illness and imply that transmissibility may precede recognizable clinical illness. Thus, careful histories and physical examinations alone will not identify all persons capable of transmitting AIDS but should be useful in identifying persons with definite AIDS diagnoses or related symptoms... Persons who may be considered at increased risk of AIDS include those with symptoms and signs suggestive of AIDS; sexual partners of AIDS patients; sexually active homosexual or bisexual men with multiple partners; Haitian entrants to the United States; present or past abusers of IV drugs; patients with hemophilia; and sexual partners of individuals at increased risk for AIDS...

Although the cause of AIDS remains unknown, the Public Health Service recommends the following actions:

1. Sexual contact should be avoided with persons known or suspected to have AIDS. Members of high risk groups should be aware that multiple sexual partners increases the probability of developing AIDS.
2. As a temporary measure, members of groups at increased risk for AIDS should refrain from donating plasma and/or blood. The recommendation includes all individuals belonging to such groups, even though many individuals are at little risk of AIDS. Centers collecting plasma and/or blood should inform potential donors of this recommendation. The Food and Drug Administration (FDA) is preparing new recommendations for manufacturers of plasma derivatives and for establishments

collecting plasma or blood. This is an interim measure to protect recipients of blood products and blood until specific laboratory results are available.

3. Studies should be conducted to evaluate screening procedures for their effectiveness identifying and excluding plasma and blood with a high probability of transmitting AIDS. These procedures should include specific laboratory tests as well as careful histories and physical examinations.

4. Physicians should adhere strictly to medical indications for transfusions, and autologous blood transfusions are encouraged.

5. Work should continue toward safer blood products for use by hemophilia patients...

As long as the cause remains unknown, the ability to understand the natural history of AIDS and to undertake preventive measures is somewhat compromised. However, the above recommendations are prudent measures that should reduce the risk of acquiring and transmitting AIDS.

Source: *MMWR* 32 (4 March 1983): 101–104.

The Surgeon General's Report

In October 1986, Dr. C. Everett Koop, surgeon general of the U. S. Public Health Service, issued a report on HIV/AIDS in the United States. The frank nature of the report and its emphasis on the epidemic as a public health problem and not a political issue took both conservatives and liberals by surprise. The following excerpt from Koop's introductory letter to the report is followed by some sections of the report itself.

Acquired Immune Deficiency Syndrome is an epidemic that has already killed thousands of people, mostly young, productive Americans. In addition to illness, disability, and death, AIDS has brought fear to the hearts of most Americans—fear of disease and fear of the unknown...

My report will inform you about AIDS, how it is transmitted, the relative risks of infection and how to prevent it. It will help you understand your fears. Fear can be useful when it helps people avoid behavior that puts them at risk for AIDS. On the other hand, unreasonable fear can be as crippling as the disease itself...

In preparing this report, I consulted with the best medical and scientific experts this country can offer. I met with leaders of organizations concerned with health, education, and other aspects of our society to gain their views of the problems associated with AIDS... This report was written personally by me to provide the necessary understanding of AIDS...

The vast majority of Americans are against illicit drugs. As a health officer I am opposed to the use of illicit drugs. As a practicing physician for more than forty years, I have seen the devastation that follows the use of illicit drugs—addiction, poor health, family disruption, emotional disturbances and death. I applaud the President's initiative to rid this nation of the curse of illicit drug use and addiction. The success of his initiative is critical to the health of the American people and will also help reduce the number of persons exposed to the AIDS virus.

Some Americans have difficulties in dealing with the subjects of sex, sexual practices, and alternate lifestyles. Many Americans are opposed to homosexuality, promiscuity of any kind, and prostitution. This report must deal with all of these issues, but does so with the intent that information and education can change individual behavior, since this is the primary way to stop the epidemic of AIDS. This report deals with the positive and negative consequences of activities and behaviors from a health and medical point of view.

Adolescent and pre-adolescents are those whose behavior we wish to especially influence because of their vulnerability when they are exploring their own sexuality (heterosexual and homosexual) and perhaps experimenting with drugs. Teenagers often consider themselves immortal, and these young people may be putting themselves at great risk.

Education about AIDS should start in early elementary school and at home so that children can grow up knowing the behavior to avoid to protect themselves from exposure to the AIDS virus. The threat of AIDS can provide an opportunity for parents to instill in their children their own moral and ethical standards.

Those of us who are parents, educators, and community leaders, indeed all adults, cannot disregard this responsibility to educate our young. The need is critical and the price of neglect is high. The lives of our young people depend on our fulfilling our responsibility.

AIDS is an infectious disease. It is contagious, but it cannot be spread in the same manner as a common cold or measles or chicken pox. It is contagious in the same way that sexually transmitted diseases, such as syphilis and gonorrhea, are contagious. AIDS can also be spread through the sharing of intravenous drug needles and syringes used for injecting illicit drugs.

AIDS is *not* spread by everyday contact but by sexual contact (penis-vagina, penis-rectum, mouth-rectum, mouth-vagina, mouth-penis). Yet there is great misunderstanding resulting in unfounded fear that AIDS can be spread by casual, non-sexual contact. The first cases of AIDS were reported in this country in 1981. We would know by now if AIDS were passed by casual, non-sexual contact...

At the beginning of the AIDS epidemic many Americans had little sympathy for people with AIDS. The feeling was that somehow people from certain groups "deserved" their illness. Let us put those feelings behind us. We are fighting a disease, not people. Those who are already afflicted are sick people and need our care as do all sick patients. The country must face this epidemic as a unified society. We must prevent the spread of AIDS while at the same time preserving our humanity and intimacy.

AIDS is a life-threatening disease and a major public health issue. Its impact on our society is and will continue to be devastating. By the end of 1991, an estimated 270,000 cases of AIDS will have occurred with 179,000 deaths within the decade since the disease was first recognized. In the year 1991, an estimated 145,000 patients with AIDS will need health and supportive services at a total cost of between $8 and $16 billion. However, AIDS is preventable. It can be controlled by changes in personal behavior. It is the responsibility of every citizen to be informed about AIDS and to exercise the appropriate preventive measures. This report will tell you how.

The spread of AIDS can and must be stopped.

In addition, the following are excerpts from Dr. Koop's report.

The Challenge of the Future

An enormous challenge to public health lies ahead of us and we would do well to take a look at the future. We must be prepared to manage those things we can predict, as well as those we cannot.

At the present time, there is no vaccine to prevent AIDS. There is no cure. AIDS, which can be transmitted sexually and by sharing needles and syringes among illicit intravenous drug users, is bound to produce profound changes in our society, changes that will affect us all.

Information and Education Only Weapons against AIDS

It is estimated that in 1991 54,000 people will die from AIDS. At this moment, many of them are not infected with the AIDS virus. With proper information and education, as many as 12,000 to 14,000 people could be saved in 1991 from death by AIDS.

AIDS Will Impact All

The changes in our society will be economic and political and will affect our social institutions, our educational practices, and our health care. Although AIDS may never touch you personally, the societal impact certainly will.

Be Educated—Be Prepared

Be prepared. Learn as much about AIDS as you can. Learn to separate scientific information from rumor and myth. The Public Health Service, your local public health officials, and your family physician will be able to help you.

Special Educational Concerns

There are a number of people, primarily adolescents, that do not yet know they will be homosexual or become drug abusers and will not heed this message; there are others who are illiterate and cannot heed this message. They must be reached and taught the risk behaviors that expose them to infection with the AIDS virus.

Anger and Guilt

Some people afflicted with AIDS will feel a sense of anger and others a sense of guilt. In spite of these understandable reactions, everyone must join the effort to control the epidemic, to provide for the care of those with AIDS, and to do all we can to inform and educate others about AIDS, and how to prevent it.

Confidentiality

Because of the stigma that has been associated with AIDS, many afflicted with the disease or who are infected with the AIDS virus are reluctant to be identified with AIDS. Because there is no vaccine to prevent AIDS and no cure, many feel there is nothing to be gained by revealing sexual contacts that might also be infected with the AIDS virus. When a community or a state requires reporting of those infected with the AIDS virus to public health authorities in order to trace sexual and intravenous drug contacts—as is the practice with other sexually transmitted diseases— those infected with the AIDS virus go underground out of the mainstream of health care and education. For this reason current public health practice is to protect the privacy of the individual infected with the AIDS virus and to maintain the strictest confidentiality concerning his/her health records.

School

Schools will have special problems in the future. In addition to the guidelines already mentioned in this pamphlet, there are other things that should be considered such as sex education and education of the handicapped.

Sex Education

Education concerning AIDS must start at the lowest grade possible as part of any health and hygiene program. The appearance of AIDS could bring together diverse groups of parents and educators with opposing views on inclusion of sex education in the curricula. There is now no doubt that we need sex education in schools and that it must include information on heterosexual and homosexual relationships. The threat of AIDS should be sufficient to permit a sex education curriculum with a heavy emphasis on prevention of AIDS and other sexually transmitted diseases.

Handicapped and Special Education

Children with AIDS will be attending school along with others who carry the AIDS virus. Some children will develop brain disease which will produce changes in mental behavior. Because of the right to special education of the handicapped and the mentally retarded, school boards and higher authorities will have to provide guidelines for the management of such children on a case-by-case basis.

Labor and Management

Labor and management can do much to prepare for AIDS so that misinformation is kept to a minimum. Unions should issue preventive health messages because many employees will listen more carefully to a union message than they will to one from public health authorities.

AIDS Education and the Work Site

Offices, factories, and other work sites should have a plan in operation for education of the work force and accommodation of AIDS patients *before* the first such case appears at the work site. Employees with AIDS should be dealt with as are any workers with a chronic illness. In-house video programs provide an excellent source of education and can be individualized to the needs of a specific work group.

Strain on the Health Care Delivery System

The health care system in many places will be overburdened as it is now in urban areas with large numbers of AIDS patients. It is predicted that during 1991 there will be 145,000 patients requiring hospitalization at least once and 54,000 patients who will die of AIDS. Mental disease (dementia) will occur in some patients who have the AIDS virus before they have any other manifestation...

State and local task forces will have to plan for these patients by utilizing conventional and time honored systems but will also have to investigate alternate methods of treatment and alternate sites for care including homecare.

The strain on the health system can be lessened by family, social, and psychological support mechanisms in the community. Programs are needed to train chaplains, clergy, social workers, and volunteers to deal with AIDS. Such support is particularly critical to the minority communities.

Mental Health

Our society will also face an additional burden as we better understand the mental health implications of infection by the AIDS virus. Upon being informed of infection with the AIDS virus, a young, active, vigorous person faces anxiety and depression brought on by fears associated with social isolation, illness, and dying. Dealing with these individual and family concerns will require the best efforts of mental health professionals.

Controversial Issues

A number of controversial AIDS issues have arisen and will continue to be debated largely because of lack of knowledge about AIDS, how it is spread, and how it can be prevented. Among these are the issues of compulsory blood testing, quarantine, and identification of AIDS carriers by some visible sign.

Compulsory Blood Testing

Compulsory blood testing of individuals is not necessary. The procedure could be unmanageable and cost prohibitive. It can be expected that many who *test* negatively might actually be positive due to *recent* exposure to the AIDS virus and give a false sense of security to the individual and his/her sexual partners concerning necessary protective behavior. The prevention behavior described in this report, if adopted, will protect the American public and contain the AIDS epidemic. Voluntary testing will be available to those who have been involved in high risk behavior.

Quarantine

Quarantine has no role in the management of AIDS because AIDS is not spread by casual contact. The only time that some form of quarantine might be indicated is in a situation where an individual carrying the AIDS virus knowingly and willingly continues to expose others through sexual contact or sharing drug equipment. Such circumstances should be managed on a case-by-case basis by local authorities.

Identification of AIDS Carriers by Some Visible Sign

Those who suggest the marking of carriers of the AIDS virus by some visible sign have not thought the matter through thoroughly. It would require testing of the entire population which is unnecessary, unmanageable and costly. It would miss those recently infected individuals who would test negatively, but be infected. The entire procedure would give a false sense of security. AIDS must and will be treated as a disease that can infect anyone. AIDS should not be used as an excuse to discriminate against any group or individual.

Source: Dr. C. Everett Koop, *Surgeon General's Report on Acquired Immune Deficiency Syndrome* (Washington, DC: U.S. Department of Health and Human Services, 1986).

Firsthand Perspectives on the Epidemic

People with AIDS (PWAs)

In 1987, the founding meeting of People with AIDS/ARC was held in Denver at the second AIDS Forum. Here the National Association of People with AIDS was organized and became the catalyst of the self-empowerment movement for all PWAs. Although it was later pointed out that the following important document excluded women with HIV/AIDS, it is nevertheless considered a milestone.

The Denver Principles

We condemn attempts to label us as "victims," which implies defeat, and we are only occasionally "patients," which implies passivity, helplessness, and dependence upon the care of others. We are "people with AIDS."
    We recommend that health care professionals

1. Who are gay, come out, especially to their patients who have AIDS.

2. Always clearly identify and discuss the theory they favor as to the cause of AIDS, since this bias affects the treatment and advice they give.
3. Get in touch with their feelings (fears, anxieties, hopes, etc.) about AIDS, and not simply deal with AIDS intellectually.
4. Take a thorough personal inventory and identify and examine their own agendas around AIDS.
5. Treat people with AIDS as whole people and address psychosocial issues as well as biophysical ones.
6. Address the question of sexuality in people with AIDS specifically, sensitively, and with information about gay male sexuality in general and the sexuality of people with AIDS in particular.

We recommend that all people

1. Support us in our struggle against those who would fire us from our jobs, evict us from our homes, refuse to touch us, separate us from our loved ones, our community, or our peers, since there is no evidence that AIDS can be spread by casual social contact.
2. Do not scapegoat people with AIDS, blame us for the epidemic, or generalize about our lifestyles.

We recommend that people with AIDS

1. Form caucuses to choose their own representatives, to deal with the media, to choose their own agenda, and to plan their own strategies.
2. Be involved at every level of AIDS decision making and specifically serve on the boards of directors of provider organizations.
3. Be included in all AIDS forums with equal credibility as other participants, to share their own experiences and knowledge.
4. Substitute low-risk sexual behaviors for those that could endanger themselves or their partners, and we feel that people with AIDS have an ethical responsibility to inform their potential sexual partners of their health status.

People with AIDS have the right

1. To as full and satisfying sexual and emotional lives as anyone else.
2. To quality medical treatment and quality social service provision, without discrimination in any form, including sexual orientation, gender, diagnosis, economic status, age, or race.
3. To full explanations of all medical procedures and risks, to choose or refuse their treatment modalities, to refuse to participate in

research without jeopardizing their treatment, and to make informed decisions about their lives.

4. To privacy, confidentiality of medical records, to human respect, and to choose who their significant others are.

5. To die and **live** in dignity.

Ryan White

Ryan White, a hemophiliac living in Kokomo, Indiana, was 13 when he was diagnosed with HIV infection, received through a contaminated transfusion of the clotting agent Factor VIII. He was subsequently denied the right to return to his school; he and his mother fought a lengthy public legal battle for Ryan's right to attend public school. Though he won in the courts, his family experienced enormous hostility and ignorance in their hometown, and after a bullet was fired into their home, they relocated to Cicero, Indiana. There, Ryan met a welcoming community and found his battle had attracted the attention of numerous celebrities, such as Michael Jackson and Elton John. Ryan was memorialized on the NAMES Project AIDS Memorial Quilt as "Educator for Life" because of his efforts to speak out about HIV/AIDS. Ryan White died on April 8, 1990, at age 18. The following is excerpted from his testimony before the Presidential Commission on AIDS in March 1988.

Testimony of Ryan White

I came face to face with death at thirteen years old. I was diagnosed with AIDS: a killer. Doctors told me I'm not contagious. Given six months to live and being the fighter that I am, I set high goals for myself. It was my decision to live a normal life, go to school, be with my friends, and enjoy day to day activities. It was not going to be easy.

The school I was going to said they had no guidelines for a person with AIDS... We began a series of court battles for nine months, while I was attending classes by telephone. Eventually, I won the right to attend school, but the prejudice was still there. Listening to medical facts was not enough. People wanted one hundred percent guarantees. There are no one hundred percent guarantees in life, but concessions were made by Mom and me to help ease the fear. We decided to meet everyone halfway... Because of the lack of education on AIDS, discrimination, fear, panic, and lies surrounded me. (1) I became the target of Ryan White jokes. (2) Lies about me biting people. (3) Spitting on vegetables and cookies. (4) Urinating on bathroom walls. (5) Some restaurants threw away my dishes. (6) My school locker was vandalized inside and folders were marked FAG and other obscenities.

I was labeled a troublemaker, my mom an unfit mother, and I was not welcome anywhere. People would get up and leave, so they would not have to sit anywhere near me. Even at church, people would not shake my hand.

This brought in the news media, TV crews, interviews, and numerous public appearances. I became known as the AIDS boy. I received thousands of letters of support from all around the world, all because I wanted to go to school… It was difficult, at times, to handle, but I tried to ignore the injustice, because I knew the people were wrong. My family and I held no hatred for those people because we realized they were victims of their own ignorance. We had great faith that, with patience, understanding, and education, my family and I could be helpful in changing their minds and attitudes…

Financial hardships were rough on us, even though Mom had a good job at G.M. The more I was sick, the more work she had to miss. Bills became impossible to pay. My sister, Andrea, was a championship roller skater who had to sacrifice too. There was no money for her lessons and travel. AIDS can destroy a family if you let it, but luckily for my sister and me, Mom taught us to keep going. Don't give up, be proud of who you are, and never feel sorry for yourself.

Women and HIV/AIDS

The National Conference on AIDS and HIV Infection in Ethnic and Racial Minorities was held in Washington, D.C., in August 1989. Phyllis Sharpe, a New York City mother and former drug user, testified at the conference about some of the unique problems facing minority women. In May 1990, Ms. Sharpe also spoke at a demonstration at the National Institutes of Health in Bethesda, Maryland, about the lack of access to drug trials for women in her situation. The following excerpts are from these two statements.

My name is Phyllis Sharpe of Brooklyn, New York. I am a victim of years of drug abuse. I have six children and two grandchildren. I am single, Black, and have very little means of finance. In February 1988, I discovered I was HIV-positive. At that time, I was still a user. The Bureau of Child Welfare was called by a family member and my youngest daughter was taken from me. This happened ten months ago. She is now two years old and is HIV-positive also… I have been drug-free since November 1988… I joined a women's support group to accept both my daughter's and my own illnesses. This group helped me put things in motion to get funds, medical care, and housing… Without an apartment, the Bureau of Child Welfare wouldn't even think of returning my daughter to me…

Being a PWA and living on a fixed income, I've been forced to experience non-treatment and poor treatment. Seeing a different doctor each appointment who asks the same questions as the one before. Never being asked or told of a drug trial for women or children. I learned of trials in a support group, but it seems as though women and children aren't included. The only medications that are offered are AZT and Bactrim... Why are these the only drugs offered?...

I have a home now, but just 10 months ago, I was still homeless. Many people who are here today are homeless right now. One thing I can tell you about the NIH—they don't have any homeless people in their trials. And they don't have trials for people who use drugs either.

Source: Statements of Phyllis Sharpe in *Ending the Silence: Voices of Homeless People Living with AIDS* (New York: National Coalition for the Homeless, June 1990), 43–44, 51.

Intravenous Drug Users

The National Commission on AIDS, formed by the U.S. Congress in 1989, heard testimony in Washington, D.C., on November 2, 1989. The following is excerpted from testimony given before the commission by Ralph Hernandez, a New York City veteran and IV drug user.

My name is Ralph Hernandez. I am a Viet Nam vet. I am homeless, and I am living with AIDS. When I went to Nam, the government told me I was putting my life at risk for my country... I became disabled and finally I got AIDS...

I was honorably discharged from the United States Army in 1974 with a service-connected disability. But I had another illness too. In Nam, I had become addicted to drugs. Even with my handicaps I went to school, I got a job with the phone company, and I supported my wife and children. The whole time I was still using drugs.

In 1987, I started getting sores on my skin and my physical appearance started deteriorating. I left my wife and started shooting up more and more. I felt too weak to go to work. Soon I lost my apartment and then my job. I tried to get into the VA hospital but they wouldn't see me because I was homeless. They wouldn't even let me into the detox program. They told me to just stop shooting...

I went to the Washington Heights Shelter. When I took my clothes off in the shower, the other homeless people kicked...me. Then they called the guards and the guards threw me out. I went to another shelter but I was afraid to stay there. So I started living in the tunnels under Grand Central Station. Even there I had to hide so no one would see the condition I was in...

The VA had lost all my papers. I had been tested there for AIDS three times, but because I am homeless, they have lost my records each time...

For six months I have been in a methadone program and I try not to use drugs any more. But the VA is still not giving me any medical treatment. I still do not have a place to live.

I wish you knew how I feel when I go on the subway and see people move away from me... I served my country in time of crisis. Now that I'm in crisis, where is my country?

I am not the only one who has experienced this. There are thousands of homeless men and women with AIDS struggling to survive... Like me, they have no place to turn to.

Source: Statement of Ralph Hernandez in *Ending the Silence: Voices of Homeless People Living with AIDS* (New York: National Coalition for the Homeless, June 1990), 11–13.

The Twin Epidemics of Substance Use and HIV

It is my firm belief that policies related to AIDS and policies related to drugs are so intertwined that commenting and really wrestling and getting to the solutions to one will impact the other, and that it is necessary to consider *both* national drug policy and national policies related to AIDS.

Source: Testimony by Baltimore Mayor Kurt Schmoke before the National Commission on AIDS, December 1990.

In this the tenth year of the HIV epidemic the nation continues to face not one epidemic, but two: the twin epidemics of substance use and HIV infection. Since the early 1980s the close and deadly link between the sharing of injection drug equipment and HIV has been well recognized. More recently, the link between non-injectable substances, such as alcohol and crack, and unsafe sexual activity which can result in the spread of HIV infection has also become glaringly evident. Yet, instead of responding to these epidemics with public health and treatment measures to cope with both, the federal government's primary response has been imprisonment and increased jail sentences, often ignoring drug/HIV relationships.

Source: National Commission on AIDS, *The Twin Epidemics of Substance Use and HIV* (Washington, DC: National Commission on AIDS, July 1991), 4.

Recommendations of the National Commission on AIDS on HIV/AIDS and Substance Use

1. Expand drug abuse treatment so that all who apply for treatment can be accepted into treatment programs. Continually work to improve the quality and effectiveness of drug abuse treatment.

Experts have stressed the absolute necessity of treatment on demand. Immediately available, effective, high-quality treatment slots are the final goal. In 1991 the White House issued a strategy on drug control which proposed that $100 million be added for treatment expansion to allow 11,000 additional treatment slots to be created. In early 1991, the National Institute of Medicine estimated that 66,000 people are currently on waiting lists for various treatment programs. The National Institute of Drug Abuse has issued even higher estimates, indicating that as many as 107,000 people are on waiting lists.

2. Remove legal barriers to the purchase and possession of injection equipment. Such legal barriers do not reduce illicit drug injection. They do, however, limit the availability of new/clean injection equipment and therefore encourage the sharing of injection equipment, and the increase in HIV transmission.

   Programs that distribute bleach and exchange needles have demonstrated the ability to get substance users to change injection practices. Further, these programs, rather than encouraging substance use, lead substantial numbers of users to seek treatment.

3. The federal government must take the lead in developing and maintaining programs to prevent HIV transmission related to licit and illicit drug use.

   Although in the rest of the developed world, medical and public health professionals have directed national drug policy to target prevention of the spread of HIV within the injecting drug user community, there has been no parallel in claiming such policy-setting responsibility here in the U.S.

4. Research and epidemiological studies on the relationships between licit and illicit drug use and HIV transmission should be greatly expanded and funding should be increased, not reduced or merely held constant. With the definite link between HIV transmission and substance use well-established, there remain questions about the effect of continued substance use on the progression of HIV disease, as well as about what behaviors place people at the greatest risk of transmission.

5. All levels of government and the private sector need to mount a serious and sustained attack on the social problems that promote licit and illicit drug use in American society. The combined epidemic of HIV and substance use has hit hardest the individuals in our society who are least equipped to deal with it—the poor. The poor of this nation, especially within communities of color, lack access to medical care, housing, food, and other basic needs. Substance use treatment and HIV education may often seem like

luxuries to people who do not know where they will sleep at night or where their next meal will come from.

Source: National Commission on AIDS, *The Twin Epidemics of Substance Use and HIV* (Washington, DC: National Commission on AIDS, July 1991), 4, 7, 8, 10–14.

Homeless People with HIV/AIDS

On March 21, 1990, the House Subcommittee on Housing and Community Development held hearings in Washington, D.C., on a bill introduced by Congressman Jim McDermott (D-WA), a physician from Seattle. The bill was designed to provide housing relief for homeless people with AIDS. Irving Porter of New York City testified at that hearing and provided a dramatic statement of the problems facing the drug user seeking treatment. Porter explained to the committee how he intentionally made himself homeless in order to get what little treatment was available.

Approximately twelve years ago my life began to fall out of control. I found myself addicted to cocaine and alcohol... In 1985, I decided to do something about my drug problems. I knew I needed residential treatment if I was going to kick my addiction, but all the drug treatment slots were full. In October of that year, I learned that a few designated drug treatment slots were available for people who were homeless. I know it sounds crazy, but the only way I knew to get the treatment I needed was to become homeless myself.

So I gave up my job as a bookkeeper and gave up my apartment as well. I then entered the New York City shelter system. Little did I know I was only compounding my problems. I was entering a system that was easy to get into but almost impossible to ever get out of...

All I wanted at this time was to be interviewed and placed in a drug program. The sooner I got the hell out of the shelter, the happier I would be. After a few days, I was sent to Daytop Village...one of the oldest drug treatment programs in the country...

While I was in drug treatment, I revealed that I was bisexual. They then tested me for HIV without my knowledge. I was told by the nurse that my immune system was shot, but I was never told that I was HIV-positive... After 21 months...I decided to leave the program... I wound up in Greenpoint Men's Shelter in Brooklyn, New York...

As time moved on, I started losing weight. I became very weak. I would lose my breath just from walking. I went to Beth Israel Hospital. I was diagnosed as having pneumonia... I signed myself out of that hospital and immediately went to Beekman Hospital, where I was diagnosed as having active tuberculosis. I was advised by the doctor to be tested for

AIDS. I was tested and the results were positive. When I was given the news, I just wanted to DIE. I was put into isolation and treated for TB...

Again I found myself living on the streets... I collapsed while standing in line for a meal and was taken to New York Hospital...

The City put me in a "welfare hotel." My hotel room is certainly better than a shelter or the streets, but it is still not the proper living situation for a person with AIDS. I have been in that same room for almost a year. I am still waiting for proper housing. I presently have to share my bathroom with about 20 people. I have to be very careful not to pick up any infections. Also there are drugs throughout the hotel, so I have to deal with a lot of temptation...

If you take a look at the statistics on homeless people who are now HIV-infected, you will see that my experience as a homeless Black male has been and will be the NEW TREND OF AIDS... Even now the city, state and federal governments would like to pretend that we don't exist.

When I first gave up my home to enter the shelter system, I didn't realize I had gotten on a merry-go-round that I couldn't stop. The people I saw trying to get into drug treatment back then are the same ones I later saw in the shelter system. The ones I saw who finally got drug treatment are the same people I see today in the hospital and in my infectious disease clinic.

When I die, my death certificate will probably say I died of AIDS. But I want the world to know the real cause: a government that saw AIDS and left it unchecked... You think AIDS will stop with us. But HIV doesn't see skin color and it can't tell a person's sexual orientation. Because you didn't care, AIDS will continue to spread.

Source: Statement by Irving Porter in *Ending the Silence: Voices of Homeless People Living with AIDS* (New York: National Coalition for the Homeless, June 1990), 36–42.

Homeless people with HIV/AIDS are predicted to become a more familiar group of the general population as the virus spreads to represent a problem of poverty. People who are already ill can lose jobs and then housing; people who are homeless can be diagnosed with the virus. Congregate shelters actually represent a health threat to HIV-infected people, and the following excerpt puts forward a number of problems the homeless person with HIV/AIDS faces.

HIV-Illness and the Homeless

In general, the homeless in America can be divided into three groups, all vulnerable to the spread of the HIV epidemic. Approximately 40 percent are chronically and severely mentally ill, receive no treatment while they live on the streets, and are subject to total health care deprivation, multiple infections, alcohol and drug addiction, and physical abuse. The fastest growing segment are poor families, whose principal wage earner has become jobless or has low-paying work. These families now account for one-third of the homeless population. The largest homeless group is comprised of single men, of whom approximately 30 percent are veterans. Many have been on the streets for several years, have become desocialized, and have drug habits or criminal histories. These are all difficult populations to reach, and persons with HIV infection in each of these groups require a stable environment in which to live, access to medical care, and education about transmission.

Two types of housing for homeless persons with HIV infection currently exist and both are in critically short supply: temporary overnight shelters and congregate living facilities that provide a permanent residence. An increasing number of HIV-infected persons stay in municipal shelters on a night-to-night basis and are required to leave during the day. For these persons in particular, access to medical care is almost non-existent. Individuals often hide their illness because discovery may mean physical and psychological abuse, or because once diagnosed, they are no longer eligible for shelter residency. In many instances, once admitted to a hospital, a homeless person cannot be released until he has a permanent address, and shelters do not qualify as official residences. Testimony before the Commission indicated that too often homeless persons with AIDS and HIV-related diseases die in the streets, having found the health care system too difficult to enter or too unresponsive to their special needs.

Persons with HIV infection may become homeless when job discrimination or the debilitating effects of the disease result in inability to work and inability to continue paying medical insurance premiums, medical bills, or rent. Witnesses before the Commission have told of being unable to obtain rental assistance and being abruptly evicted by landlords, primary tenants, or, in some instances, relatives and roommates. Testimony stated that one woman had returned from a stay in the hospital only to find herself locked out of her apartment and her belongings on the sidewalk.

Housing for homeless persons with symptomatic HIV infection is even more limited than for the general homeless population. The person with HIV infection and a damaged immune system cannot survive for very long living on streets, in subways, or city parks. Even in shelters, he or she may be exposed to infectious diseases that could prove life-threatening. Among the general New York City shelter population, for example, tuberculosis has risen at an alarming rate. The housing prospects for homeless HIV-infected women with children are even more bleak.

Adolescents who live on the streets are another homeless problem directly tied to the spread of the HIV epidemic. Many of these children work on the streets as prostitutes in order to pay for food or to support a drug addiction. Organizations that assist runaway youth provide much needed protection for these adolescents, but the problem is greater than the supply of help, and prevention messages are often too late. Dr. James T. Kennedy, Medical Director of Covenant House in New York, testified before the Commission that in a recent study of his adolescent clients, 40 percent were already HIV-infected.

The housing crisis for homeless persons with symptomatic HIV infection is greatest in our large cities, which are unable to deal with their general homeless population, and are unprepared, in terms of resources, to respond to the new problem of homeless persons with HIV-related diseases. While it is difficult to establish concrete estimates of the size of the population of homeless persons with HIV, one study estimated that as many as 1,000 to 2,000 HIV-infected people reside nightly in New York City shelters. Mr. Peter Smith, President of the Partnership for the Homeless, Inc., testified before the Commission that: New York City has no separate emergency housing shelter facilities for persons with HIV-related illnesses; the rental assistance program is inadequate; only 18 scatter-site apartments are now available for persons with AIDS; the only specialized homeless facility for persons with HIV-related illnesses, Bailey House, has 44 units; and plans for renovating city-owned abandoned buildings have not been pursued.

The Commission reviewed federal housing and medical programs for the homeless and found the following obstacles to progress:

> An accurate estimate of the size of the homeless population of persons with HIV infection is lacking. Seroprevalence studies have not been done on this difficult-to-track population. An adequate assessment of the size and scope of the problem of homelessness of persons with HIV infection is necessary to target future resources. Individuals with HIV infection may receive low priority ratings for housing subsidies due to local regulations. Construction of shelters or group residences for persons with symptomatic HIV infection has not kept pace with demand in many cities. Municipal shelters are unable to diagnose HIV infection or target medical resources to HIV-infected persons in shelters. Hospitals are often unable to discharge medically stable homeless patients because they have no permanent street address. Service needs of special populations, such as adolescents and women with children, have not been defined or estimated.

Recommendations

Federal anti-discrimination protection for persons with disabilities, including persons with HIV infection, should be expanded to cover housing that does not receive federal funds... The Department of Housing and Urban Development funding for homeless assistance programs should be increased, and funds should be made more easily available to cities and private sector organizations to build both temporary shelters and permanent residences for homeless persons with HIV infection.

Operators of all homeless shelters and residences must treat those clients who are HIV-infected in an anti-discriminatory manner, protect them from abuse, and help them seek medical assistance as needed.

The Centers for Disease Control should fund and coordinate targeted seroprevalence studies (e.g., on adolescents, women, and adult men) to be conducted by city agencies in high prevalence cities to establish the size of the homeless population of persons with symptomatic HIV infection and to help cities determine the need for services. In addition to HIV antibody status, these studies should gather information on concurrent medical problems, such as tuberculosis and drug addiction, to both collect co-factor information, and determine the need for greater medical intervention in municipal shelters. Study results including geographic breakdowns should be made available to national mayors' associations, to the Association of State and Territorial Health Officials, and to state and local officials, as appropriate.

The joint project between the National Institutes of Mental Health and the Health Resources and Services Administration on adolescent homeless youth and HIV infection should be expanded and funding increased. More programs on homeless youth should be funded.

The Department of Housing and Urban Development should provide renovation grants to public hospitals to convert underutilized acute care beds into long-term care beds for HIV-infected individuals requiring hospice or other long-term care.

The use of the Department of Housing and Urban Development funds to help finance construction and improvement of nursing homeless and related facilities should be encouraged to make additional long-term care and hospice care beds available.

The Veterans' Administration should conduct a short-term study to determine the extent of homelessness among veterans, and HIV infection in this population.

Source: *Report of the Presidential Commission on the Human Immunodeficiency Virus Epidemic* (Washington, DC: Presidential Commission, 1988), 104–107.

The Impact of HIV/AIDS on Other Aspects of Society

HIV Disease in Correctional Facilities: A Model Response

General Principles

The National Commission on AIDS recommends that policies with respect to HIV disease in prison be guided by the following basic principles:

1. The HIV epidemic in correctional facilities is part of the same epidemic the nation is experiencing outside prison walls. Interventions among prisoners will save lives and will have a significant impact upon the course of the epidemic in communities to which prisoners will return.
2. Society has a moral and legal obligation to provide prisoners with the means to prevent HIV infection, and to provide adequate medical care to infected prisoners at all stages of HIV disease.
3. Decisions regarding HIV policies should be based on sound medical and public health principles. Interventions employed in the correctional setting should be guided by the same standards of care employed in interventions targeting the general community.
4. Control and prevention of HIV infection must be viewed in the context of the need to improve significantly overall hygiene and health facilities in prisons.

Recommended Guidelines

I. Medical Care
Asymptomatic HIV infection is a serious medical condition requiring regular medical attention and in many cases aggressive treatment.

Medical, nursing, inpatient, and outpatient services for prisoners with HIV disease should, at a minimum, be equal to prevailing standards of care for people with HIV disease in the community at large.

Correctional facilities should immediately address the controllable subsidiary epidemics of sexually transmitted diseases and tuberculosis. Infection control protocols established by the U.S. Public Health Service/Centers for Disease Control should be strictly followed.

Because of the complex and rapidly changing nature of HIV treatment protocols, quality assurance mechanisms should be implemented to review periodically the adequacy and efficacy of prison medical care.

Medical information revealed in the course of treatment should be rigorously protected from disclosure to non-treating personnel.

Treatment of drug addiction should be expanded until all prisoners who request such treatment are able to receive it.

Adequate care includes, but is not limited to:

- meaningful access to HIV testing;
- regular examinations by physicians with sufficient training to diagnose and treat HIV infection and HIV related illnesses;
- a full physical examination at the time the infection is diagnosed, and subsequently as medically indicated;
- access to necessary specialist care where appropriate;
- T-cell monitoring at the intervals prescribed by the U.S. Public Health Service;
- timely, consistent, and appropriate access to necessary medications, including prophylactic drug therapies approved by the Food and Drug Administration or recommended by federal health authorities;
- access to dental care;
- access to mental health care;
- access to meaningful drug treatment on demand;
- clean, hygienic housing facilities; and
- appropriate diets.

II. Identification

Voluntary HIV testing and counseling should be available to all prisoners who request it on a confidential and/or anonymous basis. All HIV tests should be accompanied by individual pre- and post-test counseling conducted by a trained AIDS counselor observing U.S. Public Health Service/Centers for Disease Control guidelines. Test results should never be made available to any prison employee, even prison medical employee, without the specific, written informed consent of the prisoner.

Mandatory testing or screening should not be employed.

III. Information and Education

HIV education should be a high priority for all correctional facilities. Educational programs should include components targeted at reducing behaviors that place individuals at risk, alleviating fear of HIV infection and people with HIV disease, and informing everyone in the correctional setting of available medical care.

Both inmates and staff need live, interactive HIV education from a credible, properly trained educator at regular intervals. Distribution of written materials and exclusive reliance in video taped educational presentations is not sufficient. All education should be culturally sensitive and linguistically appropriate.

Education to reduce the risk of HIV infection from intravenous drug use and sexual activity should be explicit, and include clear advice about resources available in the prison setting that may be employed to reduce the risk of infection, even where these behaviors occur in violation of prison regulations or applicable law.

Condom distribution should be part of overall health promotion and HIV prevention efforts in all correctional systems.

Because prisoners may discount information provided by prison authorities, outside organizations, including health departments and AIDS service agencies, should be involved in the preparation and presentation of HIV education programs wherever possible. Inmates themselves should be trained and equipped to serve as HIV educators among their peers, with adequate supervision and support from trained HIV educators.

HIV continuing education programs developed specifically for correctional social service and medical staff should be mandatory and regularly updated. Updated HIV education should be regularly provided for staff of departments of probation and parole as well.

Support groups for prisoners living with HIV disease should be promoted and encouraged. Correctional systems should work cooperatively with community based AIDS service organizations in providing support services and counseling to bridge the gap between institutions and the community, and to provide follow-up services as inmates return to the community.

IV. Management
Discrimination and punitive treatment of people living with HIV disease discourages them from seeking education, testing, and treatment, thus, compromising efforts to prevent new HIV infections and to treat persons living with HIV disease.

Prisoners should not be isolated or housed in special units solely because of their HIV serostatus.

Prisoners with HIV disease should be permitted to participate in all prison programs and jobs for which they are otherwise qualified, including positions in food or health services in keeping with U.S. Public Health Service/Centers for Disease Control guidelines.

HIV-related information in the possession of medical providers should be released only under extraordinary circumstances to prison authorities for the benefit of the patient. Staff should be trained to protect the privacy of inmate medical data. Work rules prohibiting release of HIV-related information should be strictly enforced.

Jails and prisons should have written HIV management policies and treatment protocols that reflect the most up-to-date medical and scientific information. These policies should be reviewed frequently.

Universal precautions should be integrated into institutional procedures to limit the health risk to staff and inmates.

V. Release

HIV disease should not be a reason to punish further any prisoner. Release should not be capriciously denied merely because of HIV status.

To maintain continuity of care during the transition from prison to the community, every inmate with HIV disease should be assisted in finding medical care and support services within the community. This should include assisting prisoners to register with community based case management services prior to release where such services are available and if the prisoner so desires.

Prisons and jails should have workable early-discharge and medical furlough programs providing for the timely release of inmates whose incarceration is no longer medically appropriate.

VI. The Role of Public Health Authorities

Public health authorities must recognize that even though legal and architectural barriers have been erected between institutionalized populations and the community at large, such barriers are often illusory. Individuals move to and from institutions, return to their communities and loved ones, as new waves of entrants await confinement. We must learn that we cannot speak of the health of the nation without also addressing the health of individuals in prisons, jails and other institutions.

Prisons contain a disproportionate number of people at risk of, or infected with HIV. Public health agencies should make intervention in this setting a high priority, and should work closely with corrections officials to bring successful public health strategies—for example, education, voluntary testing and counseling, health care—to bear in prisons.

Recommendations

In addition to the model guidelines outlines above, the National Commission on AIDS makes the following specific recommendations:

1. The U.S. Public Health Service should develop guidelines for the prevention and treatment of HIV disease in all federal, state and local correctional facilities. Immediate steps should be taken to control the subsidiary epidemics of tuberculosis and sexually transmitted diseases. Particular attention should be given to the specific needs of women and youth within *all* policies.
2. Given the dearth of anecdotal and research information on incarcerated women, incarcerated youth and children born in custody, federal and state correctional officials should immediately assess and address conditions of confinement, adequacy of health care delivery systems, HIV education programs, and the availability of HIV testing and counseling, for these populations.

3. To combat the overwhelming effects which drug addiction, overcrowding and HIV disease are having on the already severely inadequate health care services of correctional systems nationwide, a program such as the National Health Service Corps should be created to attract health care providers to work in correctional systems.
4. The Department of Health and Human Services should issue a statement clarifying the federal policies on prisoners' access to clinical trials and investigational new drugs. In addition, the Food and Drug Administration, in conjunction with the Health Resources and Services Administration and the National Institutes of Health, should initiate an educational program directed toward informing inmates and health care professionals working in correctional facilities of the availability of investigational new drugs, expanded access programs, and applicable criteria for eligibility of prisoners in prophylactic and therapeutic research protocols.
5. Meaningful drug treatment must be made available on demand inside and outside correctional facilities. Access to family social services and nondirective reproductive counseling should also be made available with special emphasis on the populations of incarcerated women, youth and children born in custody.
6. Prison officials should ensure that both inmates and correctional staff have access to comprehensive HIV education and prevention programs. Particular attention should be paid to staff training on confidentiality and educating inmates about the resources available in the prison setting that may be employed to reduce the risk of infection.
7. The burden of determining and assuring standards of care has largely fallen to the courts, due, in part, to the failure of public health authorities to take a leadership role in assuring appropriate standards of health care and disease prevention for our incarcerated populations. Bar associations and entities such as the Federal Judicial Center must, therefore, establish programs to educate judges, judicial clerks, and court officers about HIV disease.

Source: *Report of the National Commission on AIDS* (Washington, DC: National Commission on AIDS, 1991), 33–37.

HIV/AIDS and the Workplace

Responding to AIDS: Ten Principles for the Workplace
National Leadership Coalition on AIDS

1. People with AIDS or HIV (Human Immunodeficiency Virus) infection are entitled to the same rights and opportunities as people with other serious or life threatening illnesses.

2. Employment policies must, at a minimum, comply with federal, state, and local laws and regulations.

3. Employment policies should be based on the scientific and epidemiological evidence that people with AIDS or HIV infection do not pose a risk of transmission of the virus to coworkers through ordinary workplace contact.

4. The highest levels of management and union leadership should unequivocally endorse nondiscriminatory employment policies and educational programs about AIDS.

5. Employers and unions should communicate their support of these policies to workers in simple, clear, and unambiguous terms.

6. Employers should provide employees with sensitive, accurate, and up-to-date education about risk reduction in their personal lives.

7. Employers have a duty to protect the confidentiality of employees' medical information.

8. To prevent work disruption and rejection by coworkers of an employee with AIDS or HIV infection, employers and unions should undertake education for all employees before such an incident occurs and as needed thereafter.

9. Employers should not require HIV screening as part of pre-employment or general workplace physical examinations.

10. In those special occupational settings where there may be a potential risk of exposure to HIV (for example, in health care, where workers may be exposed to blood or blood products), employers should provide specific, ongoing education and training, as well as the necessary equipment, to reinforce appropriate infection control procedures and ensure that they are implemented.

HIV/AIDS and Health Care Workers

In early 1991, CDC's *Morbidity and Mortality Weekly Report* published an account of possible infection of several patients of Dr. David Acer of Stuart, Florida. By far it was this case and the attendant publicity given to 23-year-old patient Kimberly Bergalis, who came forward publicly, that reversed the public's previous conception of the danger in a patient–health care worker situation as being that of transmission *to* a health care worker.

Update: Transmission of HIV Infection during an Invasive Dental Procedure—Florida

Possible transmission of Human Immunodeficiency Virus (HIV) infection during an invasive dental procedure was previously reported in a young woman patient (patient A) with acquired immunodeficiency syndrome (AIDS)... Patient A had no identified risk factor for HIV infection and was infected with a strain of HIV closely related to that of her dentist... A follow-up investigation had identified four additional patients of the dentist who are infected with HIV. Laboratory and epidemiological investigation has been completed on three of these patients; two are infected with strains closely related to those of the dentist and patient A but not to strains from other persons residing in the same geographic area as the dental practice. The follow-up investigation included review of medical records of the dentist and interviews of former staff on the infection-control procedures of the dental practice...

Epidemiological Investigation of the Dentist's Patients

Following the initial report, the dentist wrote an open letter to his former patients, which prompted 591 persons to be tested for HIV antibody at the Florida Department of Health and Rehabilitative Services (HRS) county public health units; two (patients B and C) were seropositive. In addition, one infected patient (patient D) was identified by HRS by matching the list of available names of the dentist's former patients with the state's AIDS surveillance records, and another (patient E) contacted CDC to report that she was HIV-infected and a former patient of this dentist. Although the exact number of patients in this dental practice is unknown, approximately 1100 additional persons who may have been patients of the dentist and who could be located have been contacted by HRS to offer counseling and HIV-antibody testing; of these persons, 141 have been tested, and all are seronegative.

Medical History of the Dentist

Review of the dentist's medical records revealed that he was diagnosed with symptomatic HIV infection in late 1986, and AIDS in September 1987... He performed invasive procedures on patient B after he was diagnosed with AIDS, including the brief period when he was receiving antiretroviral therapy, and on patient C both before and after he was diagnosed with symptomatic HIV infection...

Investigation of the Dental Practice

The office employees of the dentist were interviewed regarding infection control and other work practices of the dental office. Of the 14 employees, eight had been tested for HIV antibody; all were negative... Interviews revealed no written policy or training course on infection-control principles or practices provided for staff by the dentist and that no office protocol existed for reporting or recording injuries... The dentist could not be interviewed before his death regarding his care of these patients.

Staff members reported that barrier precautions had been introduced into the practice by early 1987 and that all staff, including the dentist, wore latex gloves and surgical masks for patient-care activities. Staff reported that they changed gloves and washed their hands between most patient contacts; occasionally, however, they washed gloves rather than changed them between patient contacts. Masks reportedly were changed infrequently. Staff reported that the dentist's use of gloves and mask and handwashing practices were similar to their own...

Staff reported that by 1987 all surgical instruments were autoclaved... The dental practice has no written protocol or consistent pattern for operatory cleanup and instrument reprocessing.

Editorial note: Based on the following considerations, this investigation strongly suggests that at least three patients of a dentist with AIDS were infected with HIV during their dental care: 1) the three patients had no other confirmed exposures to HIV; 2) all three patients had invasive procedures performed by an HIV-infected dentist; and 3) DNA sequence analyses of the HIV strains from these three patients indicate a high degree of similarity of these strains to each other and to the strain that had infected the dentist...

Although barrier precautions were reportedly used, these techniques were not always consistent or in compliance with recommendations...

Transmission might also have occurred by the use of instruments or other equipment that had been previously contaminated with blood from either the dentist or a patient already infected by the dentist... This mode of transmission may be less likely than direct blood-blood transfer during an invasive procedure, because HIV is present in blood at low concentrations, does not survive in the environment for extended periods, and has not demonstrated resistance to heat or commonly used chemical germicides...

The precise risk for HIV transmission to patients during invasive procedures is not known but is most likely very low. Although AIDS has been recognized in the United States since 1981, the cases described here are the first in which transmission has been reported...

On June 14, 1991, the CDC reported that two additional patients were believed to have been infected by the dentist.

Source: *MMWR* 40 (18 January 1991): 21–27.

Responding to the Epidemic

Much has changed during the first decade of the HIV/AIDS epidemic in the United States. Medical and scientific knowledge, though still far from perfect or complete, more advanced. Many groups have organized to address the effects of seropositivity and AIDS in their own communities; the volunteer sector has taken the lead where government has not, and U.S. public opinion has evolved.

Established by the U.S. Congress, the National Commission on AIDS (NCOA) spent the years 1989–1991 traveling the country to learn about the epidemic. The commission held hearings, made site visits, and consulted with people with AIDS as well as with medical and scientific experts. The commissioners heard from over 1,000 people, including those infected with HIV, service providers, volunteers, and others. Then, in September 1991, just after the death from AIDS of Commissioner Belinda Ann Mason of Kentucky, the group released the report *America Living with AIDS: Transforming Anger, Fear, and Indifference into Action*. The following recommendations of the NCOA represent its ideas on incorporating all the needs around and facets of the epidemic into effective action for the future.

Developing National Policy

A comprehensive national HIV plan should be developed with the full participation of involved federal agencies and with input from national organizations representing various levels of government to identify priorities and resources necessary for preventing and treating HIV disease. The federal government should establish a comprehensive national HIV prevention initiative.

The federal government should fund the Ryan White CARE Act at the fully authorized level.

The federal government should develop an evaluation and technical assistance component for all federally funded HIV-related programs.

Elected officials at all levels of government have the responsibility to be leaders in this time of health care crisis and should exercise leadership in the HIV epidemic based on sound science and informed public health practices.

Access to Health Care

Government should assure access to a system of health care for all people with HIV disease; universal health care coverage should be provided for all persons living in the United States to ensure access to quality health care services. At a minimum, a system of care for all people with HIV disease should include a package of continuous and comprehensive medical and social services designed to enhance quality of life and minimize hospital-based care. Case management programs should be available to coordinate such care and should include: voluntary, anonymous, confidential HIV antibody testing and counseling; education and counseling to foster behavioral change; comprehensive primary and long-term care; psychological care; drug treatment; social services, including housing and income maintenance.

Medicaid should cover all low-income people with HIV disease. Medicaid payment rates for providers should be increased sufficiently to ensure adequate participation in the Medicaid program.

Congress and the Administration should work together to adequately raise the Medicaid cap on funds directed to the Commonwealth of Puerto Rico to ensure equal access to care and treatment.

Social Security Disability Insurance (SSDI) beneficiaries who are disabled and have HIV disease or another serious chronic health condition should have the option of purchasing Medicare during the current two-year waiting period.

States and/or the federal government should pay the continuing health insurance premiums for low-income people with HIV disease who have left their jobs and cannot afford to pay the health insurance premium.

The Department of Health and Human Services should conduct a study to determine the policies of third-party payers regarding the payments of certain health service costs that are provided as part of an individual's participation in clinical trials conducted in the development of HIV-related drugs.

Drug Trials, Therapies, and Other Treatments

The Secretary of Health and Human Services should direct the National Institutes of Health, the Health Care Financing Administration, and the Health Resources and Services Administration to work together to develop a series of recommendations to address the obstacles that keep many people from participating in HIV-related clinical trials, as well as the variables that force some people to seek participation in trials because they have no other health care options.

HIV-related services should be expanded to facilities where underserved populations receive health care and human services, in part to ensure their increased participation in trials of investigational new therapies.

Policies should be developed now to address future plans for the distribution of AIDS vaccines and the ethical and liability issues that will arise when vaccines become available.

Current efforts at the National Institutes of Health (NIH) to expand the recruitment of underrepresented populations in the AIDS Clinical Trials Group should be continued and increased.

The Food and Drug Administration should aggressively pursue all options for permitting the early use of promising new therapies for conditions for which there is no standard therapy or for patients who have failed or are intolerant of standard therapy.

The following interim steps to improve access to expensive HIV-related drugs should be taken:

(a) adequately reimburse for the purchase of drugs required in the prevention and treatment of HIV disease, including clotting factor for hemophilia;

(b) undertake, through the Department of Health and Human Services, a consolidated purchase and distribution of drugs used in the prevention and treatment of HIV disease;

(c) amend the Orphan Drug Act to set a maximum sales cap for covered drugs.

Education and Research

Congress should remove the government restrictions that have been imposed on the use of funds for certain kinds of HIV education, services, and research.

HIV education and training programs for health care providers should be improved and expanded and better methods should be developed to disseminate state-of-the-art clinical information about HIV disease, as well as drug and alcohol use, to the full range of health care providers.

Greater priority and funding should be given to behavioral, social science, and health services research.

The U.S. Public Health Service should expand and promote comprehensive programs for technical assistance and capacity building for effective long-term prevention efforts.

The National Institutes of Health should develop a formal mechanism for disseminating state-of-the-art treatment information in an expeditious and far-reaching manner.

Implementation of the Americans with Disabilities Act should be carefully monitored, and states and localities should evaluate the adequacy of existing state and local antidiscrimination laws and ordinances for people with disabilities, including people living with HIV disease.

Drug Use and Treatment

The federal government should expand drug abuse treatment so that all who apply for treatment can be accepted into treatment programs. The federal government should also continually work to improve the quality and effectiveness of drug abuse treatment.

Legal barriers to the purchase and possession of drug injection equipment should be removed.

Support for Community-Based Organizations and Volunteers

All levels of government should join forces with the private sector in providing long-term support to community-based organizations.

Federal, state, and local entities should provide support for training, technical assistance, supervisory staff, and program coordination to acknowledge and support the family members, friends, and volunteers who are an integral part of the care system of a person with HIV disease.

Source: *America Living with AIDS* (Washington, DC: National Commission on AIDS, 1991), 127–134.

Notes

1. Randy Shilts, *And the Band Played On: Politics, People, and the AIDS Epidemic* (New York: St. Martin's Press, 1987), xxi, xxii.

2. Ibid., 147.

3. Ibid., 142.

4. Ibid., 83.

5. Ibid., 183. See generally chapters 17 and 18.

6. Ibid., 206–207.

7. Ibid., 220–221.

6

HIV/AIDS and the Law

AS THE HIV/AIDS EPIDEMIC HAS EVOLVED, it has become more apparent that it touches virtually every aspect of daily life. Consequently, the states have begun to address the specific public issues the epidemic raises through state law. The major areas of law-making during the 1989, 1990, and 1991 sessions at the state level are illustrated in Table 4-12 in Chapter 4, "Facts and Statistics."

Chronology of Significant Federal Legislation since 1982

Following is a chronological summary of federal legislation on HIV/AIDS from 1982 to 1991.

1982	$5.6 million is allocated to research. These are the first allocated federal funds made available.
1984	$150,000 in targeted funds is made available to community-based organizations.
1985	The National Institutes of Health (NIH) receive a major increase in research funding.
1986	$47 million is added to federal spending to create what would become the AIDS Clinical Trials Group.

1987   The Helms Amendment passes the Senate, 94 to 2. This measure prohibits federal funding for HIV/AIDS education work that "encourages or promotes homosexual sexual activity."

Also, $30 million is appropriated to help poor Americans purchase AZT.

1988   HIV/AIDS prevention and research programs are established with the passage of the Health Omnibus Programs Extension (HOPE) Act.

1989   The Helms Amendment barring persons with HIV from entering the country is added to an appropriations bill.

1990   The Americans with Disabilities Act is passed; it bars discrimination against anyone with a disability, including HIV. The Americans with Disabilities Act (ADA) became effective in stages beginning in January 1992, and the law has an important impact on the issue of discrimination against HIV-infected people. The law prohibits discrimination against persons with disabilities, including persons infected with HIV, in all employment practices, including job application procedures, hiring, firing, advancement, compensation, and training.

The ADA also prohibits discrimination that is based on a relationship or an association. This protects individuals in situations where there is a threat to them because of unfounded assumptions about their relationship to a person with a disability. It also protects a person from action brought on by bias about certain disabilities. For instance, a person's hiring or continued employment could not be threatened because of the possibility that a spouse's illness would require the employee to take frequent time off. Also, individuals are protected from discrimination resulting from the knowledge that non-work time is spent being a buddy to a person with AIDS (PWA).

Also, the Ryan White Comprehensive AIDS Resources (CARE) Act (PL 101-381) is passed. This $350 million measure allows direct federal grants for the first time to 16 cities hit hardest by HIV/AIDS. About $200 million of the total funding represented level funding for already existing programs. Previously, federal funds were targeted largely to preventive measures rather than health care services.

1990
cont.

Title I of CARE provides direct funding to the cities that have more than 2,000 reported cases of AIDS or a higher incidence per capita than .0025. Title I is authorized in fiscal year 1991 (FY 91) at $275 million but funded at $87.8 million.

In FY 92, 18 cities are eligible for Title I funds. The 1992 revision of the CDC AIDS definition may also affect funding eligibility.

Title II funds the establishment of statewide care consortia; grants for home-based and community-based care; health insurance coverage continuation; and treatments. It is funded at 32 percent of the authorized level.

Title III funds counseling, testing, and early intervention, jointly administered by CDC and the Health Resources Services Administration (HRSA).

Title IV provides for pediatric demonstration projects, establishment of research priorities, and emergency response employee notification. Title IV was not funded for FY 91.

Also, $156 million is authorized as part of the AIDS Housing Opportunities Act to improve housing choices for people with HIV illness.

The 1990 Immigration Reform Act makes the secretary of Health and Human Services responsible for listing illness that would exclude immigrants, reversing the Helms Amendment. (In 1991, HIV was kept on the list, despite massive protest and resulting in the cancellation of the next international AIDS conference, planned for Boston in 1992.)

Source: AIDS Action Council, 1991.

Selected Legal Cases

The HIV/AIDS epidemic has profoundly affected many of the major institutions of this society: the nation's health care system, the schools, the prison system, the blood supply, the insurance industry. No other single disease in the history of the United States has resulted in as much litigation, and that litigation centers on some of the most important issues in the nation's judicial system: the right to privacy, freedom of expression, individual liberty, the right to know. HIV/AIDS touches our most personal relationships, as well as the routines of employment and previously anonymous encounters, such as blood transfusions.

Legal cases on HIV/AIDS can occur at several levels of the judicial system and in other public agencies. The federal, state, and local courts hear these cases, as do state and local human rights commissions and other administrative agencies. The following are summaries of just a few cases that have significance either because of the issues addressed or because of the outcome of the case. There are many other cases on many other aspects of the law. Complex cases can stay in the judicial system for years before a final decision is rendered, but these cases do give an idea of both the broad range of topics covered in such cases and the complaints heard by human rights agencies.

Discrimination Issues

Baxter v. City of Belleville, Illinois, 720 F. Supp. 720 (S.D. III. 1989)

This case first used the 1988 Fair Housing Act amendments to protect people with disabilities, including HIV-infected people. Charles Baxter was stopped by the city administration from opening a nonprofit residence for PWAs in need of housing. The American Civil Liberties Union (ACLU) argued that this was a violation of federal law, and the court found that the discrimination was based almost solely on "misapprehensions" about HIV transmission. The court found that the city could not prevent Baxter from obtaining the special permit needed for the house and agreed to allow the house's opening.

Bogard v. White, Clinton Circuit Court No. 86-144, Indiana; ACLU Amicus Curiae Brief April 9, 1986 Court's Finding of Fact and Order April 10, 1986 Findings of Special Education Appeals Board, February 14, 1986

Ryan White was a hemophiliac who entered the seventh grade at Western Middle School in Kokomo, Indiana, in August 1984. In December, he was hospitalized with pneumonia and diagnosed as HIV infected. He was too ill to keep up with school and prepared to repeat a grade in the fall of 1985. However, the school superintendent refused to allow Ryan in school; instead, he was connected to his classmates by speakerphone. Seven months later, a Board of Special Education Appeals ordered that Ryan be admitted to school, subject to recent state guidelines on the presence of HIV-infected children in school. Hours after his return to school, Ryan was ordered out of class, when a state court granted other parents an injunction staying the decision of the appeals board. The injunction was subsequently dissolved, and Ryan returned to school. His case had attracted national publicity and the interest of celebrities and activists, and after the final court decision, when the Whites faced continued hostility in the Kokomo community, they were able to turn to prominent supporters to assist them in moving from Kokomo to Cicero, Indiana.

Buler v. Southland Corporation,
7-11 Stores, Cir. Ct., Balt. MD. Sup. Ct. January 27, 1989

Buler had worked in the 7-11 for nine months, performing a variety of duties as a sales clerk. The manager ordered him to be tested for HIV, and he refused. He submitted when threatened with the loss of his job, and his test was positive. The manager suggested Buler kill himself and told him he would not be permitted to work in the store. Additionally, the manager told Buler he would prevent Buler from drawing unemployment and shared Buler's diagnosis with other employees, as well as with Buler's friends and family. Buler was fired and was unable to find work. He subsequently entered a psychiatric hospital for voluntary treatment; he later lived in a shelter for the homeless. The commission found that the company had unfairly discriminated against Buler and ordered him reinstated with back pay and benefits. In addition, the company was ordered to revise its employment policy to prevent discriminatory treatment of handicapped individuals.

Chalk v. U.S. District Court of California,
Orange County Superintendent of Schools, 840 F.2d 701
(9th Cir. 1988)

Chalk was a teacher of hearing-impaired students who was transferred from his classroom to an administrative position because of his diagnosis. His pay remained the same. Chalk argued that his medical condition permitted his continued presence in the classroom and that he was "otherwise qualified" to work. The court ruled in his favor, finding that a person with a contagious disease can be "otherwise qualified" to work if, with some reasonable accommodation, that person can perform job duties without exposing others to risk. To reach the decision, a court must review the nature, duration, and severity of the risk of transmission of the disease, as well as the probability that it would be transmitted and cause harm. Such a review must be based on up-to-date medical judgments and must consider the opinions of public officials. The court found that HIV infection did not constitute a threat to the students and that Chalk would be irreparably harmed psychologically by being taken out of the classroom; this harm could not be compensated.

Paul F. Cronan v. New England Telephone Company, 41 FEP 1273 (Mass. Super. Ct. 1986)

Paul Cronan had worked for the phone company for 12 years and was diagnosed in May 1985 with ARC. He was under a doctor's care. After repeated requests, he admitted to a supervisor the nature of his illness because he was in fear of losing his job. A promise of confidentiality was subsequently broken when his diagnosis was disclosed to management and other employees. Advised of negative reactions by co-workers and in fear, Cronan did not seek to return to work and was placed on indefinite disability. A few months later, he was diagnosed with AIDS. The court found that there were grounds for a claim of invasion of privacy and that Cronan had a handicap under the terms of the law. As part of the settlement that was reached, the company made a $30,000 donation to AIDS education work and prepared an educational brochure for workers. Cronan subsequently returned to work in October 1986, and some of his co-workers staged a walk-out in protest.

Doe v. Dolton Elementary School District No. 148, 694 F. Supp. 440 (N.D. Ill. 1988)

The school board ordered home education for a boy who was HIV infected and had ARC. However, there was no medical or other evidence to show that the child should be kept out of a regular classroom, and the court found that irreparable harm would be done to the child if he was denied a mainstream education. To balance the interests of the child and the public, the court ordered that the child be allowed to attend class and take part in extracurricular events. However, the court ordered that the results of monthly medical examinations be forwarded to the court and the school district, that the child be examined weekly by the school nurse, that the school follow CDC guidelines, and that HIV education be provided to the faculty and staff by the school district. In addition, the child was not to participate in any sports, and his identity was to be revealed to faculty and staff in confidence.

Estate of Campanella v. Hurwitz, No. 87-203PA
(N.Y.C. Comm. on Human Rts., July 31, 1991)

The New York City Human Rights Commission heard this case involving a claim against a dentist who refused to treat a gay man with HIV. An administrative law judge ruled that human rights laws cover such HIV discrimination in medical and dental offices and that a refusal to treat a person with AIDS was not justified medically and was not acceptable legally. Further, the judge stated that use of universal precautions—rather than discrimination against patients—is the best means to ensure a safe practice environment.

Iacono v. Town of Huntington Security Division, et al.
New York State Division of Human Rights; 1989 complaint

Iacono was a security guard at a commuter rail station; he was on sick leave from February to July 1987 and was diagnosed with AIDS in March 1987. In May, when he was certified by his physician as ready to return to work, he contacted a supervisor and also told the supervisor he had AIDS. He was advised not to share this information, not to worry about his job, and to see the town doctor before returning to work. Iacono had to wait seven weeks to be seen by the doctor and then returned to work. He was reassigned, his publicly owned vehicle was taken away, he was told to purchase his own gas, and he was given a radio for his own use. He was sent to a work location without heat or sanitary facilities. In January 1988, he was suspended without pay, and in May he was fired. The state agency found that Iacono had been discriminated against on the basis of his handicap.

Martinez v. School Board of Hillsborough County, Florida,
711 F. Supp. 1066 (M.D. Fla. 1989)

The plaintiff was a neurologically handicapped and incontinent child with AIDS whose mother sought a place for her in a training class for the mentally handicapped. Under the Education of All Handicapped Children Act (EAHCA), the school district was required to provide a free, appropriate, public education in the least restrictive environment possible. The lower court found that, because there was some possibility of HIV transmission, the child could attend class by observing from a glass cubicle to be constructed by the school district. The appellate court sought to balance the child's rights under EAHCA with the rights of the other students and worked for a compromise. The school district was told to build within the classroom another room with a large picture window permitting the transmission of sound; this solution would permit the child to learn and observe while eliminating the possibility of infection in either direction. Both the child's parents and other parents would be allowed into the observation room if they absolved the school board of liability for injury.

People v. 49 West 12 Tenants Corporation, Index No. 43604/83 (Sup., Ct. N.Y. Cty. 1984)

Dr. Joseph Sonnabend, one of New York City's leading physicians treating people with HIV/AIDS, was refused a continuation of the lease on his office. The Supreme Court issued a preliminary injunction preventing Dr. Sonnabend's eviction, and the parties agreed to settle. The defendant agreed not to refuse access to the doctor's patients, not to discriminate against the doctor because of the disabilities of his patients, and not to engage in any other discriminatory action based on disability.

Poff v. Caro, 542 A.2d 900 (N.J. Super L., 1988)

Three homosexuals filed a complaint with the Department of Human Rights when a landlord would not rent to them. The landlord feared the potential tenants would be infected with HIV and cause his family to be infected. The court found that persons at-risk of HIV infection are part of the protected class under laws protecting the handicapped from discrimination.

Ray v. School District of DeSoto County, 666 F. Supp. 1524 (M.D. Fla. 1987)

The Ray family had lived in Arcadia, Florida, for several generations. The three hemophiliac Ray brothers contracted HIV from use of blood products, and they were denied access to public school due to their HIV status. The court ruled that the boys would suffer irreparable harm by being denied a classroom education and that they presented little or no threat to the public. The boys were already suffering emotionally from their exclusion.

The court ordered that the boys be allowed into school, instructed that CDC guidelines be followed carefully, and prohibited the boys' participation in sports. The boys and their parents were ordered to be tested for HIV every six months, with the results reported to the court. In addition, the court ordered that the boys observe a high standard of hygiene, cover all sores and lesions, and avoid any school incident where

HIV transmission was possible. Further, the court ordered comprehensive sex education instruction for the boys and suggested that this be extended to the entire school system. The school board was also ordered to provide HIV/AIDS education for parents. After the court ruled, the parents and the school district reached a settlement that called for the Rays to be paid more than $1 million over a period of several years.

Subsequently, some members of the local community formed the Citizens against AIDS in Schools Committee and organized a successful boycott of the Ray brothers' school. The mayor removed his son from the school; the Rays received death threats. On August 28, 1987, Louise and Clifford Ray's home was burned down.

Raytheon Company v. Fair Employment and Housing Commission, Estate of Chadbourne, California Superior Court, Santa Barbara County, 261 Cal. Rptr. 197 (Cal .App. 2 Dist. 1989)

The deceased party Chadbourne had been a quality control analyst for a defense company; the company agreed he had been a satisfactory employee. Chadbourne worked closely with other employees and shared an office with five others. He developed *Pneumocystis carinii* pneumonia (PCP) and was diagnosed with AIDS; his physician informed the company that Chadbourne would be able to return to work when he had recovered. The company refused to allow him to return. Chadbourne instead volunteered at an AIDS center and at an addiction program. His estate sued for back pay, but the company argued that it had acted to protect other employees. After a lengthy proceeding, the state agency found that Chadbourne had a handicap under the law and was "otherwise qualified" to work. It found that the company's beliefs about HIV transmission were ill-founded and that the company had discriminated against Chadbourne.

T. v. A Financial Services Co., NY Sup. Ct. 1988

T. worked in a large investment banking firm as a member of the travel department; he had a diagnosis of AIDS or ARC and had Kaposi's sarcoma (KS). T. had been absent from work for medical appointments and was asked by a supervisor whether he had AIDS. He gave a factual answer. Because of his KS lesions, T. suffered frequent cuts on his face. On one occasion, he was sent home. Subsequently, he was placed on disability for a month because of a second incident. When he returned to the office, he was told that he was only allowed to touch his own computer and phone equipment and that any subsequent cuts would result in his being sent home. The court found that these procedures constituted unlawful discrimination and that any such restrictions would have to apply to all employees. Instead, the court ordered that T. was to report to the health station of the company in the event of a cut, and all employees were required to take an AIDS education program.

Thomas v. Atascadero Unified School District, 662 F. Supp. 376 (C.D. Cal. 1987)

Ryan Thomas was a kindergartener who had received an HIV-infected blood transfusion following his premature birth. After a lengthy administrative procedure, he was admitted to class with other children whose parents had consented for their children to be his classmates. Ryan was provided with a separate, locked bathroom. He subsequently bit another child and was suspended. The school board voted to bar him from school and provide him with a tutor. The court ruled that Ryan did not pose a risk to his classmates, as biting was not a scientifically established mode of transmission of the virus. Ryan was allowed to attend school under CDC guidelines, and the court found that he could be disciplined or suspended for other conventional reasons in the future.

Testing Issues

Estate of Behringer v. Medical Center, No. L88-2550 (N.J. Super. Ct., Apr. 25, 1991)

In the wake of publicity surrounding the Florida dentist's possible HIV transmission to five of his patients, this decision attracted attention because of its departure from the federal government's standard of "significant risk" for determining the employability of disabled persons. A New Jersey judge ruled that it was appropriate for an HIV-positive surgeon to be barred from practice at the Princeton Medical Center. The surgeon had sued after his serostatus had been made widely available in his place of employment. The judge also stated that surgeons were required to disclose any risk factor that a patient might want to know prior to an invasive procedure, ignoring the fact that HIV risk is not quantifiable in this situation. The court's ruling suggested that the routes of HIV transmission are not firmly established, threatened other antidiscrimination rulings, and seemed to suggest that HIV-positive surgeons could be deprived of their livelihood on apparently slender justification.

Doe v. Westchester County Medical Center, New York State Department of Health, Dec. 9, 1988

Pharmacist John Doe was first hired by the medical center in 1986 and reported for a pre-employment physical. A nurse from another part of the facility told the physician that Doe had been a patient at the hospital more than a year before and was HIV positive. The Medical Center subsequently refused to give Doe the pharmacist's job. The Office of Civil Rights of the Department of Health and Human Services ruled that the employer's position violated Section 504 of the 1973 Rehabilitation Act. The hospital appealed the ruling but lost a decision by a three-judge civil rights review board in September 1992. In the first federal AIDS-related civil rights enforcement action, the Bush administration ordered the termination of more than $100 million a year in Medicaid and Medicare payments (about 40 percent of the hospital's budget) to the hospital until the plaintiff was offered the job and back pay.

Glover v. Eastern Nebraska Community Office of Retardation, 867 F.2d 461 (8th Cir. 1989)

In the first such case to be ruled on in the nation, the requirement of an HIV antibody test for employees of a mental health facility in Nebraska was challenged successfully by the ACLU. The U.S. district court ruled that the testing policy violated the employees' right to privacy.

Leckelt v. Board of Commissioners of Hospital District 1, et al., E.D. La., Apr. 14, 1989 (1989 U.S. Dist.)

This was the first lawsuit to challenge required HIV testing for health care workers. Leckelt was a surgical, emergency, and intensive care nurse at Terrebonne General Medical Center; his partner, Potter, had died of AIDS. The U.S. district court first ruled that the hospital had a basis for requiring Leckelt to be tested in accordance with hospital policy and for firing him when he refused. A pending appeal of the case was argued in 1990.

Other Issues

Thomas Bradley v. Empire Blue Cross and Blue Shield, NY Sup. Ct., N.Y. Cty., No. 15290/90

Tom Bradley and his twin brother, Bob, were both schoolteachers in a small Long Island community. Tom sought to compel his insurer to pay for a bone marrow transplant that his doctors believed was an effective therapy for advanced HIV infection. The procedure is a standard one for immune deficiency, but Blue Cross regarded it as "experimental" and declined to pay. The New York State Supreme Court (the trial court) granted a preliminary injunction ordering the insurer to cover the cost of the treatment. However, Tom had an infection that would not allow for the possibility of the transplant. Blue Cross appealed the decision. Bradley died in late September 1991.

Gay Men's Health Crisis (GMHC) et al. v. Sullivan, Sec'y. HHS, S.D.N.Y., Oct. 28, 1988

GMHC is one of the oldest AIDS service organizations in the nation; several organizations joined to file this complaint against the language of the Helms Amendment, which restricted the use of federal funds for educational materials or similar activities where the "promotion or encouragement" of homosexuality could be construed. The legislation also required that material be "inoffensive to most educated adults" to be acceptable, even where those people are not part of the group for whom the materials are intended. The groups claimed that these restrictions made it difficult to produce positive and medically accurate educational material aimed at specific audiences. The court ruled that the federal government must show that these regulations have a public health purpose; CDC has proposed new rules that still contain the word "offensive." In May 1992, a federal judge held the rule to be an unconstitutional restriction of free speech.

Mixon v. Grinker, No. 14392/88 (NY Sup. Ct., filed July 28, 1988)

This class action suit sought medically appropriate housing—including a private sleeping accommodation and private sanitary facilities—for persons who are HIV-seropositive and homeless. Conditions in the city shelters and on the streets endanger people with HIV/AIDS, according to the suit, and placement in a shelter is not only inadequate but also harmful to their health.

Porter v. Axelrod
NY Sup. Ct., N.Y. Cty., filed Nov. 26, 1990

This New York case challenges the state's standards of care for residential health care facilities for persons with HIV/AIDS. The case charges the state with weakening its guidelines on HIV counseling, education, and prevention and permitting the Roman Catholic Archdiocese to obtain permits for two residential facilities for persons with HIV. Under the standards adopted by the state, those facilities are not required to provide various on-site medical services. At the center of this controversy are the questions of whether safe sex practices should be taught to residents and whether gynecological services should be available to women residents, including family planning education and counseling on reproductive choices.

S.P., et al. v. Sullivan, S.D.N.Y., No. 90-CIV-6294-MGC

This class action lawsuit, decided in mid-1991, pointed out the difficulties associated with CDC's case definition of AIDS. The definition relied on research that largely excludes anyone except gay men and does not accept illness and disability commonly seen in women, children, IV drug users, and others without access to health care. The Social Security Administration (SSA) relied on this definition and used it to deny the plaintiffs' disability benefits or to make them wait lengthy periods before qualifying. The federal government took the position that the SSA's regulations permitted a case-by-case consideration of applicants outside the definition, but the court found that such consideration does not in fact occur, leaving the CDC definition to prevail.

Wiggins v. Maryland,
315 Md. 232, 554 A.2d 356 (1989)

Wiggins was tried and convicted of murder; he was thought to be HIV infected because of the number of participants in his trial who were drug users and/or homosexuals. Because of his serostatus, court personnel wore rubber gloves during his trial, bound him, and remained a certain distance from him. Wiggins argued on appeal that these measures deprived him of a fair trial. The Maryland Court of Appeals agreed and granted him a new trial.

7

Organizations, Government Agencies, and Hotlines

HUNDREDS OF ORGANIZATIONS HAVE sprung up around the country to address diverse issues and problems presented by HIV/AIDS. In addition, many existing organizations have added HIV/AIDS components to their programs, as they analyze the influence of the epidemic or as they identify a need for action. Listed below are some of the major groups that fit these descriptions, along with their publications or products. Few of the publications listed below are included elsewhere in this book.

Many of these groups are national organizations; some address only the needs of specific populations. A few have been chosen because they do unique work. There are many more in every state or community, and many of the groups listed can provide direction in finding additional groups, as can the hotlines.

The second section lists major federal programs and agencies that are involved in issues of HIV/AIDS. Virtually every federal agency is affected by this epidemic, but those listed are most heavily involved. Also included are international resources.

The third section enumerates state departments of public health, AIDS agencies, and state hotlines; the final section lists national hotlines.

Organizations

ACT UP: AIDS Coalition to Unleash Power

ACT UP is an activist organization founded in New York City in 1987 by gay white men seeking to influence government policy on the epidemic through use of the media and confrontational direct action strategies, including civil disobedience. ACT UP is a decentralized organization with chapters around the country that are committed to participatory democracy, no identified leaders, no hierarchical structure, and access to information by all. ACT UP chapters can be located through gay and lesbian newspapers and gathering places, political clubs, HIV/AIDS service organizations, and university groups.

AIDS Action Council (AAC)
1875 Connecticut Avenue, NW
Washington, DC 20009
(202) 986-1300
Daniel Bross, Executive Director

This lobbying organization represents other AIDS service organizations and provides information on federal legislation and policy. The AIDS Action Foundation (AAF) is its tax-exempt affiliate.

PUBLICATIONS: "AIDS Action Alert" (AAC) and "AIDS Action Update" (AAF).

AIDS National Interfaith Network
300 I Street, NE, Suite 400
Washington, DC 20002
(202) 546-0807
Rev. Kenneth T. South, Executive Director

This coalition of ministries and religious organizations shares information and resources and represents the interfaith community on public policy issues in Congress.

PUBLICATIONS: "Interaction," "Special Edition."

AIDS Treatment Resources (ATR)
259 West 30th Street
New York, NY 10001
(212) 268-4196
(212) 268-4199, Fax
James E. D'Eramo, Executive Director

ATR provides information on experimental AIDS treatments and drug trials in New York, New Jersey, Philadelphia, and at the National Institutes of Health. ATR works to improve clinical research by advocating wider access to trials for minorities, women, children, IV drug users, and hemophiliacs. ATR publishes materials in English, Spanish, and Creole to reach those communities hardest hit by HIV-illness and least represented in drug trials and gives free workshops on experimental drugs and clinical trials. Publications are free to people with HIV or AIDS.

PUBLICATIONS: *Directory of AIDS Clinical Trials* (quarterly); "Deciding to Enter an AIDS/HIV Drug Trial"; "Should I Join an HIV/AIDS Clinical Drug Trial?"

American Bar Association (ABA)
AIDS Coordination Project
1800 M Street, NW
Washington, DC 20036
(202) 331-2248
Michelle Zavos, Coordinator

Coordinates HIV/AIDS-related activities and acts as a clearinghouse.

PUBLICATIONS: *The Directory of Legal Resources for People with AIDS and HIV;* quarterly newsletter.

American Civil Liberties Union AIDS Project
132 West 43rd Street
New York, NY 10036
(212) 944-9800
William B. Rubenstein, Director

The ACLU AIDS Project undertakes precedent-setting litigation, public policy advocacy, and public education on civil liberties issues raised by the epidemic. These issues include discrimination, confidentiality, public health policy, and access to care.

PUBLICATIONS: *Epidemic of Fear: A Survey of AIDS Discrimination in the 1980's and Policy Recommendations for the 1990's; AIDS and the Law Legal Docket;* assorted publications on testing and counseling issues.

American Civil Liberties Union National Prison Project
1875 Connecticut Avenue, NW, Suite 410
Washington, DC 20036
(202) 234-4830
(202) 234-4890, Fax
Judy Greenspan, Director

The project focuses a component of its work on HIV/AIDS issues in prisons.

PUBLICATIONS: *AIDS and Prisons: The Facts for Inmates and Officers.*

American Dental Association
211 East Chicago Avenue
Chicago, IL 60611
(312) 440-2500
Thomas J. Ginley, Executive Director

The professional organization for dentists provides guidelines for practice and education for its members.

PUBLICATIONS: *Journal of the American Dental Association (JADA)* (monthly); *ADA News* (semimonthly).

American Foundation for AIDS Research (AmFar)
1515 Broadway, Suite 3601
New York, NY 10036
(212) 719-0033
(212) 719-0712, Fax
Robert H. Brown, Executive Director

5900 Wilshire Boulevard
2nd Floor East Satellite
Los Angeles, CA 90036
(213) 857-5900
(213) 857-5920, Fax

As the largest private sector organization involved in AIDS research and education, AmFar funds biomedical research on AIDS where it identifies gaps in research and education, conducts educational programs, and supports innovative projects.

PUBLICATIONS: *Educating AIDS,* annotated review and bibliography of the range of educational resources on HIV/AIDS; *AIDS/HIV Experimental Treatment Directory* (quarterly); *AmFAR Report; AIDS Clinical Trial Handbook; AIDS Information Resources Directory* (annual); *AIDS Clinical Care* (monthly); *AIDS Education: A Business Guide;* "AIDS Targeted Information Newsletter" (monthly).

American Medical Association (AMA)
Council on Scientific Affairs/Panel on AIDS
535 North Dearborn Street
Chicago, IL 60610
(312) 645-5000

AMA is the professional organization for physicians. The organization provides guidelines for delivery of physician services and education for its members.

PUBLICATIONS: *Journal of the American Medical Association* (*JAMA*) (monthly).

American Public Health Association (APHA)
1015 Fifteenth Street, NW
Washington, DC 20005
(202) 789-5600

The world's largest organization of public health professionals, APHA endeavors to influence public health policy and to disseminate information on public health issues. APHA also is the U.S. distributor of World Health Organization (WHO) publications.

PUBLICATIONS: *Preventing AIDS: A Guide to Effective Education for the Prevention of HIV Infection; American Journal of Public Health* (monthly); *The Nation's Health* (monthly).

American Red Cross
National Headquarters
1730 E Street, NW
Washington, DC 20006
(202) 639-3223
Elizabeth H. Dole, President

The Red Cross's most central role in regard to the HIV/AIDS epidemic is in the administration of its 53 blood centers across the nation; half the nation's blood supply comes from the Red Cross. The Red Cross is currently in the midst of a two-year national revamping of its collection, processing, and delivery system.

PUBLICATIONS: The Red Cross prepares and distributes a wide variety of videos, posters, brochures, and other materials through its local chapters.

Association for the Care of Children's Health (ACCH)
7910 Woodmont Avenue, Suite 300
Bethesda, MD 20814
(301) 654-6549

ACCH supports the emotional and developmental needs of children by providing educational resources to health care professionals, researchers, and parents. ACCH's "Commitment to Caring" Pediatric AIDS Campaign focuses on supporting families of children with HIV.

PUBLICATIONS: *Children and the AIDS Virus: A Book for Children, Parents, and Teachers; Children with HIV Infection and Their Families: Organizing a Community Response; Family-Centered Care for Children with HIV Infection: Checklists; Pediatric AIDS: A Time of Crisis* (video); "ACCH News"; *Children's Health Care* (quarterly).

ATN Publications
P.O. Box 411256
San Francisco, CA 94141
(800) TREAT-1-2
(415) 255-0588
(415) 255-4659, Fax

PUBLICATIONS: "AIDS Treatment News"; *The HIV/AIDS Book: Information for Workers.*

B'nai B'rith International
Commission on Community Volunteer Services
1640 Rhode Island Avenue, NW
Washington, DC 20036
(202) 857-6580
Harvey Gerstein, Chair

B'nai B'rith International is the Jewish service and education organization.

PUBLICATIONS: *AIDS: We Care,* an education and action packet.

Body Positive
2095 Broadway, Suite 306
New York, NY 10023
(212) 721-1619
Paul Wychules, Executive Director

Body Positive provides information and support for people who test positive for the HIV virus in the form of seminars, support groups, public gatherings, a volunteer-staffed hotline, and social events.

PUBLICATIONS: *the body positive* (monthly).

California Prostitutes Education Project (CAL-PEP)
811 Clay Street
Oakland, CA 94607
(510) 874-7850
Gloria Lockett, Executive Director

CAL-PEP does well-regarded work in street outreach and education for persons in commercial sex work. It also offers a vocational reorientation program.

Center for Population Options (CPO)
National Initiative on Adolescent Aids and HIV Prevention
1025 Vermont Avenue, NW, Suite 210
Washington, DC 20005
(202) 347-5700
Wanda Wigfall-Williams, Project Director

CPO seeks to improve the quality of life for adolescents; its HIV prevention program focuses on the risk-taking, experimental behavior of youths. CPO's Teens for AIDS Prevention (TAP) program emphasizes teens as peer educators and advocates reaching other teens.

PUBLICATIONS: *Out of the Shadows: Building an Agenda and Strategy for Preventing HIV/AIDS in Street and Homeless Youth; Peer Education: Teaching Teens about AIDS and HIV Infection Prevention; Adolescents, AIDS, and HIV: Guidelines for Review; Resources for Educators; Reaching High-Risk Youth through Model AIDS Education Programs; Guide for Implementing TAP; Options* (quarterly).

Center for Women Policy Studies (CWPS)
National Resource Center on Women and AIDS
2000 P Street, NW, Suite 508
Washington, DC 20036
(202) 872-1770
Leslie R. Wolfe, Executive Director

CWPS is a policy research and advocacy organization, focusing on health, education, and economic issues affecting women.

PUBLICATIONS: *More Harm Than Help,* a policy report on rape survivors and mandatory HIV testing for rapists; *The 1991 Guide to Resources on Women and AIDS; Fighting for Our Lives* (video).

Child Welfare League of America (CWLA)
Task Force on Children and HIV Infection
440 First Street, NW, Suite 310
Washington, DC 20001
(202) 638-2952
David S. Liederman, Executive Director

A national federation of over 600 public and voluntary organizations, CWLA addresses issues affecting children and their families. In 1987, CWLA and the American Academy of Pediatrics co-founded the Pediatric AIDS Coalition. The coalition now consists of over 20 social services, child health, and advocacy organizations working to educate Congress, the public, and the press about children with HIV infection.

PUBLICATIONS: *Report of the CWLA Task Force on Children and HIV Infection: Initial Guidelines; Serving HIV-Infected Children, Youth, and Their Families: A Guide for Residential Group Care Providers; Miami's Attention to AIDS; Courage to Care: Responding to the Crisis of Children with AIDS;* and several videos, including *With Loving Arms* and *Hugs Invited.*

Design Industries Foundation for AIDS (DIFFA)
150 West 26th Street
New York, NY 10001
(212) 580-3311
Russ Radley, Executive Director

In 1984, leaders from the design, architecture, and furnishings industries organized DIFFA to raise and distribute funds nationally to fight HIV/AIDS.

Funders Concerned about AIDS
130 West 42nd Street
New York, NY 10036
Michael Seltzer, Executive Director

Funders Concerned about AIDS is one of several affinity groups of representatives from foundation and corporate funders who work together on a particular issue.

PUBLICATIONS: *A Funder's Guide to AIDS Grantmaking: Action Strategies.*

Gay Men's Health Crisis (GMHC)
P.O. Box 274
132 West 24th Street
New York, NY 10011
(212) 807-6655
Tim Sweeney, Director

GMHC is one of the oldest service organizations for people with HIV/AIDS.

PUBLICATIONS: "Treatment Issues" (newsletter).

Global AIDS Policy Coalition (GAPC)
International AIDS Center
Harvard School of Public Health
665 Huntington Avenue
Boston, MA 02115
(617) 432-4316
Dr. Jonathan Mann, Coordinator

GAPC is an international network for AIDS policy and program research.

PUBLICATIONS: *AIDS in the World 1992.*

Health Policy Advisory Center (Health/PAC)
853 Broadway, Suite 1607
New York, NY 10003
(212) 614-1660
Nancy McKenzie, Executive Director

Health/PAC is a public interest center advocating for appropriate, accessible health care for all, with an emphasis on the crisis in care for poor and minority people.

PUBLICATIONS: *Health/PAC Bulletin* (quarterly).

Human Rights Campaign Fund (HRCF)
P.O. Box 1396
Washington, DC 20077
(202) 628-4160
(202) 347-5323, Fax
(202) 639-8735, HRCF NET computer bulletin board
Tim McFeeley, Executive Director

HRCF combines the activities of campaigning, legislative lobbying, and grassroots organizing to raise the concerns of gays and lesbians in national politics and the legislative process. One component of that effort is work on AIDS-related issues.

PUBLICATIONS: "Momentum" (monthly newsletter).

Intergovernmental Health Policy Project (IHPP)
AIDS Policy Center
George Washington University
2021 K Street, NW, Suite 800
Washington, DC 20006
(202) 872-1445

IHPP is a university-based research program that focuses on state health laws and programs. The AIDS Policy Center acts as an information and resource center for state government agencies, research centers, planning agencies, and interest groups.

PUBLICATIONS: *A Summary of AIDS Laws* (annual editions from 1983 to 1992); *AIDS: A Public Health Challenge—State Issues, Policies, and Programs;* "Intergovernmental AIDS Reports" (10 times per year).

Lambda Legal Defense and Education Fund
666 Broadway
New York, NY 10012
(212) 995-8585
(212) 995-2306, Fax
Thomas B. Stoddard, Executive Director

606 South Olive Street, Suite 580
Los Angeles, CA 90014
(213) 629-2728
(213) 629-9022, Fax

The oldest legal advocacy organization for gay and lesbian people, Lambda also concentrates on carefully chosen civil rights litigation arising out of HIV/AIDS issues and on the policymaking of administrative agencies, especially in the area of discrimination.

PUBLICATIONS: *Living with AIDS;* "Lawyers, Clients, and AIDS"; *AIDS Legal Guide; AIDS Bibliography;* "Lambda Update" (quarterly); "AIDS Update" (6 times per year).

The NAMES Project
The QUILT: An International AIDS Memorial
The NAMES Project Foundation
2362 Market Street
San Francisco, CA 94114
(415) 863-1966
(415) 863-0708, Fax
David Lemos, Executive Director

The Quilt, started by San Francisco activist Cleve Jones in 1987 in memory of a friend, now covers many acres; the project receives thousands of new panels annually from friends, family members, and others; each square is worked in memory of someone who died of AIDS.

PUBLICATIONS: *Common Threads* (video).

National Association of PWA's (NAPWA)
P.O. Box 34056
Washington, DC 20043
(202) 898-0414
(202) 898-0414, TDD
(202) 898-0435, Fax

NAPWA is the only national organization directed by and primarily serving people with AIDS. Founded in 1983, NAPWA serves as a national clearinghouse of information and technical assistance for HIV-positive individuals and AIDS service organizations. Its focus is on information, training, and advocacy, and the organization operates a speakers' bureau.

PUBLICATIONS: "NAPWA News" (monthly); NAPWA Link (computer bulletin board).

National Coalition of Hispanic Health and Human Service Organizations (COSSHMO)
AIDS Education Project
1030 Fifteenth Street, NW, Suite 1053
Washington, DC 20005
(202) 371-2100
Concha Orozco, Project Director

Dedicated to improving the health and psychosocial well-being of the nation's Hispanic population, COSSHMO conducts national demonstration programs, coordinates research, and serves as a source of technical assistance, information, and policy analysis.

PUBLICATIONS: *The COSSHMO Reporter* (quarterly); *AIDS—A Guide for Hispanic Leadership* (English and Spanish); *AIDS Service Directory for Hispanics.*

National Conference of State Legislatures (NCSL)
HIV/AIDS Project
1560 Broadway, Suite 700
Denver, CO 80202
(303) 830-2200
(303) 863-8003, Fax
Tracey Hooker, Policy Specialist

NCSL's HIV/AIDS Project is funded by CDC to provide state legislatures and their staffs with up-to-date information from colleagues, experts, and government officials. The project operates an information clearinghouse, sponsors meetings, and offers other resources.

PUBLICATIONS: *HIV/AIDS Project News; State Legislative Reports; HIV/AIDS Facts to Consider;* "HIV/AIDS Project News" (regular newsletter); *Adolescents and AIDS; Protecting Health Care Workers from HIV Infection; AIDS Education Funding.* NCSL also offers LEGISNET, a database of state policy reports and issue briefs.

National Council of Churches (NCC)
AIDS Task Force
475 Riverside Drive, Room 572
New York, NY 10015
(212) 870-2385

NCC works ecumenically to provide guidance, leadership, and resources for congregations addressing HIV/AIDS.

PUBLICATIONS: *AIDS: A Pastoral Opportunity,* a packet of materials on pastoral care and worship, news stories, references, and statements from the major denominations. Also includes the addresses of other major religious HIV/AIDS offices and projects.

National Council of La Raza (NCLR)
AIDS Center
810 First Street, NE, Suite 300
Washington, DC 20002
(202) 289-1380
Norma Lopez, Director

NCLR is an umbrella group for more than 100 community-based Hispanic organizations. The AIDS Center offers training, technical assistance, network development, and needs assessment.

National Gay and Lesbian Task Force (NGLTF)
1517 U Street, NW
Washington, DC 20009
(202) 332-6843
Urvashi Vaid, Executive Director

NGLTF is a clearinghouse of information and provides education and advocacy on HIV/AIDS-related issues.

PUBLICATIONS: *Task Force Report* (bimonthly).

National Gay Rights Advocates
540 Castro Street
San Francisco, CA 94114
(415) 863-9156

This public interest law firm litigates in cases that have broad implications for public policy, such as insurance discrimination, quarantine, and civil liberties cases.

PUBLICATIONS: *AIDS Practice Manual.*

National Hemophilia Foundation
Hemophilia and AIDS/HIV Network for the Dissemination of
  Information (HANDI)
The SoHo Building
110 Greene Street, Suite 406
New York, NY 10012
(800) 42-HANDI
(212) 431-8541
(212) 431-0906, Fax
Alan P. Brownstein, Executive Director

This nonprofit national health agency is exclusively devoted to the health issues of hemophiliacs and others with blood disorders and complications; HANDI is the foundation's information center for local chapters in over 40 states.

PUBLICATIONS: "What You Should Know about Hemophilia"; "What Women Should Know about HIV Infection, AIDS and Hemophilia"; "Living with HIV: Adolescents with Hemophilia"; "Adults with Bleeding Disorders"; "Talking with Your Child"; "Hemophilia Newsnotes" (quarterly newsletter); *HANDI Quarterly* (quarterly).

National Lawyers Guild AIDS Network
558 Capp Street
San Francisco, CA 94110
(415) 824-8884
Eileen Hansen, Executive Director

The AIDS Network was founded to involve the legal community in the epidemic of discrimination caused by HIV/AIDS. Lawyers, legal workers, law students, and other participants are linked to AIDS service organizations to assist the service organizations in their work.

PUBLICATIONS: *AIDS Practice Manual;* "The Exchange" (periodic).

National Leadership Coalition on AIDS
1730 M Street, NW, Suite 905
Washington, DC 20036
(202) 429-0930
B. J. Stiles, President

Established in 1987, the Leadership Coalition brings together corporations, labor, trade, and professional associations, as well as key civic, voluntary, religious, gay, and ethnic groups, to address the crisis of AIDS.

PUBLICATIONS: *Business and Labor Speak Out on AIDS; AIDS and the Workplace: Resources for Workers, Managers, and Executives; The ADA and HIV: What Employers Need to Know Now; AIDS: Risk, Prevention, and Understanding; Small Business and AIDS: How AIDS Can Affect Your Business; Responding to AIDS: Ten Principles for the Workplace.*

National Minority AIDS Council (NMAC)
300 I Street, NE, Suite 400
Washington, DC 20002
(202) 544-1076
(202) 544-0378, Fax
Paul Akio Kawata, Executive Director

Minority communities have been disproportionately affected by HIV/AIDS. NMAC works to assist ethnic and racial minority communities with up-to-date information, technical assistance, and other resources. NMAC is a membership organization providing regional conferences through Project Health, Education, and AIDS Leadership (HEAL), focusing on microcomputer technology, financial planning and management, and volunteer program development. Project VITAL (Volunteer Information, Technical Assistance, and Leadership) reaches minority community organizations to develop resources for volunteer programs. Materials are available in English and Spanish.

PUBLICATIONS: *Technical Assistance Manual for Volunteer Program Development; Computer Technical Assistance Manual;* "NMAC Update"; "NMAC HEALer."

National Native American AIDS Prevention Center
3515 Grand Avenue, Suite 100
Oakland, CA 94610
(800) 283-2437
(415) 444-2051
(415) 444-1593, Fax

The center provides outreach to Native American communities, training, technical assistance, a national hotline, and a national clearinghouse. It operates the Native American AIDS Media Consortium to provide current information and camera-ready copy to Native American media, and it also organized the National Native Community AIDS Network.

PUBLICATIONS: *Seasons* (quarterly), statistics on HIV/AIDS among Native Americans; *Raven's Guide,* prevention resources including a directory of Native projects; videos.

National Network of Runaway and Youth Services
Safe Choices Project
1400 I Street, NW, Suite 330
Washington, DC 20005
(202) 682-4114
Jay Coburn, Director

The National Network represents more than 900 organizations serving runaway, homeless, and other youth in high-risk situations.

PUBLICATIONS: *The Safe Choices Guide; To Whom Do They Belong: Runaway, Homeless and Other Youth in High-Risk Situations in the 1990s;* "Network News" (newsletter); "Policy Reporter." The National Network also sponsors YOUTHNET, a computerized information system.

National Organizations Responding to AIDS (NORA)
2033 M Street, NW, Suite 802
Washington, DC 20036
(202) 293-2886
(202) 296-1292, Fax

NORA is a national coalition of over 100 groups that was convened by the AIDS Action Council in 1987 to more effectively address public policy issues. Member organizations represent medical, mental health, public health, legal, education, and social service professionals. Religious, civil rights, labor, and gay and lesbian communities are involved, as well as people with AIDS and organizations that serve them.

National Pediatric HIV Resource Center (NPHRC)
Children's Hospital of New Jersey
15 South Ninth Street
Newark, NJ 07107
(800) 362-0071
(201) 268-8251

A joint project of the University of Medicine and Dentistry–New Jersey Medical School and the Children's Hospital, NPHRC is funded in part by the Maternal and Child Health Bureau. NPHRC offers technical assistance, consultation, and training for health care and social service professionals who care for children with HIV and their families.

National School Boards Association
HIV and AIDS Education Project
1680 Duke Street
Alexandria, VA 22314
(703) 838-6722
David Demchuk, Coordinator

Local school board members from the states, possessions, and District of Columbia make up this organization, which provides support and a voice for the school oversight bodies of the nation.

PUBLICATIONS: *Reducing the Risk: A School Leader's Guide to AIDS Education; Leadership for AIDS Education,* a training curriculum for school board members; and a national report, *HIV Prevention Education in the Nation's Public Schools.* The organization also provides *The NSBA HIV and AIDS Resource Database,* containing sample school board policies, legal updates, and model curricula.

Pediatric AIDS Coalition
1331 Pennsylvania Avenue, NW, Suite 721 North
Washington, DC 20004
(800) 336-5475
(202) 662-7460
Pete Willson, Co-chair

The Pediatric AIDS Coalition is composed of 32 national organizations advocating for children, adolescents, families, and service providers affected by HIV/AIDS.

PUBLICATIONS: *Legislative Agenda.*

Pediatric AIDS Foundation
1311 Colorado Avenue
Santa Monica, CA 90404
(213) 395-9051

This foundation raises money for basic research on pediatric HIV/AIDS.

Project Inform (PI)
1965 Market Street, Suite 220
San Francisco, CA 94103
(415) 558-8669
Martin Delaney, Executive Director

Delaney started PI in 1985 to collect information on HIV/AIDS therapies and improve access to those treatments for PWAs. PI works to educate those at-risk, seeks early testing and aggressive measures for the asymptomatic, works to influence public policy on treatments and their availability, and initiates research not being done elsewhere.

PUBLICATIONS: *PI Perspective* (quarterly journal); *Strategies for Survival.*

PWA Coalition
31 West 26th Street
New York, NY 10010
(212) 532-0290
William Case, Executive Director

The PWA Coalition is mainly staffed by people with AIDS (PWAs) and provides current information on treatments, support groups, and other services. It is a major component of the self-empowerment movement for people most directly affected by HIV. Community Research Initiative (CRI), a community-based organization that supports clinical drug trials with pharmaceutical sponsorship, is a subsidiary of the coalition.

PUBLICATIONS: "PWA Coalition Newsline" (newsletter); "SIDAhora" (Spanish newsletter).

PWA Prison Project
All Care, Inc.
961 Clarkson Street, Suite 304
Denver, CO 80218

This national organization provides education and organization guidelines on prison issues for inmates and staff.

PUBLICATIONS: PWA resource directory on prison issues.

Robert Wood Johnson Foundation (RWJ)
College Road, P.O. Box 2316
Princeton, NJ 08543
(609) 452-8701
Steven Schroeder, President

RWJ is the nation's largest health care philanthropic organization and has a major component dedicated to HIV/AIDS funding.

PUBLICATIONS: *Advances* (newsletter); publications on grants awarded.

San Francisco AIDS Foundation
P.O. Box 6182
San Francisco, CA 94101

PUBLICATIONS: *Bulletin of Experimental Treatments for AIDS (BETA).*

Service Employees International Union, AFL-CIO
1313 L Street, NW
Washington, DC 20005
(202) 898-3200
John J. Sweeney, International President

This union represents workers in many of the front-line occupations exposed to the HIV virus: health care workers, emergency response workers, and public safety personnel.

PUBLICATIONS: *HIV/AIDS and the Health-Care Worker; The HIV/AIDS Book: Information for Workers; The AIDS Book for School Workers; AIDS: Everyone's Concern.*

U.S. Conference of Mayors
AIDS/HIV Program
1620 I Street, NW
Washington, DC 20006
(202) 293-7330
J. Thomas Cochran, Executive Director

PUBLICATIONS: "AIDS Information Exchange" (bimonthly newsletter).

Federal Programs and Agencies

AIDS Clinical Trials Information Service (ACTIS)
P.O. Box 6421
Rockville, MD 20850
(800) TRIALS-A, U.S. and Canada
(301) 217-0023, International
(800) 243-7012, TTY/TDD
(301) 738-6616, Fax

ACTIS can be reached 9:00 A.M. to 7:00 P.M. EST, Monday through Friday. A Spanish-speaking health specialist is available. ACTIS is a Public Health Service collaborative project provided by the Centers for Disease Control, the Food and Drug Administration, the National Institute of Allergy and Infectious Diseases, and the National Library of Medicine. The bilingual ACTIS hotline puts callers in contact with health specialists who can describe the purpose of specific clinical trials and their eligibility requirements, as well as how to contact the testing sites. Calls are confidential. Callers can also directly access this information through the databases of the National Library of Medicine, AIDSTRIALS and AIDSDRUGS.

Alcohol, Drug Abuse, and Mental Health Administration (ADAMHA)
5600 Fishers Lane, Room 12C-15
Rockville, MD 20857
(301) 443-3783

ADAMHA includes the National Institute of Mental Health (NIMH), the National Institute on Drug Abuse (NIDA), and the National Institute on Alcohol Abuse and Alcoholism (NIAAA). ADAMHA performs 85 percent of the research on biomedical and behavioral aspects of alcoholism, drug abuse, and mental health.

Centers for Disease Control (CDC)
National AIDS Information and Education Program
Executive Park 26-E25
1600 Clifton Road, NE
Atlanta, GA 30333
(404) 639-3311
William L. Roper, M.D., M.P.H., Director
James W. Currant, M.D., M.P.H., Director, Division of HIV/AIDS

CDC is a component of the Department of Health and Human Services. CDC's national program was created to inform and educate the U.S. public about HIV/AIDS. The major components of the program are "America Responds to AIDS," CDC's national media campaign; the National AIDS Hotline; and the National AIDS Information Clearinghouse.

PUBLICATIONS: *Morbidity and Mortality Weekly Report* (*MMWR*) (weekly); *HIV/AIDS Surveillance* (monthly); *America Responds to AIDS Materials Catalog; CDC Plan for Preventing Human Immunodeficiency Virus*

(HIV) Infection: A Blueprint for the 1990s; CDC HIV/AIDS Prevention Fact Book 1990.

Department of Veterans Affairs (VA)
VA Central Office
AIDS Program Office
810 Vermont Avenue, NW
Washington, DC 20420
(202) 233-3631
Anthony J. Principi, Acting Administrator of Veterans Affairs

VA hospitals across the nation see 7 percent of all HIV/AIDS patients.

Food and Drug Administration (FDA)
5600 Fishers Lane
Rockville, MD 20857
(301) 443-3285
David A. Kessler, M.D., Commissioner of Food and Drugs

This federal consumer protection agency is responsible for evaluating and approving new therapies. The FDA grants permission to pharmaceutical companies to test experimental drugs and biologic products on humans, monitors the progress of those trials, and reviews the results. FDA also inspects the more than 2,500 registered blood collection establishments that collect more than 11 million units of blood annually.

PUBLICATIONS: *FDA Consumer* (10 times per year).

Health Care Financing Administration (HCFA)
U.S. Department of Health and Human Services
6325 Security Boulevard
Baltimore, MD 21207
(301) 966-3000
Gail R. Wilensky, Administrator

HCFA plays a major role in health care financing for people with HIV/AIDS and is responsible for administering the Medicare program and the federal portion of the Medicaid program.

Health Resources Services Administration (HRSA)
5600 Fishers Lane
Rockville, MD 20857
(301) 443-3377

This agency of HHS focuses on the delivery of health services.

National AIDS Hotline
(800) 342-AIDS, Toll-free hotline;
(800) 344-SIDA, Spanish-language hotline;
(800) AIDS-TTY, TTY line

This hotline is part of the Centers for Disease Control's (CDC) National AIDS Information and Education Program. The hotline provides confidential information and referrals to the public 24 hours a day.

National AIDS Information Clearinghouse (NAIC)
P.O. Box 6003
Rockville, MD 20850
(800) 458-5231, Toll-free reference line
(301) 217-0023, International calls
(800) 243- 7012, TTY-TDD
(301) 738-6616, Fax

Services are available 9:00 A.M. to 7:00 P.M. EST, Monday through Friday. Spanish and French language referral specialists are available. A service of the U.S. Department of Health and Human Services, Public Health Service, and Centers for Disease Control, NAIC offers HIV/AIDS information, resources, and publications for educators, public health professionals, employers, and others in businesses, community-based organizations, service agencies, and other settings. Reference specialists use information databases in the areas of funding, educational materials, school health education, and resources to help callers. These databases are further described in the "Nonprint Materials" section of Chapter 8.

PUBLICATIONS: **Pamphlets:** *AIDS and You; AIDS Prevention Guide; Caring for Someone with AIDS; Condoms and Sexually Transmitted Diseases; Eating Defensively: Food Safety Advice for Persons with AIDS; HIV Infection and AIDS; How You Won't Get AIDS; Surgeon General's Report on AIDS; Tuberculosis; What about AIDS Testing?; Voluntary HIV Testing and Counseling* (all available in English or Spanish); and *Understanding AIDS* (also available in Braille, Asian languages, and Haitian/Creole). **Resource Guides:** *AIDS and Deafness Resource Directory; AIDS and the Workplace; Directory of AIDS-Related Databases and Bulletin Boards; Catalog of HIV/AIDS Materials for Professionals;* and *User Guide to National AIDS Information Clearinghouse Services.* **Reports:** *Morbidity and Mortality Weekly Report (MMWR)* (weekly), *HIV/AIDS Surveillance Report* (monthly); and *The National AIDS Information Clearinghouse Conference*

Calendar (quarterly). **Also:** Assorted posters, display boards, and fact sheets are available. **Videos:** *AIDS Health Fraud; Eating Defensively,; and I Have AIDS: A Teenager's Story.*

National AIDS Program Office
Hubert H. Humphrey Building
200 Independence Avenue, SW, Room 738G
Washington, DC 20201
James Allen, M.D., Director

This Public Health Service component focuses on coordination and integration of prevention and control efforts.

National Commission on AIDS (NCOA)
1730 K Street, NW
Washington, DC 20006
(202) 254-5125
(202) 254-3060, Fax
June E. Osborn, M.D., Chair

NCOA was created by Congress in 1989 and convened a series of hearings and site visits around the nation. It has issued a series of provocative reports that call on the federal government to take increasingly more specific action to stem the epidemic.

PUBLICATIONS: *Failure of U.S. Health Care System to Deal with HIV Epidemic; Leadership, Legislation, and Regulation; Research, the Workforce and the HIV Epidemic in Rural America.*

National Institute of Allergy and Infectious Diseases (NIAID)
9000 Rockville Pike
Bethesda, MD 20892
(301) 496-4000
Dr. Anthony Fauci, Director

NIAID has the major responsibility for funding federally sponsored AIDS clinical trials and supports a national network of AIDS Clinical Trials Units to enroll patients.

National Institutes of Health (NIH)
9000 Rockville Pike, Building 31, Room 7A32
Bethesda, MD 20892
(301) 496-5717
Dr. Bernadine Healy, Director

NIH is the federal government's primary biomedical research agency, performing clinical and laboratory studies as well as supporting the work of scientists in universities, medical schools, and hospitals.

National Library of Medicine (NLM)
8600 Rockville Pike
Bethesda, MD 20892
(301) 496-4000

NLM serves as a reference library to supplement local, national, and other resources. NLM provides online services to users worldwide who are seeking information from its databases.

PUBLICATIONS: *AIDS Bibliography* (monthly).

Office of Minority Health
U.S. Public Health Service
Hubert H. Humphrey Building
200 Independence Avenue, SW
Washington, DC 20201
(202) 245-0020

HIV/AIDS, cancer, cardiovascular illness, diabetes, substance use, infant mortality, and violence all affect minorities disproportionately. This Public Health Service office focuses on these problems.

Social Security Administration (SSA)
1500 Woodlawn Drive
Baltimore, MD 21241
(301) 965-7675
Gwendolyn S. King, Commissioner

SSA is responsible for handling disability claims.

U.S. Department of Health and Human Services (HHS)
Hubert H. Humphrey Building
200 Independence Avenue, SW
Washington, DC 20201
(202) 245-6867
Louis Sullivan, M.D., Secretary

HHS is the health policy agency of the federal government.

U.S. Public Health Service (PHS)
5600 Fishers Lane
Rockville, MD 20857
(301) 443-4000
Dr. Antonia Novello, Surgeon General

PHS is a component of HHS and has responsibility for issues and problems affecting the public health, including the reporting, control, and spread of disease.

World Health Organization (WHO)
Global Programme on AIDS
1211 Geneva 27
Switzerland

WHO is an international agency addressing health issues around the world.

PUBLICATIONS: *Guide to Planning Health Promotion for AIDS Prevention and Control; Guidelines on Sterilization and Disinfection Methods Effective against Human Immunodeficiency Virus (HIV); Prevention of Sexual Transmission of Human Immunodeficiency Virus; Bulletin of the World Health Organization* (bimonthly); *World Health Forum* (quarterly); *Weekly Epidemiological Record* (weekly); *AIDS Health Promotion Exchange* (quarterly).

State AIDS Coordinators and Hotlines

Alabama Department of Health
AIDS Branch
434 Monroe Street
Montgomery, AL 36130
(800) 228-0469
(205) 242-5838

Alaska Department of Health
AIDS Health Program
P.O. Box 240249
Anchorage, AK 99524
(800) 478-AIDS
(907) 561-4406

Arizona Department of Health
AIDS Program Office
Department of Health Services
3008 North 3rd Street
Phoenix, AZ 85012
(800) 342-AIDS
(602) 230-5819

Arkansas Department of Health
AIDS Coordinator
4815 West Markham Street
Little Rock, AR 72205
(800) 445-7720
(501) 661-2315

California Department of Health
Office of AIDS
714-744 P Street/P.O. Box 942732
Sacramento, CA 94234
(800) 876-AIDS (S. CA)
(800) 922-AIDS (N. CA)

Colorado Department of Health
AIDS Program
4210 East 11th Street, Room 221
Denver, CO 80220
(800) 252-AIDS
(303) 331-8320

Connecticut Department of Health
AIDS Program
150 Washington Street
Hartford, CT 06106
(800) 342-AIDS
(203) 566-2048

Delaware Division of Public Health
AIDS Coordinator
Jesse Cooper Building
Federal and Water Streets
Wilmington, DE 19901
(800) 422-0429
(302) 739-3033

D.C. Government
Office of AIDS Activities
1600 L Street, NW, Suite 700
Washington, DC 20036
(202) 673-3679
(202) 332-AIDS

Florida Department of Health and Rehabilitative Services
AIDS Program Administrator
1317 Winewood Boulevard
Building 2
Tallahassee, FL 32399
(800) FLA-AIDS
(904) 487-2478

Georgia Department of Infectious Diseases
878 Peachtree Street, NE
Atlanta, GA 30309
(800) 551-2728
(404) 894-5307

Hawaii Department of Health
STD and AIDS Prevention Branch
3627 Kilauea Avenue, Room 306
Honolulu, HI 96816
(808) 735-9010
(808) 922-1313

Idaho Bureau of Communicable Disease Prevention
STD/AIDS Program Supervisor
450 West State Street
Boise, ID 83720
(208) 334-6526

Illinois Department of Health
Infectious Diseases, AIDS Activity Section
100 West Randolph Street, Room 6-600
Chicago, IL 60601
(800) 243-2437
(217) 814-4846

Indiana State Board of Health
Division of Acquired Disease
1330 West Michigan
P.O. Box 1964
Indianapolis, IN 46206
(800) 848-AIDS
(317) 633-8406

Iowa Department of Public Health
AIDS Education
Lucas Building, Third Floor
Des Moines, IA 50319
(800) 532-3301
(515) 281-4938

Kansas Department of Health and Environment
Office of Health Education
109 SW 9th Street, Suite 605
Topeka, KS 66612
(800) 232-0109
(913) 296-5586

Kentucky Department for Health Services
AIDS Health Education
275 East Main Street
Frankfort, KY 40621
(800) 654-AIDS
(502) 564-3418

Louisiana Department of Health and Hospitals
Room 615
P.O. Box 60630
New Orleans, LA 70160
(800) 992-4379
(504) 568-5005

Maine Department of Human Services
Office of AIDS Programs
State House, Station 11
Augusta, ME 04333
(800) 638-6252
(207) 289-3747

Maryland Department of Health and Mental Hygiene
AIDS Administration
201 West Preston Street, Room 308
Baltimore, MD 21201
(800) 638-6252
(301) 225-6707

Massachusetts Department of Public Health
AIDS Programs and Health Resources
150 Tremont Street, 11th Floor
Boston, MA 02111
(800) 235-2331
(617) 727-0368

Michigan Department of Health
Special Office on AIDS Prevention
3423 North Logan Street
Lansing, MI 48906
(800) 872-AIDS
(517) 335-8371

Minnesota Department of Health
AIDS Program
717 SE Delaware Street
Minneapolis, MN 55440
(800) 248-AIDS
(612) 623-5363

Mississippi Department of Health
AIDS Prevention
Box 1700
Jackson, MS 39215
(800) 826-2961
(601) 960-7723

Missouri Department of Health
Bureau of AIDS Prevention
1730 East Elm
P.O. Box 570
Jefferson City, MO 65101
(800) 533-AIDS
(314) 751-6149

Montana Department of Health—AIDS Program
Cogswell Building
Helena, MT 59260
(800) 537-6187
(406) 444-4740

Nebraska Department of Health
AIDS Program
301 Centennial Mall South/Box 95007
Lincoln, NE 68509
(800) 782-AIDS
(402) 471-2937

Nevada State Health Division
State AIDS Coordinator
505 East King Street, Room 104
Carson City, NV 89710
(702) 687-4804

New Hampshire Public Health Service
6 Hazen Drive
Concord, NH 03301
(800) 872-8909
(603) 271-4576

New Jersey Division of AIDS Prevention and Control
363 West State Street, C.N. 360
Trenton, NJ 08625
(800) 624-2377
(609) 984-6000

New Mexico Department of Health
AIDS Prevention Program
1190 St. Francis Drive
Santa Fe, NM 85702
(800) 545-AIDS
(505) 827-0086

New York State Department of Health
AIDS Institute
Empire State Plaza, Corning Tower, Room 342
Albany, NY 12237
(800) 541-AIDS
(518) 474-7542

North Carolina Division of Epidemiology
AIDS Control Program
Box 27687
Raleigh, NC 27611
(800) 535-AIDS
(919) 733-7301

North Dakota Department of Health
State AIDS Coordinator
State Capitol Building
Bismarck, ND 58505
(800) 472-2180
(710) 224-2378

Ohio Department of Health
AIDS Activity Unit
P.O. Box 118
Columbus, OH 43266
(800) 332-AIDS
(614) 466-0295

Oklahoma Department of Health
STD/HIV Division
1000 10th Street
Oklahoma City, OK 73152
(800) 535-AIDS
(405) 271-4636

Oregon State Health Division
HIV Program Manager
800 Oregon Street
Portland, OR 97207
(800) 777-AIDS
(503) 731-4029

Pennsylvania Department of Health
Bureau of HIV/AIDS
Box 90
Harrisburg, PA 17108
(800) 692-7254
(717) 783-0479

Commonwealth of Puerto Rico
Department of Health
Call Box STD
Caparra Heights Station
San Juan, PR 00922
(809) 765-1010

Rhode Island Department of Health
AIDS/STD Division
3 Capitol Hill, Cannon Building
Providence, RI 02908
(401) 277-6502
(401) 277-2362

South Carolina Department of Health
AIDS Project
2600 Bull Street
Columbia, SC 29201
(800) 322-AIDS
(803) 734-4110

South Dakota Department of Health
AIDS Program
523 East Capital
Pierre, SD 57501
(800) 592-1861
(605) 773-3364

Tennessee Department of Health and Environment—Disease Control
AIDS Program
C-2 221 Cordell Hull Building
Nashville, TN 37247
(800) 525-AIDS
(615) 741-7500

Texas Department of Health
AIDS Division
1100 West 49th Street
Austin, TX 78756
(800) 248-1091
(512) 458-7209

Utah Bureau of HIV/AIDS Prevention
Box 16660
Salt Lake City, UT 84116
(800) 537-1046
(801) 538-6096

Vermont AIDS Program
60 Main Street
Box 70
Burlington, VT 05486
(800) 882-AIDS
(802) 863-7286

Virgin Islands Department of Health
AIDS Program
Charles Harwood Complex
Christiansted, VI 00820
(809) 773-1311

Virginia Department of Health
AIDS Education and Information
109 Governor Street #722
Richmond, VA 23219
(800) 533-4148
(804) 225-4844

Washington Department of Social and Health Services—Office on AIDS
Mail Stop LJ-17B
Olympia, WA 98504
(800) 272-AIDS
(206) 586-0427

West Virginia Department of Health
AIDS Prevention Program
1900 Kanawha Boulevard East
Charleston, WV 25305
(800) 642-8244
(304) 348-2950

Wisconsin Division of Health AIDS/HIV Program
1414 East Washington Street, Room 241
Madison, WI 53701
(800) 334-AIDS
(608) 266-9853

Wyoming Division of Health and Medical Services—AIDS Prevention Program
Hathaway Building, 4th Floor
Cheyenne, WY 82002
(800) 327-3577
(307) 777-5800

National Hotlines

AIDS Clinical Trials Information Service (ACTIS)
(800) TRIALS-A; (800) 243-7012, TTY/TDD

Offers information on the availability of the drug AZT.

AIDS Crisisline
(800) 221-7044

Operated by the National Gay and Lesbian Task Force, this hotline provides information and referrals to local AIDS services anywhere in the United States.

AIDS Technical Assistance Hotline
(800) 878-AIDS

This hotline is operated by the Safe Choices Project of the National Network of Runaway and Youth Services. It provides information on developing programs, finding materials, and putting on workshops and trainings.

AZT Federal Hotline
(800) 843-9388

Centers for Disease Control (CDC) Recordings

CDC operates the following recorded messages, with the most recent HIV/AIDS statistics updated monthly.

(404) 330-3020: Total number of cases, cases distributed by age group and racial/ethnic background.

(404) 330-3021: Cases distributed by gender.

(404) 330-3022: Highest numbers of cases distributed among the states and metropolitan areas; projections of cases to 1993.

National AIDS Hotline
(800) 342-AIDS
(800) 344-7432, Spanish-language line
(800) 243- 7889, TTY line

This hotline is part of the Centers for Disease Control's (CDC) National AIDS Information and Education Program. The hotline provides confidential information and referrals to the public 24 hours a day.

National AIDS Information Clearinghouse
(800) 458-5231
(800) 874-2572, Clinical trials
(800) 243-7012, TTY-TDD

National Cancer Institute AIDS Information
(800) 4-CANCER

National Institute of Drug Abuse
(800) 662-HELP

National Native American AIDS Hotline
(800) 283-AIDS

This hotline is available Monday through Friday, 9:00 A.M. to 5:00 P.M. Pacific time.

National Sexually Transmitted Diseases Hotline
(800) 227-8922

This hotline is operated by the American Social Health Association.

Project Inform
(800) 822-7422

Provides experimental drug information.

8

Reference Materials

IN THE YEARS SINCE 1981, much has been written about the scientific and medical aspects and history of the HIV/AIDS epidemic, as well as its social, political, and economic impact on our country. Primary sources for many books and bibliographies have been the wealth of national and international scientific, medical, and public health professional journals that have reported major developments on the subject, along with the newsletters of service and advocacy organizations around the nation. Yet, even though it has been present in our lives for a decade, the nature of HIV/AIDS is such that developments of all kinds continue on a regular basis, outdating even the most recent publications. Further, many of the frequently used primary sources are not readily available for the general reader or are simply overwhelming in number or content.

The following selected bibliography has been assembled with all these considerations in mind. The topic areas cover a wide variety of subject matter, and the entries have been chosen with an interest in the quality and accuracy of the information that is conveyed, as well as a concern for their accessibility and their ability to serve as paths to other current sources of information. These resources offer information for readers interested in either general or specific knowledge about HIV/AIDS. In addition, many of the organizations listed in Chapter 7 make available publications of their own that are not listed here.

Print Materials

Reference Books

Abrams, Donald I., M.D., and Michael H. Grieco, M.D., eds. **AIDS/HIV Treatment Directory: Experimental and Approved Agents and Methods.** Compiled and published by the American Foundation for AIDS Research (AmFAR). New York and Los Angeles: American Foundation for AIDS Research, 1991. ISSN 0898-5030.

A quarterly publication of AmFAR that contains information on HIV treatments, treatments for opportunistic infections, compassionate use programs, and an extensive glossary and list of publications.

Baker, Ronald A., Jeffrey M. Moulton, and John Charles Tighe, eds. Foreword by Mathilde Krim. **Early Care for HIV Disease.** San Francisco: San Francisco AIDS Foundation, 1991. 108p. $9.95.

Early health evaluation is the focus of this book, which has sections on drug trials, experimental therapies, and specific body parts and systems. Resource listings, including hotlines, treatment publications, minority HIV projects, and a glossary, are included.

Eidson, Ted, ed. **The AIDS Caregivers Handbook.** New York: St. Martin's Press, 1988. 331p. $11.95. ISBN 0-312-02350-2.

HIV/AIDS is a debilitating and cyclical disease that can require constant care at some points and little intervention at others. In addition, people with HIV infection must make personal decisions about their use of alternative or experimental therapies, which may require commitments of time and resources. This book addresses many of these issues, as well as those faced by the caregiver alone: stress, burnout, grief. An extensive resource listing provides information on videos, audiocassettes, workshops, and other helpful materials.

The Foundation Center. **AIDS Funding.** Washington, DC: The Foundation Center, 1991. 175p. $60. ISBN 0-87954-243-8.

This guide to giving by foundations and charitable organizations contains profiles of donors and the grants they have made on HIV/AIDS issues. Grants range from the large to the small and are aimed at research, education, services, and other uses.

Halleron, Trish, Janet Pisaneschi, and Margi Trapani, eds.
Learning AIDS: An Information Resources Directory. New York:
American Foundation for AIDS Research (AmFAR), 1989.
Distributed by R. R. Bowker. 270p. $24.95. ISBN 0-9620363-1-5.

A wealth of information has flooded the market to educate the public
on HIV/AIDS; some of it, unfortunately, uses scare tactics and inaccurate information to make its point. Other material fails to communicate effectively with its audience. Who can know which is the best
program to use? Where can a group find materials that address its
particular concerns or appear in a foreign language, yet still know
that the materials are technically correct and appropriate for the
audience's cultural background and educational level?

This special and valuable resource covers every type of material:
audiotapes, books, manuals, brochures, catalogs, computer services,
directories, instructional materials, microfilm, slides, pamphlets, pe-
riodicals, policy statements, posters, public service ads, reports, films,
and videos. Materials are assessed for their content and their ability
to reach their audience. Some are recommended; some are not.
Materials in more than 16 languages are evaluated, and extensive
information is provided so consumers can contact suppliers or find
materials aimed at their specific situations.

Lingle, Virginia A., and M. Sandra Wood. **How To Find
Information about AIDS.** New York: Harrington Park Press, 1992.
290p. $14.95. ISBN 0-918393-99-X.

Unannotated listings of organizations, health departments, research
institutions, hotlines, computerized resources, printed information,
and audiovisual producers are provided in this slightly dated but
affordable resource.

McCormack, Thomas. **The AIDS Benefits Handbook.** New Haven,
CT: Yale University Press, 1990. 357p. $10. ISBN 0-300-04721-5.

People affected by HIV/AIDS increasingly fall into two groups with
very different life experiences: poor people who are likely to have
some prior experience in negotiating the maze of paperwork, eligibility requirements, interviews, appointments, and waiting periods
necessary for public benefits of any kind, and people with little
previous interaction with public agencies. As individuals in these
groups grapple with disability or failing health brought on by
HIV/AIDS—as well as a possible accompanying loss of job or income
and housing and a need for medical care or food for themselves or

family members—they suddenly have a common goal of gaining access to what they need. This comprehensive, step-by-step book is a necessary guide to doing just that; it also contains helpful appendices of state-specific information, national organizations, a glossary, and bibliography.

Malinowsky, H. Robert, and Gerald J. Perry. **AIDS Information Sourcebook.** Phoenix, AZ: Oryx Press, 1991. 316p. $39.95. ISBN 0-89774-598-1.

The third edition of this reference book provides an unannotated bibliography of other resources, as well as a chronology of key events, a directory of organizations, and selected tables of information.

Media Network. **Seeing through AIDS.** New York: Media Network, 39 West 14th Street, New York, NY 10011, (212) 929-2663, 1989. 39p. $7.50.

This alphabetical reference to over 70 films and videos includes selections ranging from three-minute films to full-length productions. Resources for all kinds of audiences are included, along with helpful indexing and tips on running a film screening.

National Gay Rights Advocates and the National Lawyers Guild AIDS Network. **AIDS Practice Manual: A Legal and Educational Guide, 2d ed.** San Francisco: National Gay Rights Advocates, 1988. 200p. ISBN 0-9602188-0-7.

This guide provides topical references for legal issues impacted by HIV/AIDS.

National Lawyers Guild AIDS Network. **AIDS Practice Manual, 3d ed.** $90. ISBN 0-9602-1887-4.

This manual treats the many key issues influenced by HIV/AIDS and provides other legal resources. Specific state laws and state handicap discrimination laws are covered, as well as model jury selection questions. Also included are resource lists; a medical and public health overview; and facts on personal and estate planning, care of children, public assistance, and debtor's rights.

Terl, Alan H. **AIDS and the Law: A Basic Guide for the Nonlawyer.** Philadelphia: Hemisphere Publishing Company, 1992. 180p. $18.50. ISBN 1-56032-219-5.

Legal issues surrounding the epidemic are discussed here. Public benefits, confidentiality issues, consumer fraud, and criminal law are covered, as well as a variety of discrimination issues.

University Publishing Group. **AIDS Reference and Research Collection.** Frederick, MD: University Publishing Group, 1988. $315.

This commercial publisher produces several AIDS-related newsletters. This four-volume work includes an extensive bibliography, copies of relevant editions of *Morbidity and Mortality Weekly Report,* excerpts from hearings and reports, and a listing of AIDS services and organizations.

Watstein, Sarah. **AIDS and Women: A Sourcebook.** Phoenix, AZ: Oryx Press, 1991. 160p. $36.50. ISBN 0-89774-577-9.

This extensive reference book focuses on just one group affected by HIV/AIDS: women. Detailed appendices include videos, a list of organizations, a glossary, and resources for research.

Monographs

Altman, Dennis. **AIDS in the Mind of America.** Garden City, NY: Anchor Press/Doubleday, 1986. 228p. $8.95. ISBN 0-385-19524-9.

Altman, a gay political scientist, examines the social, political, and psychological impact of the epidemic. He focuses on the fear and stigma attached to the new disease, as well as on the struggles for power and money in the scientific and medical communities.

American Civil Liberties Union (ACLU) AIDS Project. **AIDS and the Law Legal Docket.** New York: ACLU, 132 West 43rd Street, New York, NY 10036. July 1990. 36p. $5.

This monograph summarizes the work of the ACLU and its state projects on HIV/AIDS cases. Included are case summaries on confidentiality, discrimination, criminal justice, education, medical access, and prisons.

————. **Epidemic of Fear.** New York: ACLU, 132 West 43rd Street, New York, NY 10036. 1990. 146p. $20.

This survey of AIDS discrimination cases in the 1980s and ACLU policy recommendations for the 1990s reflects the results of canvassing more than 250 service organizations. The report covers the characteristics of those experiencing discrimination, as well as the types of cases pursued. There is an extensive state-by-state description of available discrimination law.

Anderson, Gary, ed. **Courage to Care: Responding to the Crisis of Children with AIDS.** Washington, DC: Child Welfare League of America, 1990. 416p. $15.95. ISBN 0-87868-401-8.

The Public Health Service estimated that there would be 270,000 cases of CDC-defined AIDS by the end of 1991; 3,000 of those would be pediatric cases. This volume of more than two dozen essays from practitioners, social workers, and others involved in the lives and care of children with HIV/AIDS is published by one of the foremost child welfare organizations in the nation.

Andrulis, Dennis P. **Crisis at the Front Line: The Effect of AIDS on Public Hospitals.** New York: Priority Press Publications, 1989. 93p. $8.95. ISBN 0-87078-266-5.

Andrulis argues that the HIV/AIDS crisis has not brought on a crisis in the health care delivery system but instead has exposed the major flaws in the existing system.

Bateson, Mary Catherine, and Richard Goldsby. **Thinking AIDS: The Social Response to the Biological Threat.** Reading, MA: Addison-Wesley Publishing Company, 1988. 153p. $7.95. ISBN 0-685-22770-7.

The immune system of society is the focus of the authors, who are, respectively, an anthropologist and a biologist. They examine the social costs of the exclusion and despair that have characterized the HIV/AIDS epidemic.

Bayer, Ronald. **Private Acts, Social Consequences: AIDS and the Politics of Public Health.** New York: Free Press, 1989. 288p. $22.95. ISBN 0-02-901961-3.

Maintaining that the onset of HIV/AIDS has created a number of political questions, the author explores the politics of privacy, safety, identification, exclusion, control, persuasion, and public health.

Cartland, Cliff. **You Can Protect Yourself and Your Family from AIDS.** Old Tappan, NJ: Fleming H. Revell, 1987. 192p. $8.95. ISBN 0-8007-5262-7.

This professional journalist provides medical and scientific information in a straightforward book that is aimed at parents.

Dalton, Harlan, Scott Burris, and the Yale AIDS Law Project, eds. **AIDS and the Law: A Guide for the Public.** New Haven, CT: Yale University Press, 1987. 382p. $10.95. ISBN 0-300-0478-4.

The HIV/AIDS epidemic has shown that the law's presumption of the existence of a "reasonable person" does not always hold up; the epidemic has aroused a level of public emotion and concern that sometimes runs counter to scientific and medical knowledge. Consequently, complex legal issues have surfaced in several areas. This anthology of 20 articles covers some of the major topics, including medical, private sector, and government responses as well as the impact of the epidemic on institutions, health care, and groups such as the gay and lesbian community, people of color, and IV drug users. It includes a particularly helpful introductory section on law for nonlawyers that offers useful reading on its own.

Falco, Mathea, and Warren I. Cikins, eds. **Toward a National Policy on Drug and AIDS Testing.** Washington, DC: Brookings Institution, 1989. 81p. $10.95. ISBN 0-8157-2733-X.

As part of the Brookings Dialogues on Public Policy, two conferences on drug testing and HIV/AIDS were held in 1987–1988. The major addresses, by National Commission on AIDS chair Dr. June Osborn, life insurance executive Russel Iuculano, and Harvard psychiatrist Dr. Norman Zinberg, are included here.

Fumento, Michael. **The Myth of Heterosexual AIDS.** New York: Basic Books, 1990. 426p. $22.95. ISBN 0-465-09803-7.

Conservative thinker Michael Fumento, who was relieved of his duties as AIDS analyst at the U.S. Commission on Civil Rights after a one-year tenure, argues that politicized science is behind the specter of the epidemic. He asserts that HIV/AIDS does not pose a significant threat to heterosexuals but that "special interest" groups of homosexuals have magnified its impact.

Griggs, John, ed. **Simple Acts of Kindness.** New York: United Hospital Fund, 1989. 122p. $5. ISBN 0-934459-56-8.

The front lines of service in the last decade have been populated by volunteers. People running meal programs, acting as buddies, operating hotlines, and working in clinics and other settings have helped to make available much needed services as well as a compassionate presence for those who have felt marginalized by society. This book explores the phenomenon of volunteerism in the age of HIV/AIDS.

Grmek, Mirko D. Translated by Russell C. Maulitz and Jacalyn Diffin. **History of AIDS: Emergence and Origin of a Modern Pandemic.** Princeton, NJ: Princeton University Press, 1990. 400p. $29.95. ISBN 0-691-08522-8.

This extremely thorough history of disease looks at virology, microbiology, and immunology in depth. The book includes an extensive bibliography.

Hein, Karen, M.D., and Theresa Foy Digeronimo. **AIDS: Trading Fears for Facts: A Guide for Teens.** Mount Vernon, NY: Consumers Union of the United States, 1989. 196p. $3.95. ISBN 0-890-43269-4.

This straightforward paperback has been widely distributed to teens, and it includes factual information on HIV transmission, sexual practices, drug use, testing, and treatment. Question-and-answer formats are used in each topic. A section on national and local information resources and hotlines is also included, as is a comprehensive glossary.

Hyde, Margaret O., and Elizabeth Forsyth, M.D. **AIDS: What Does It Mean to You?** New York: Walker and Company, 1987. 116p. $6.95. ISBN 0-8027-6747-8.

Suited for the slightly older student and good reader, this book addresses more complicated issues surrounding HIV/AIDS, including historical information on plagues in other times, the epidemic of fear accompanying HIV, and global aspects of the disease. The book includes the text of former Surgeon General C. Everett Koop's report on HIV.

————. **Know about AIDS.** New York: Walker and Company, 1990. 102p. $12.95. ISBN 0-8027-6920-9.

The revised version of this popular book that focuses on risk behaviors is aimed at teenagers. The contents cover the basics of global HIV/AIDS, told in a series of illustrative anecdotes interspersed with factual material.

Johnson, Earvin "Magic." **What You Can Do To Avoid AIDS.** New York: Time Books, 1992. 192p. $3.99. ISBN 0-8129-2063-5.

This book, by the retired basketball star who announced that he had HIV in late 1991, is aimed at adolescents. It contains factual information on HIV/AIDS and explicit advice on safer sexual practices. The book is also available on cassette.

Kinsella, James. **Covering the Plague: AIDS & the American Media.** New Brunswick, NJ: Rutgers University Press, 1990. 299p. $22.95. ISBN 0-8135-1481-9.

To many observers, the HIV/AIDS epidemic has taken shape in the public's mind largely through the media coverage it has received. Thus, with each characterization of HIV as being the disease of a particular group, it has taken longer for the public to recognize the urgent need for education and prevention. This book analyzes the media's role in the epidemic.

Kirp, David L., et al. **Learning by Heart: AIDS and Schoolchildren in America's Communities.** New Brunswick, NJ: Rutgers University Press, 1989. 304p. $14.95. ISBN 0-8135-1609-9.

Few aspects of the spread of HIV have received so much media attention as the highly publicized cases of schoolchildren seeking to remain part of their own everyday world. Some have been barred from their classrooms; some have kept up with their education without a pause. In a series of easily read case studies, this book presents the variety of circumstances and outcomes that were shaped so differently by the law, popular opinion, and concerned parents. Included is the case of Ryan White in Indiana.

Kübler-Ross, Elisabeth. **AIDS: The Ultimate Challenge.** New York: Collier Books, 1987. 330p. $4.95. ISBN 0-02-567170-7.

This well-known psychiatrist previously authored pioneering work on death and dying issues. She unsuccessfully sought to open a facility for children with AIDS in a small Virginia community where she lives. Here she writes about the particular questions of death and grief that accompany AIDS.

Nichols, Eve K. **Mobilizing against AIDS.** Cambridge, MA: Harvard University Press, 1989. 387p. $12.95. ISBN 0-674-57762-0.

This comprehensive introductory look at HIV/AIDS offers helpful appendices, the 1987 CDC case definition, and an explanation of existing tests. It also focuses on prevention issues and includes the Public Health Service guidelines on counseling. The book contains a useful chronology of research advances.

Nourse, Alan E., M.D. **AIDS.** New York: Franklin Watts, 1989. 159p. $12.90. ISBN 0-531-10662-4.

The world of viruses is explored here in depth, as is the story of the discovery of HIV. Nourse, who has written many books for adolescents, also addresses prevention and risk-reduction issues in straightforward language.

Nussbaum, Bruce. **Good Intentions: How Big Business and the Medical Establishment Are Corrupting the Fight against AIDS.** New York: Atlantic Monthly Press, 1991. 352p. $10.95. ISBN 0-14-016000-0.

The interaction between pharmaceutical manufacturers, such as AZT's Burroughs Wellcome, and the medical/scientific research establishment has been a source of controversy, especially with Burroughs charging tens of thousands of dollars annually to PWAs taking AZT.

Quackenbush, Marcia, and Sylvia Villarreal, M.D. **Does AIDS Hurt? Educating Young Children about AIDS.** Santa Cruz, CA: Network Publications (ETR), 1988. 150p. $14.95. ISBN 0-941816-52-4.

Both authors have backgrounds in public health education on HIV/AIDS. This book is actually aimed at parents, teachers, and other caregivers who work with children to age ten, and it provides concrete ideas on how to broach necessary topics at different stages of development, as well as how to "read" the questions children might ask. There are very helpful ideas on addressing these topics if a family member, friend, or classmate is at-risk or infected with HIV. The book ends with a guide to further resources on child development, parent/child sex education, children's attitudes on chronic illness and death, family life and health education curricula, child sexual abuse, drug abuse, and HIV/AIDS in the schools.

Richardson, Diane. **Women and AIDS.** New York: Routledge, 1988. 183p. $11.95. ISBN 0-416-01751-7.

Special issues and medical problems confront women who are HIV infected. Not the least of these are the facts that a partner or child may also be ill and that women's manifestations are little recognized in the medical system. This book offers an examination of HIV/AIDS among women worldwide and gives special attention to lesbians with HIV, caring for PWAs, issues for women living with HIV, policies and prevention issues, and a resource listing.

Schwartz, Linda. **AIDS Answers for Teens.** Santa Barbara, CA: Learning Works, 1989. 32p. $4.95. ISBN 0-88160-155-1.

This oversize paperback is formatted in a question-and-answer style and is intended for classroom use.

Shilts, Randy. **And the Band Played On: Politics, People, and the AIDS Epidemic.** New York: St. Martin's Press, 1987. 653p. $24.95. ISBN 0-312-00994-1.

Widely viewed as the definitive documentary study of how AIDS developed into a major health and social issue in the United States, Shilts's carefully crafted and very readable book tells his version of the beginning of the infection from pre-1980 identification as a gay disease to the mid-1980s, when it became a political and social issue as well as a health problem. Shilts brings to life the players, the politics, and the suffering of the early years.

Wachter, Oralee. **Sex, Drugs, and AIDS.** New York: Bantam Books, 1987. 76p. $3.95. ISBN 0-553-34454-4.

Based on the popular video of the same name, this book is aimed at teens.

Woodruff, John O., Diane Doherty, and Jean Garrison Athey, eds. **Troubled Adolescents and HIV Infection.** Washington, DC: CASSP Technical Assistance Center, Georgetown University, 1989. 144p.

This monograph by professionals working with troubled adolescents addresses the risks, education programs, and interventions necessary for abused children, system youth, runaways, and other at-risk youth.

Pamphlets and Newsletters

American Dental Association. **Facts about AIDS for the Dental Team.** Chicago: American Dental Association, 1991. 14p.

While the focus on health care workers has often been on physicians and nurses, attention has shifted to dental practices as well with several publicized cases of HIV transmission. This report outlines the issues faced in dental practices.

James, John S. **AIDS Treatment News.** Issues 1–75. Berkeley, CA: Celestial Arts, 1989. 522p. $12.95. ISBN 0-89087-553-7.

AIDS Treatment News is a highly regarded biweekly newsletter on experimental and conventional treatments and therapies for HIV/AIDS. It was started by John S. James in San Francisco in 1986, drawing on his background in statistical computer programming in medical research. Articles are researched from medical journals, computerized databases, and interviews with those following or developing treatments. The first 75 issues of the newsletter are included in this volume, along with pertinent updates on information in the articles. The book is heavily indexed, and articles carry reference information for contacting those involved.

National Coalition of Advocates for Students. **Criteria for Evaluating an AIDS Curriculum.** Boston: National Coalition of Advocates for Students, 1988. 23p. Also in Spanish.

This short booklet contains valuable information on evaluating and shaping curriculum content for teaching HIV/AIDS, as well as helpful information on stages of child development, working with adolescents, conducting staff training, and securing parental and community involvement.

Government Documents and Reports

Congressional Information Service (CIS). **CIS/INDEX.**

Since the beginning of the epidemic in 1981, there have been dozens of congressional hearings, reports, and pieces of legislation on every aspect of the HIV/AIDS crisis. CIS publishes a monthly index of all hearings, reports, committee prints, and other papers issued on this and other subjects. An index, abstracts, and legislative history are printed and also available on microfiche in many libraries. Individual libraries selectively collect the paper copies of these documents. Other methods of acquiring such material are listed in the "Nonprint Materials" section of this chapter.

Institute of Medicine, National Academy of Sciences. **Confronting AIDS: Directions for Public Health, Health Care, and Research.** Washington, DC: National Academy Press, 1989. 374p. $24.95. ISBN 0-309-03699-2.

A strong scientific basis provides the framework for this volume that examines the status of the epidemic, its predicted future course, the care of PWAs, future research needs, and the international aspects of the epidemic. A final chapter covers many concrete recommendations from the Institute of Medicine (IOM). The book has several useful appendices based on CDC documents and a comprehensive glossary.

National Commission on AIDS (NCOA). **America Living with AIDS.** Washington, DC: National Commission on AIDS, 1991. 165p. ISBN 0-16-035859-0.

NCOA has issued a number of reports notable for their provocative content and assertions concerning federal responsibility. After two years of hearings, site visits, and research, NCOA issued this comprehensive study.

—————. **Failure of U.S. Health Care System to Deal with HIV Epidemic.** Washington, DC: National Commission on AIDS, 1989. 9p.

This NCOA report focuses on the impact of HIV/AIDS on the U.S. health care system.

—————. **HIV Disease in Correctional Facilities.** Washington, DC: National Commission on AIDS, March 1991. 43p.

More and more people are being sent to prison or receiving lengthy mandatory sentences for drug-related offenses, and the nation's corrections institutions are disproportionately filled with poor and minority people, putting them at high risk for HIV/AIDS. This report paints a grim picture of the epidemic behind prison walls.

—————. **Leadership, Legislation, and Regulation.** Washington, DC: National Commission on AIDS, 1990. 9p.

Several key aspects of public policy on HIV/AIDS are examined in this report.

—————. **Research, the Workforce and the HIV Epidemic in Rural America.** Washington, DC: National Commission on AIDS, 1990. 20p.

NCOA focuses on three diverse issues in addressing HIV/AIDS in this report. HIV/AIDS is growing rapidly in rural areas, and few researchers have examined it. NCOA issued this report on the need for services and education.

—————. **The Twin Epidemics of Substance Use and HIV.** Washington, DC: National Commission on AIDS, July 1991. 26p.

With fully one-third of reported AIDS cases among adults and adolescents linked to IV drug use, with crack use being a formidable cofactor to unsafe sexual practices, and with 70 percent of pediatric AIDS cases being related to drugs, the connection between drug use and the HIV/AIDS epidemic is strong. This NCOA report contains important findings on the need for drug treatment on demand, as well as an approach to substance use that focuses on public health measures and not ideology.

Pan American Health Organization. **AIDS: Profile of an Epidemic.** Washington, DC: Pan American Health Organization, 1989. 382p. ISBN 9-275-1151-4-1.

The international HIV/AIDS epidemic parallels the U.S. one but differs in some fundamental ways. This anthology of articles paints a picture of HIV/AIDS in other parts of the world.

Presidential Commission on the Human Immunodeficiency Virus. **Report of the Presidential Commission on the Human Immunodeficiency Virus Epidemic.** Washington, DC: Presidential Commission, 1988. 220p.

The Watkins Commission was appointed by President Ronald Reagan to study the HIV/AIDS epidemic. Its recommendations are contained in this report.

U.S. Conference of Mayors. **Local AIDS Services: The National Directory.** Washington, DC: U.S. Conference of Mayors, 1990. 233p. $15.

This directory, sponsored by the Conference of Mayors, DIFFA, NAPWA, and the Fund for Human Dignity, lists state and local projects as well as national organizations. A section on minority service organizations also is included.

U.S. Department of Health and Human Services (HHS). **AIDS Litigation Project: A Survey of Federal, State, and Local Cases before Courts and Human Rights Commissions.** Washington, DC: U.S. Government Printing Office, 1990. 172p. $9.50.

This report analyzes the litigation brought on HIV/AIDS issues at all levels of the judicial and human rights system.

————. **Community-Based AIDS Prevention: Studies of IV Drug Users and Their Sexual Partners.** Washington, DC: HHS, 1991. 455p. GPO 1990-2871-820/44113.

These case studies from a 1989 conference on community-based efforts to prevent HIV transmission focus on research on outreach and intervention efforts with IV drug users and their partners.

————. **Surgeon General's Report on Acquired Immune Deficiency Syndrome.** Washington, DC: HHS, 1986. 36p.

This report, by former Surgeon General C. Everett Koop, is excerpted elsewhere in this book.

U.S. General Accounting Office (GAO). **AIDS: Health Services in Five Communities.** Washington, DC: GAO, 1989. 72p. Free. GAO/HRD-89-120.

This report examines payment for services and delivery of services in five communities hard hit by HIV/AIDS: Baltimore; Philadelphia; New Haven, Connecticut; New Orleans; and Seattle.

————. **AIDS Education: Gaps in Coverage Still Exist.** Washington, DC: GAO, 1990. Free. GAO/T-HRD-90-26.

Although most teens have received basic information on HIV/AIDS, this report found that significant gaps in education still exist.

————. **AIDS Education: Programs for Out-of-School Youth Slowly Evolving.** Washington, DC: GAO, 1990. 20p. Free. GAO/HRD-90-111.

Runaways, homeless youth, migrant youth, and youth involved with institutional systems are at particularly high risk for use of drugs and alcohol as well as for high-risk sexual behavior. This report examines how programs to reach these youth are operating.

————. **AIDS Education: Public School Programs Require More Student Information and Teacher Training.** Washington, DC: GAO, 1990. Free. GAO/HRD-90-103.

About 20 percent of new cases reported to CDC are among people in their twenties, effectively showing that these individuals were probably infected as teenagers. Consequently, HIV education takes on an important role in reducing further infection in this age group.

————. **Defense Health Care: Effects of AIDS in the Military.** Washington, DC: GAO, 1990. Free. GAO/HRD-90-39.

The Department of Defense implemented a service-wide policy of HIV testing for all active duty military personnel, reserve personnel, and applicants for service in 1985. It also planned comprehensive education programs, a policy for retaining HIV-positive active duty service members, and measures to provide necessary health care to infected personnel. This report examines these steps for effectiveness.

————. **Drug Abuse: The Crack Cocaine Epidemic.** Washington, DC: GAO, 1991. Free. GAO/HRD-91-55FS.

Crack cocaine use has been strongly linked to unsafe sexual practices with multiple partners, often in exchange for drugs or money. This raises critical issues for women who may become HIV-infected and pregnant, as well as for those who cannot obtain treatment. Although there is no reliable figure on the extent of crack use, this parallel epidemic must be addressed if there is to be significant progress in public health.

————. **Drug Abuse: Research on Treatment May Not Address Current Needs.** Washington, DC: GAO, 1990. Free. GAO/HRD-90-114.

Though drug use grew dramatically during the 1980s, research results on drug use treatments did not. Little is known about treatments for new drugs, and matching patients with appropriate treatments remains a problem.

————. **Drug-Exposed Infants: A Generation at Risk.** Washington, DC: GAO, 1990. Free. GAO/HRD-90-138.

No reliable figures are available to estimate how many infants are born drug-exposed because of their mother's substance use, but both infants and mothers can be at-risk for HIV/AIDS. The federal government's drug control agency suggests that 100,000 or more infants may be at-risk, though other researchers estimate the number may be several times higher. Such infants have many costly health problems, and, as this report finds, their circumstances could be altered drastically if more drug treatment were available for women at risk.

————. **Drug Treatment: Some Clinics Not Meeting Goal of Prompt Treatment for Intravenous Drug Users.** Washington, DC: GAO, 1990. Free. GAO/HRD-90-80BR.

About 20 percent of AIDS cases are linked to shared needles in IV drug use, and additional cases result from infected users having unprotected sexual intercourse. Treatment for IV drug users is thus important not only for curbing drug use alone but also for halting the spread of HIV infection. Yet treatment facilities remain inadequate to meet demand and do not currently comply with federal requirements.

————. **Rural Drug Abuse: Prevalence, Relation to Crime, and Programs.** Washington, DC: GAO, 1990. 72p. Free. GAO/PEMD-90-24.

With HIV-infection rates rising quickly in rural areas, this report examines the use of drugs in those same areas. The surprising finding of the report is that total substance use rates are about the same in rural and nonrural areas.

————. **Teenage Drug Use: Uncertain Linkages with Either Pregnancy or School Dropout.** Washington, DC: GAO, 1991. Free. GAO/PEMD-91-3.

About 20 percent of new HIV/AIDS cases are among people just out of their teens, meaning that they probably were infected during their teenage years. Further, the risk of pregnancy as an accompaniment to unsafe sexual practices and drug use is an area of great concern. This report examines possible connections between drug use and other trends among teens.

World Health Organization (WHO). **Guidelines for the Development of a National AIDS Prevention and Control Programme.** Geneva, Switzerland: WHO, 1988. 32p. ISBN 92-4-12100-1-X.

This WHO report looks at macro-level prevention and control issues.

Anthologies

The ACT UP/NY Women and AIDS Book Group. **Women, AIDS & Activism.** Boston: South End Press, 1990. 295p. $7. ISBN 0-89608-394-2.

This anthology of articles by the activist ACT UP group focuses entirely on the often-neglected issues facing women with HIV/AIDS. Articles cover safe sex, HIV testing, drug treatment and drug trials, public policy, and activism.

Alyson, Sasha. **You Can Do Something about AIDS.** Boston: Stop AIDS Project, 1988. 126p. Free. ISBN 0-945-97200-8.

Contributors ranging from Abigail Van Buren to Whoopi Goldberg to former White House Press Secretary Jody Powell wrote short essays for this paperback project of the publishing industry. The contents cover many viewpoints on personal involvement as well as educational and service projects for schools, congregations, and workplace groups.

Brickner, Philip W., et al. **Under the Safety Net: The Health and Social Welfare of the Homeless in the United States.** New York: W. W. Norton, 1990. 439p. $27.95. ISBN 0-393-02885-2.

This anthology of more than two dozen articles on homeless health care is the result of national street and shelter outreach programs for the homeless. The book includes useful essays on the health problems of homeless people with HIV/AIDS, tuberculosis, and substance abuse problems.

Brown, Lawrence D., ed. **Health Policy and the Disadvantaged.** Durham, NC: Duke University Press, 1991. 212p. $13.60. ISBN 0-8223-1142-9.

As more and more poor people are hit by the HIV/AIDS epidemic— either through IV drug use, sex with an infected partner, or perinatal transmission—their lack of access to necessary health care is easily highlighted. This anthology of readings focuses on the juncture of specific disadvantaged groups—the homeless, people with HIV/AIDS, the uninsured, substance users—and the necessity to implement adequate health care policies.

Clarke, Loren K., and Malcolm Potts, eds. **The AIDS Reader: Documentary History of a Modern Epidemic.** Boston: Branden Publishing Company, 1988. 350p. $17.95. ISBN 0-8283-1918-9.

All aspects of the epidemic are covered in this first volume of a planned series. More than 50 articles are reprinted here.

Crimp, Douglas, with Adam Rolston. **AIDS Demographics.** Seattle, WA: Bay Press, 1990. 141p. $13.95. ISBN 0-941920-16-X.

AIDS Coalition to Unleash Power (ACT UP) has been an influential activist force in the fight against HIV/AIDS. To make its point, it has frequently drawn on the skilled resources of artists and writers, who have created its forceful and sometimes controversial graphic statements. This book reproduces some of ACT UP's best art and essays.

Fee, Elizabeth, and Daniel M. Fox, eds. **AIDS: The Burdens of History.** Berkeley: University of California Press, 1988. 362p. $12.95. ISBN 0-520-06396-1.

AIDS has caused enormous suffering and death in a relatively short period of time, yet another way of viewing the epidemic involves analyzing the impact of the disease on society. This book of essays examines the historical questions of quarantine and plague, physician responsibility, and disease as punishment for sin.

Gostin, Lawrence O., ed. **AIDS and the Health Care System.** New Haven, CT: Yale University Press, 1990. 299p. $12.95. ISBN 0-300-04720-7.

Health care policies, prevention and education, treatment, patients' rights, public health issues, and concerns of health care workers are some of the subjects covered in this book. Gostin has assembled 16 essays, including one by former Surgeon General C. Everett Koop, to survey the range of issues affecting the HIV/AIDS epidemic and the health care system.

Graubard, Stephen R., ed. **Living with AIDS.** Cambridge, MA: MIT Press, 1989. 463p. $14.95. ISBN 0-262-57079-3.

This collection of 20 essays focuses on the social history and impact of the epidemic, as well as its public policy implications. In addition, there is a section devoted to the international aspects of HIV/AIDS.

McKenzie, Nancy F., ed. **The AIDS Reader: Social, Political, Ethical Issues.** New York: Meridian/Penguin, 1991. 597p. $13.95. ISBN 0-452-01072-1.

Just as HIV-illness seeks out the vulnerabilities of the body, the epidemic itself has highlighted social prejudices, unresponsive institutions, and a flawed health care system. This anthology brings together more than 30 essays and articles by leading researchers, scholars, and scientists to explore these questions.

O'Malley, Padraig, ed. **The AIDS Epidemic: Private Rights and the Public Interest.** Boston: Beacon Press, 1989. 566p. $12.95. ISBN 0-8070-0601-7.

The essays in this volume first appeared as a special issue of the *New England Journal of Public Policy.* The essays cover every aspect of the epidemic, as well as personal stories by individuals touched by HIV/AIDS.

Russell, Letty M. **The Church with AIDS: Renewal in Time of Crisis.**
Louisville, KY: Westminster/John Knox Press, 1990. 223p. $10.95.
ISBN 0-664-25111-0.

Although religious belief about sexual practices, homosexuality, and
other issues has been a controversial source of criticism of people with
HIV/AIDS, all communities of faith contain PWAs. This anthology of
articles by both ordained clergy and academics reflects the efforts of
the Church of Christ to address the spiritual needs of all members in
the age of AIDS.

Scientific American. **The Science of AIDS.** New York: W. W.
Freeman and Company, 1989. 135p. $11.95. ISBN 0-7167-2036-1.

This collection of articles originally published in *Scientific American*
magazine includes some of the foremost international scientists involved in researching HIV. Covered here are the origins of the virus,
molecular biology, epidemiology, clinical and cellular aspects, therapies, and vaccines.

Siegel, Larry, M.D. **AIDS and Substance Abuse.** New York:
Harrington Park Press, 1988. 206p. $17.95. ISBN 0-918393-59-0.

A variety of researchers and clinical experts contributed to this anthology, which explores basic questions of the connection between
substance use and HIV infection and progression. Essays explore
whether drugs and alcohol depress the immune system, whether they
increase the risk of primary infection with HIV, and whether they
contribute to the progression to AIDS.

Sontag, Susan. **Illness as Metaphor and AIDS and Its Metaphors.**
New York: Anchor/Doubleday, 1989. 183p. $8.95. ISBN
0-385-26705-3.

This volume combines the two famous essays of Sontag's that address
the punitive meaning attached to illness in our society. In the first,
written in 1978, she reveals the social stigma attached to cancer. She
wrote about AIDS in 1989 to look at the thinking behind the "plague"
title given the illness.

Personal Accounts

Berrigan, Daniel. **Sorrow Built a Bridge: Friendship and AIDS.**
Baltimore, MD: Fortkamp Publishing Company, 1990. 231p.
$14.95. ISBN 1-879175-04-5.

Longtime peace activist Father Daniel Berrigan here recounts his relationships with 14 people with AIDS.

Callen, Michael. **Surviving AIDS.** New York: HarperCollins, 1991. 256p. $9.95. ISBN 0-06-092125-0.

One of the most public of long-term survivors of HIV, Callen has testified before Congress, written a popular song, recorded an album, and self-published a PWA magazine. In addition, he co-founded the People with AIDS Coalition and the Community Research Initiative.

————. **Surviving and Thriving with AIDS, Volume I: Hints for the Newly Diagnosed.** New York: PWA Coalition, 1987. 160p. $10. ISBN 0-317-93646-8.

————. **Surviving and Thriving with AIDS, Volume II: Collected Wisdom.** New York: PWA Coalition, 1988. 368p. $20. ISBN 0-317-93647-6.

These two volumes, compiled by PWA Michael Callen, contain detailed and helpful information for other PWAs.

Connor, Steve, and Sharon Kingman. **The Search for the Virus: The Scientific Discovery of AIDS and the Quest for a Cure.** New York: Viking/Penguin, 1989. 278p. $8.95. ISBN 0-14-011397-5.

The anatomy of HIV is discussed in detail here, and the authors also tell the story of the race both for the discovery of the virus and for the credit for the achievement.

Cox, Elizabeth. **Thanksgiving: An AIDS Journal.** New York: Harper Perennial, 1990. 230p. $8.95. ISBN 0-06-092041-6.

Cox kept this journal during the years 1985–1987, while her husband, Keith Avedon, fought HIV/AIDS. Avedon died in 1990.

Fortunato, John E. **AIDS: The Spiritual Dilemma.** San Francisco: Harper & Row, 1987. 156p. $8.95. ISBN 0-06-250338-3.

Psychotherapist Fortunato has written widely on AIDS and gay issues. Here he discusses his own experiences in listening to the stories of those with HIV/AIDS and exploring the spiritual impact the epidemic has had on him.

Gallo, Robert. **Virus Hunting: AIDS, Cancer, and the Human Retrovirus.** New York: Basic Books, 1991. 352p. $22.95. ISBN 0-465-09806-1.

Dr. Robert Gallo, the discoverer of the human retrovirus and former co-discoverer of HIV, tells the story of his own life here. Gallo, one of the most powerful scientists in the nation, gives an authentic view of a science lab at work.

Glaser, Elizabeth, and Laura Palmer. **In the Absence of Angels.** New York: G. P. Putnam's Sons, 1991. 304p. $21.95. ISBN 0-399-13577-4.

Elizabeth Glaser, wife of a popular television star, received a contaminated blood transfusion that gave her and two of her children HIV. This memoir tells the story of her family's struggle with this reality, as well as her establishment of the Pediatric AIDS Foundation.

Koop, C. Everett. **Koop: The Memoirs of America's Family Doctor.** New York: Random House, 1991. 342p. $22.50. ISBN 0-394-57626-8.

Dr. C. Everett Koop was one of the nation's leading pediatric surgeons when he was nominated in 1981 by President Ronald Reagan to be the surgeon general. His vigorous work to educate Americans about HIV/AIDS and the need for sex education in the schools gave him his reputation as an effective surgeon general.

Kramer, Larry. **Reports from the Holocaust: The Making of an AIDS Activist.** New York: St. Martin's Press, 1989. 291p. $10.95. ISBN 0-312-03921-2.

Kramer is a well-known writer who helped start Gay Men's Health Crisis (GMHC) in early 1982 and was controversial in the gay community for advising men to stop having sex to halt the epidemic. In 1987 he called for the angry advocacy that gave birth to ACT UP. In this volume are collected letters, speeches, columns, and other personal documents he wrote on the epidemic.

Monette, Paul. **Borrowed Time: An AIDS Memoir.** New York: Avon Books, 1988. 342p. $8.95. ISBN 0-380-70779-9.

Nominated for the 1988 National Book Critics Circle Award, this book dramatically offers a personal account of one man's 19-month–long struggle with AIDS.

National Coalition for the Homeless. **Ending the Silence: Voices of Homeless People Living with AIDS.** New York: National Coalition for the Homeless, June 1990. 80p. $5.

This anthology of statements from homeless people with HIV/AIDS represents their testimony about their lives and need for care and services in many settings.

Peavey, Fran. **A Shallow Pool of Time.** Philadelphia: New Society Publishers, 1991. 168p. $11.95. ISBN 0-317-93395-7.

This account of an HIV-positive woman facing her diagnosis raises many of the questions faced by all women during the HIV/AIDS epidemic.

Petrow, Steven. **Dancing against the Darkness: A Journey through America in the Age of AIDS.** New York: Free Press, 1991. 288p. $18.95. ISBN 0-669-24309-4.

Petrow, of the San Francisco AIDS Foundation, tells the stories of more than 40 people whose lives have been touched by HIV/AIDS.

Tilleraas, Penny. **Circle of Hope: Our Stories of AIDS, Addiction, and Recovery.** New York: Harper & Row, 1990. 364p. $10.95. ISBN 0-06-255412-3.

Issues of continuing substance use and its influence on the immune system are important for the general health of all HIV-infected people. In addition, many exclusively gay and lesbian recovery programs have started to help people progress in an environment that supports their identity. A product of the Hazelden recovery program in Minnesota, this book offers the stories of two dozen PWAs who became part of the recovery community.

White, Ryan, and Ann Marie Cunningham. **Ryan White: My Own Story.** New York: Dial Books, 1991. 277p. $16.95. ISBN 0-8037-0977-3.

Young Ryan White, a hemophiliac, was diagnosed with HIV at the age of 13, after he had received a contaminated transfusion of the clotting agent Factor VIII. He was subsequently refused permission to return to his school, and he and his family undertook a very public court battle that ultimately proved successful. Ryan's battle, and his educational work in schools and for AIDS groups, attracted the attention of celebrities who became his friends. Here he tells his story, accompanied by family photos.

Whitmore, George. **Someone Was Here.** New York: Plume/Penguin, 1988. 211p. $8.95. ISBN 0-452-26237-2.

The human dimension of the epidemic is portrayed here, through the telling of the stories of several people with HIV/AIDS, their caregivers, and their family members, friends, and lovers. The book combines the intimacy of a novel with the documentary power of journalism.

Photographic Works

Nixon, Nicholas, photographer. Text by Bebe Nixon. **People with AIDS.** Boston: David R. Godine, 1991. 160p. $25. ISBN 0-87923-886-0.

Fifteen individuals with AIDS, their family members, and their friends volunteered to work with photographer Nicholas Nixon as he chronicled their life-and-death struggles with the disease.

Photographers + Friends United Against AIDS. **The Indomitable Spirit.** New York: Harry N. Abrams, 1990. 96p. $24.95. ISBN 0-801-09245-52.

In 1990, the photography exhibit "The Indomitable Spirit" was assembled to "celebrate human strength, compassion, and endurance in the face of challenge and adversity." The show was produced by the organization Photographers + Friends, which unites the diverse elements of the photographic community—commercial, art, fashion, and sports photographers; photojournalists; and artists and scientists who use photography in their work.

Ruskin, Cindy. **The Quilt: Stories from the NAMES Project.** New York: Simon and Schuster, 1988. 160p. $22.95. ISBN 0-671-66597-9.

This photography book, with images by Matt Herron, tells the story of the NAMES Project Quilt.

Fiction and Poetry

Klein, Michael, ed. **Poets for Life: Seventy-Six Poets Respond to AIDS.** New York: Crown Publishers, 1989. 244p. $18.95. ISBN 0-517-57242-7.

Poet Michael Klein wrote to more than 500 American poets to gather work on HIV/AIDS for this volume. Much of it has never before appeared in print. Included are works by June Jordan, Adrienne Rich, Brad Gooch, and Paul Monette, with essays by the late Joe Papp and by Bishop Paul Moore.

Kramer, Larry. **The Normal Heart.** New York: New American Library, 1985. 123p. $7.95. ISBN 0-452-25798-0.

Writer Larry Kramer was one of the first to address the AIDS crisis through literature. He helped start Gay Men's Health Crisis in New York City and his call for an outpouring of anger over government indifference prompted the formation of the activist group ACT UP. This impassioned and angry play about the early years of the epidemic depicts public officials, as well as compassionately drawn gay men and their family members.

Osborn, M. Elizabeth, ed. **The Way We Live Now: American Plays & the AIDS Crisis.** New York: Theatre Communications Group, 1990. 282p. $14.95. ISBN 1-55936-005-4.

This anthology of plays concerned with HIV/AIDS as protagonist includes work by William M. Hoffman, Lanford Wilson, Harvey Fierstein, Susan Sontag, and Terence McNally.

Nonprint Materials

Films and Videos

Many films and videos have been produced as part of the HIV/AIDS education effort, and their diversity reflects the range of audiences that need to be reached: students, members of health professions, racial and ethnic minorities. Films and videos offer needed flexibility for working with small groups or introducing topics not covered by other media. Because the federal government's televised public service advertising campaign has been accompanied by little educational coverage by the television networks that reach most people, there has been an enormous need to reach people where they are and educate them, whether in the classroom or the workplace. Further, because HIV/AIDS cuts across so many lines in our society, all educational materials must offer people images with which they can identify. The cultural behavior depicted must be consistent with their own, whether the product is aimed at white middle-class youth or Hispanic women.

The American Foundation for AIDS Research (AmFAR), a national nonprofit educational and research organization, has rated hundreds of educational materials to determine which meet its criteria for recommendation. Among its qualifications are:

1. Content. The material must be current and accurate, and medical and scientific information must be presented factually. The material must be appropriate to the audience.
2. Instructional Design. The film clearly states its objectives and seeks to increase knowledge, change attitudes and behavior, and build skills for the audience. It uses fundamentals of good instruction and communication and has a language level appropriate for the audience. The material is organized, accessible, stimulating, and concise.
3. Technical Quality. The film has a high standard of technical production, uses effective visual techniques, and is easy to use.
4. Other Factors. There are appropriate support materials to accompany the film, and they are consistent with the film's objectives. The product is reasonably priced, is part of a larger health study program, and requires a thoroughly trained instructor. It is also important to keep in mind that older films will use older statistics and may not include medical/scientific advances.

Because AmFAR has taken the lead in identifying quality, factual, and effective educational tools among the many that are available, and because not all available products are either appropriate or factual, their recommendations of the following products are indicated in the text. No material has been included that specifically did not win a recommendation by AmFAR, although there are films and videos listed that were not reviewed in the last AmFAR rating guide. The guide itself is listed in the reference section of this book. No feature-length films with HIV/AIDS-related themes are listed here; several are available for rental through video stores. In addition, many of the organizations listed in Chapter 7 produce or distribute videos.

Answers about AIDS
Type: VHS 1/2", Umatic 3/4"
Length: 16 min.

Cost:	Purchase $19.95 (1/2"), $24.95 (3/4")
Sources:	American Red Cross local chapters
Date:	1987
Language:	English

An introductory look at HIV/AIDS issues, this film provides factual coverage of elementary science and transmission issues.

Black People Get AIDS, Too

Type:	Video
Length:	23 min.
Cost:	Purchase $350
Source:	Multicultural Prevention Resource Center
	1540 Market Street, Suite 320
	San Francisco, CA 94102
	(415) 861-2142
Date:	1987
Language:	English

This film offers an overview of HIV/AIDS basics and is suited to well-educated and adult audiences. It presents many facts orally, but also uses charts and one-on-one interviews. Topics discussed include high-risk behaviors, testing, prevention and protection, and the need for education.

Blood Transfusion Risks and Benefits

Type:	VHS 3/4"
Length:	9 min.
Cost:	Purchase $119, rental $25/day
Source:	American Association of Blood Banks National Office
	1117 North Nineteenth Street, Suite 600
	Arlington, VA 22209
	(703) 528-8200
Date:	1987
Language:	English

The risks and benefits of blood transfusions in the age of HIV/AIDS are explained in this film, which discusses how to reduce the chance of contracting the virus from blood products. The film presents the basic facts about the disease and describes how autologous blood transfusions can work for some surgery. AmFAR recommends this film.

Don't Forget Sherrie

Type:	VHS 1/2", Umatic 3/4"
Length:	30 min.
Cost:	Purchase $19.95 (1/2"), $24.95 (3/4")
Sources:	American Red Cross local chapters
Free loan copy available from:	Modern Talking Picture Service
	Film Scheduling Center
	5000 Park Street North
	St. Petersburg, FL 33709
	(800) 243-MTPS; (813) 546-0681, Fax
Date:	1989
Language:	English

When teenage Sherrie dies of AIDS after experimenting with intravenous drugs, her friends confront the issues presented by the deadly disease. Her former boyfriend and his new girlfriend are particularly affected. Minority youth are depicted in this film, which features former U.S. Surgeon General C. Everett Koop and is recommended by AmFAR.

Images: Crisis on AIDS

Type:	VHS 3/4"
Length:	30 min.
Cost:	Purchase $95, rental $50/2 weeks
Source:	New Jersey Network
	1573 Parkside Avenue CN777
	Trenton, NJ 08625
	(609) 530-5015
Date:	1987
Language:	English; Spanish subtitles

In this segment of a television show, the state's health commissioner talks about fighting HIV/AIDS in the intravenous drug-using community. The impact of the disease in the state is discussed, as well as issues of mandatory testing and confidentiality, and effective education programs. AmFAR recommends this film for all audiences.

A Letter from Brian

Type:	VHS 1/2", Umatic 3/4"
Length:	30 min.
Cost:	Purchase $19.95 (1/2"), $24.95 (3/4")
Sources:	American Red Cross local chapters

Free loan copy available from: Modern Talking Picture Service
Film Scheduling Center
5000 Park Street North
St. Petersburg, FL 33709
(800) 243-MTPS; (813) 546-0681, Fax
Date: 1987
Language: English

When a teenage girl receives a letter from her old boyfriend, she must confront the threat of HIV disease. This film features former Surgeon General C. Everett Koop and is recommended by AmFAR.

No Nos Enganemos
Type: VHS
Length: 22 min.
Cost: Purchase $24.95
Source: Los Angeles County Department of
Health Services
2901 South Hope Street Annex
Los Angeles, CA 90007
(213) 744-3837
Date: 1987
Language: Spanish

Still photos and the voice of a narrator make this video documentary-like in presentation. The focus is a Latino physician in his office and giving a talk for local residents and patients. Among the topics covered are the basic science of how HIV debilitates the immune system, the myth of casual contact, how infected persons need not have any apparent symptoms, how individuals are affected differently, and how the virus can be transmitted through sexual activity and IV drug use. AmFAR recommends this film.

Ojos Que No Ven/Eyes That Fail To See
Type: VHS
Length: 52 min.
Cost: Purchase $356, rental $75/2 weeks
Source: Instituto Familiar De La Raza—Latino
AIDS Project
2515 Twenty-fourth Street #2
San Francisco, CA 94110
(415) 647-5450
Date: 1988
Language: Spanish

This film covers primary factual material while making the point that everyone must live and love safely to reduce the risk of HIV.

'Til Death Do Us Part

Type:	VHS
Length:	16 min.
Cost:	Purchase $355
Source:	Durrin Films/New Day Films
	1748 Kalorama Road, NW
	Washington, DC 20009
	(202) 387-6700
Date:	1988
Language:	English

The Everyday Theatre Youth Ensemble of Washington is shown presenting a play about the basic facts of HIV/AIDS. The film does not offer prevention information but does cover women at-risk and IV drug use. The film delivers its message through music, poetry, rap, and dance; it is recommended by AmFAR. A discussion guide is available.

What Is AIDS?

Type:	16mm film, VHS, videodisc
Length:	16 min.
Cost:	Purchase $435 (film), $335 (video),
	$295 (videodisc)
Source:	Coronet/MTI Film & Video
	108 Wilmot Road
	Deerfield, IL 60015
	(800) 621-2131; (708) 940-3640, Fax
Date:	1988
Language:	English

In a serious but sensitive presentation, two 12-year-olds learn how the body fights a virus. The film employs a baseball "analogy" with the body's defense team rallying against the germ team. The film does not address HIV prevention measures, but it does generally describe how sexual activity and the use of needles can be avenues for contracting the virus. This film won a ribbon at the American Film and Video Festival and a recommendation from AmFAR.

Computer Databases and Other Resources

Computerized resources of all kinds have become an important tool in sharing and gaining information about HIV/AIDS. Rapidly changing material can be updated quickly, anonymity can be maintained, and resources can be used at any hour and for relatively low costs. Below are just a few of the computer resources available; many organizations listed in Chapter 7 have their own bulletin boards or databases, as do many federal agencies.

AIDSQUEST ONLINE
AIDSWeekly
P.O. Box 830409
Birmingham, AL 35283
(800) 633-4931
(205) 995-1567
(205) 995-1588, Fax

This interactive database accompanies the *AIDSWeekly* newsletter and is available at no extra cost to newsletter subscribers. It provides an online version of the newsletter, a comprehensive review of published research on drugs and therapies, a database of periodical information, a database of research presented at conferences, AIDS-related articles from CDC's *Morbidity and Mortality Weekly Report,* a calendar of upcoming meetings, and descriptions of other databases.

AIDSTRIALS
Computerized AIDS Information Network (CAIN)
1213 North Highland Avenue
Los Angeles, CA 90038
(213) 464-7400

CAIN is an online network with the capability for both communications services (electronic mail, forum, and conferencing) and database services. The latter includes calendar, electronic publications, research library, and services resources. CAIN provides access to monthly medical and educational abstracts, up-to-date statistics, drug studies, selected journal articles and newsletters, popular press stories, and a monthly calendar of conferences, trainings, and meetings. All information is reviewed by a professional advisory panel. CAIN is available 24 hours a day to anyone with a computer, a modem, and telecommunications software; users may choose to remain anonymous. Membership and set-up fee costs are $49.95, and there are additional charges for hourly use of the system.

LEGISNET
National Conference of State Legislatures (NCSL)
1560 Broadway, Suite 700
Denver, CO 80202
(303) 830-2200
(303) 863-8003, Fax

LEGISNET is NCSL's information system on state policy issues, reports, and publications. Over 100 HIV/AIDS materials are available to LEGISNET subscribers and state legislatures. Material may be accessed directly by the user or by requesting a search by NCSL staff.

NAPWA Link
National Association of People with AIDS (NAPWA)
P.O. Box 34056
Washington, DC 20043
(202) 898-0414
(202) 898-0435, Fax
(800) 926-2792, NAPWA Link
(703) 998-3144, NAPWA Link local access
This computerized information and communications bulletin board of NAPWA contains current information and resources on HIV/AIDS. Services are available on different subscription plans for users. NAPWA operates a clipping service, keyword search, local resource directory, glossary, drug interaction database, "Ask-A-Doc" service, online conferences, and electronic mail.

National AIDS Information Clearinghouse (NAIC)
P.O. Box 6003
Rockville, MD 20850
(800) 458-5231; (301) 217-0023, International
(800) 243-7012, TTY/TDD
(301) 738-6616, Fax

NAIC maintains four information databases that experienced reference specialists can access for callers. Databases are:

1. The Resources Database, containing descriptions of more than 15,000 organizations providing HIV/AIDS services and resources
2. The Educational Database, including a collection of more than 7,500 hard-to-locate educational materials
3. The AIDS School Health Education Database, produced by CDC's Division of Adolescent and School Health, offers citations and annotations of resources for professional educators
4. The Funding Database provides information on funding possibilities for community-based organizations, including application, eligibility, and deadline information

Other Government Information Resources

Congressional Information Service (CIS) Documents on Demand
4520 East-West Highway, Suite 800
Bethesda, MD 20814
(800) 638-8380

This service provides paper or microfiche copies of congressional hearings, reports, committee prints, and documents, as well as complete legislative histories for all current and historical documents from the U.S. Congress. To order documents, provide the CIS publication year and access number, which are available through the *CIS/Index*, published monthly and available in libraries.

Government Document Cataloging Service (GDCS)

All publications indexed by the U.S. Government Printing Office from June 1976 to the present month are carried on this CD-ROM service. Title, author, and subject searches are available, with all supporting bibliographic detail provided on the format and content of the requested document, as well as the "SUDOC" (Superintendent of Documents) number necessary to find shelved material. Available in libraries.

Glossary

A WIDE ARRAY OF MEDICAL, SCIENTIFIC, AND PUBLIC HEALTH terms is used in the discussion of HIV/AIDS. Some have to do with sexual practices or drug use; some simply describe testing procedures, drug trials, or legal issues. At least some will be unfamiliar to any average reader.

Three mini-glossaries in Chapter 4, "Facts and Statistics," cover terms used in discussing HIV/AIDS and its transmission, testing, and drug therapies and drug trials. Those terms are basic to an understanding of HIV/AIDS as discussed in much of the literature; the terms are not repeated in this glossary. In the following section are some of the other most commonly used terms, including references to specific sexual practices. Many are used in this book, but others will be found in using the resources described. Though this list is by no means comprehensive and does not include many technical and scientific terms, it provides a basis for general understanding of some of the terms encountered.

abstinence Refraining from, as in abstinence from sexual activity or from the use of drugs.

Acquired Immune Deficiency Syndrome (AIDS) The final stage of a series of specific health conditions and problems and opportunistic infections (OI) caused by a virus (HIV) that can be passed from person to person chiefly through sexual contact, through the sharing of syringes used for intravenous drug injection, or through transmission from an infected mother to her unborn child. In AIDS, the body's natural immune system is suppressed and allows for the active presence of microorganisms that otherwise would be fought off by the immune system. The acronym *AIDS* was first used by the Centers for Disease Control (CDC) in late 1982 to name cases of illness that were first reported in 1981.

Acyclovir An antiviral agent approved to treat herpes simplex and varicella-zoster infections. It is also under investigation for use against cytomegalovirus (CMV).

aerosolized pentamidine   This drug, administered by inhalation of a fine mist, is approved for use against one of the primary fatal infections of AIDS, *Pneumocystis carinii* pneumonia. Injectable pentamidine is also used.

AIDS (Acquired Immune Deficiency Syndrome)   Infection with the Human Immunodeficiency Virus (HIV) is manifested by a depressed immune system that is overtaken by one or more of the diseases defined by Centers for Disease Control (CDC).

AIDS Clinical Trial Group (ACTG)   Medical centers that are taking part in the evaluation of treatments for HIV-related infections. These sites, of which there were 46 in 1991, are sponsored by the National Institute of Allergy and Infectious Diseases.

AIDS virus   A popular and widely used but inaccurate term for the Human Immunodeficiency Virus (HIV), the virus that leads to AIDS.

AL-721 (Active Lipid)   This antiviral drug is used to treat conditions related to AIDS. The drug was developed from an egg-based compound and affects membrane fluidity without being toxic. It was tested in France and Israel and was popular as a self-administered therapy in the mid-1980s, but did not meet with institutional success once AZT became available.

alpha interferon   The body makes small amounts of this hormone-like protein. It is produced in laboratory settings to treat Kaposi's sarcoma.

amebiasis   Infection with amoebas, including *Entamoeba histolytica*. Such infections are common among PWAs.

Amphotericin-B   An antifungal medication used to treat cryptococcal meningitis.

Ampligen   A drug still in trials that may be an immunomodulator and an antiviral.

anal intercourse   The sexual practice in which a man inserts his penis in his partner's rectum.

anemia   A condition in which there are a reduced number of red blood cells.

anorexia   A loss of appetite that is a neuropsychological disorder. Commonly referred to as an eating disorder.

antibiotic   A type of drug used to fight bacterial infection.

antibody   The body's immune system develops this special protein in the blood when a foreign substance is present; it is the body's defense against illness. Specific antibodies are developed by the body to fight various infections.

antibody-positive   This term refers to the result of a blood test that shows that person has been exposed to a particular infection at some time and developed antibodies to it.

antigen This substance, when introduced into the body, provokes the production of an antibody that will specifically react to it.

antiviral drug A medication that will halt the work of a virus before it multiplies or damages other cells.

antivirals These agents may be effective in treating AIDS; they are being studied in experiments to see if they halt the work of the virus or kill it entirely.

anus The opening of the lower end of the bowel.

ARC (AIDS-Related Complex) This term has not been defined or recognized by CDC, but is used frequently in the literature to describe symptoms found in some persons with HIV. It is also used to describe symptomatic HIV infection. Some of the symptoms are recurring fever, weight loss, fungal infection in the mouth and throat, and swollen lymph nodes.

asymptomatic Having no symptoms. Persons infected with HIV may not have symptoms for years.

autologous Having to do with the same organism or its parts. An autologous blood transfusion involves a person donating his or her own blood for later transfusion back into his or her own body.

AZT Azidothymidine, an antiviral and the first prescription drug approved in 1987 by the Food and Drug Administration (FDA) for use in prolonging life. The drug was approved for use before testing was completed; testing was done only on male subjects. AZT and another drug, ddT, are members of the same nucleoside family. AZT has a high cost and has shown extreme toxicity, as well as a loss of effectiveness over time. Research released in early 1992 showed that the drug did not prolong the life of users.

Bactrim This antibiotic has been effective in treating *Pneumocystis carinii* pneumonia (PCP). The drug has notable side effects.

beta-2 microglobulin test Physicians use this test to study the immune status of patients with HIV.

biopsy A surgical procedure where a sample of tissue is removed for examination.

bisexual A person who is sexually attracted to both males and females.

blood count This laboratory test determines the number of red blood cells, white blood cells, and platelets in the blood at a given time.

boarder baby An infant who is medically able to go home but lives in the hospital because he or she has no place to go. The number of boarder babies has risen with HIV/AIDS. Many boarder babies contracted HIV from their mothers. In some cases, a baby's mother has died. In other cases, because of a mother's drug use, homelessness, or illness, the baby cannot go home. In some communities, litigation compels a search for a foster home so that the baby does not remain in the hospital.

body or bodily fluids A euphemism to describe semen, blood, saliva, urine, and other fluids found in the body and central to the discussion of HIV transmission.

bone marrow This soft material at the center of the bone serves as the site of red blood cell production.

campylobacter A bacterial infection caused by contact with infected animals or contaminated food or water.

cancer Several diseases in which abnormal cells grow out of control in the body, destroy surrounding tissues, and may spread to other parts of the body.

candidiasis (*Candida albicans*) Also known as "thrush" in the mouth, this treatable yeast infection is common in persons with immune suppression and causes a fungus-like growth in the mouth, sinus cavity, esophagus, and vagina.

carcinogen Any substance that produces cancer.

case control study An epidemiological study that uses persons with a particular problem (cases) with others who do not have that problem (controls). The two groups may be matched for other factors, such as age, race, or occupation.

case definition The official Centers for Disease Control (CDC) definition of AIDS.

casual contact Ordinary daily activity. For instance, HIV cannot be transmitted by shaking hands with someone who has it, by using a telephone touched by a person with HIV, or by sitting in a classroom with a child who has HIV.

catheter A line installed semipermanently in the body to inject or remove fluids.

CD4 Also known as T4, CD4 is a protein in T-lymphocyte helper cells. HIV first infects cells by becoming attached to CD4 molecules. HIV destroys T4-cells, and a T4-cell count is one laboratory means of assessing the status of the immune system.

CD8 Also known as T8, CD8 is a protein in T-lymphocyte suppressor cells. The ratio between CD4 and CD8 cells is another important means of judging the viability of a person's immune system.

Centers for Disease Control (CDC) A federal government agency responsible for infectious disease control. The agency is located in Atlanta, Georgia, and operates under the U.S. Public Health Services, a part of the U.S. Department of Health and Human Services.

cervical cancer The second most common malignancy of the reproductive organs in women. It is seen at higher rates among poor women, women who have their first sexual experience at a relatively early age, and women with multiple sex partners. Cervical cancer is not part of the CDC diagnostic framework for AIDS, but has been characterized as a common component of HIV/AIDS in women.

cervix The neck of the uterus.

chemotherapy Treatment of the body with drugs that fight cancer.

clean needles Usually refers to syringes used for injection of drugs. Clean needles reduce the chance of passing HIV via blood that accumulates in the syringe. A clean needle can also be one that has been sterilized with bleach after being previously used.

clinical trial A research study in which new therapies are tested in humans. Therapies are tested in humans after they have been tried in animals and laboratory studies.

cofactors Scientific, medical, psychosocial, or other conditions that exist simultaneously and influence the progress or likelihood of a disease or condition.

cohort In any research study, a group of subjects that has a common statistical factor.

colitis Inflammation of the colon.

communicable disease A disease that can be spread from one person to another.

Community-Based Clinical Trial (CBCT) Primary care physicians working closely with patients in an accompaniment to conventional research studies.

compassionate use A means of using an investigational new drug before there is much established data on its capacity to produce results. Drugs must generally be given free of charge to patients by the companies manufacturing them. The FDA gives specific approval for each drug used this way.

Compound Q A highly purified protein made from root tubers that is being investigated in drug trials to inhibit HIV replication in both acute and chronic infections.

condom A shield placed over the penis during sexual intercourse. Condoms may be made of latex or sheep's intestine, though only latex condoms prevent the spread of HIV. The condom acts like a bag to collect semen, thus also acting as a birth control device and to prevent transmission of other sexual diseases. Condoms are also known as "gloves," "French letters," and "rubbers."

contact tracing A public health measure used in sexually transmitted diseases. Current and previous sexual partners are contacted by public health officials, who may or may not identify the other partner.

contagious disease An illness that can be spread through casual contact.

crack A very addictive smokable drug derived from cocaine. Crack is frequently traded for sex, making its use an indicator of frequent and multiple sexual partners, as well as a likely source of unsafe sexual practices.

cryptococcosis (*Cryptococcus neoformans*) A yeast-like fungus that is very life-threatening and ordinarily attacks the brain and lungs.

cryptosporidiosis A parasitic infection based in the intestines and causing chronic severe diarrhea. The parasite is transmitted by direct contact with an infected animal or through contaminated food or water.

cunnilingus The use of the tongue or mouth on a woman's genitals during sexual activity.

cytomegalovirus (CMV) A pathogen that is a member of the herpes virus family. Almost all AIDS patients have been infected with CMV, and it is being investigated as a cofactor in the sequence of events that leads to AIDS. Infection occurs directly though the mucous membranes, or via tissue or blood. Sites of infection are widespread in the body, but frequently include the retina and the colon.

ddC (dideoxycytidine) A potent HIV inhibitor drug being tested in vitro in drug investigations.

ddI (dideoxyinosine) An HIV inhibitor approved for use in 1991. ddI was the second drug approved by FDA to fight HIV, and it can be administered only for patients who cannot take the first approved drug (AZT) or who did not improve while taking it. As part of the process to speed development of new drugs, ddI was approved before all the research studies were completed. Studies are expected to be complete in early 1992.

dementia The loss of mental ability that is one of the symptomatic illnesses of AIDS. It is characterized by decreased concentration, loss of interest, and slowed motor abilities. At its end-stage, it can result in a nearly vegetative state.

dental dam A latex square that can protect against the transmission of HIV when placed over the vagina, clitoris, or anus during sexual activity.

dextran sulfate An antiviral that has inhibited HIV in test tube studies. It will be studied further but is in use in the drug "underground."

diagnosis An analysis of a patient's medical history.

diaphragm A form of birth control that uses a latex cap to cover the cervix during and immediately after sexual intercourse.

directly observed therapy A practice in the management of tuberculosis care in which a health care provider's role is to witness the patient taking medication.

DNA Deoxyribonucleic acid, the protein that carries genetic information in a cell. HIV can enter the DNA of a cell and use its structure to reproduce itself.

double blind A component of a drug trial in which neither the subjects nor the researchers know which subjects are receiving a test drug and which are receiving placebos or other substances. The structure is based on a belief that this promotes faster and more objective results, because neither party has expectations about the outcome.

drug-resistant tuberculosis Recent strains of tuberculosis that are impervious to one or more of the 13 commonly used antibiotics employed to treat the disease.

efficacy Ability to produce results. Investigational drugs are assessed for their efficacy in treating specific infections, for instance.

ejaculation The discharge of semen from the male's penis during sexual intercourse or other stimulation.

ELISA Enzyme-Linked Immunosorbent Assay, a simple blood test that can measure antibodies to HIV. Because this test can produce some false positive results, the test is repeated when positive and confirmed with a more sophisticated test, the Western blot test.

encephalitis nflammation of the brain.

endemic Disease in certain areas or groups of people.

enteritis Inflammation of the intestine.

enzyme This substance causes chemical reactions in the body to take place at an accelerated rate.

epidemiology The scientific and medical study of the incidence, distribution, and control of disease.

Epstein-Barr virus A virus found in the nose and throat. It causes mononucleosis and may cause chronic fatigue syndrome. It has been seen in lymphadenopathy, Kaposi's sarcoma (KS), and other opportunistic infections.

erythrocytes These red blood cells carry oxygen to the other cells of the body.

Erythropoietin A drug approved for treatment of severe anemia that can accompany AZT use. The drug is based on a naturally occurring compound and stimulates red blood cell production.

etiology The study of factors that cause disease.

expanded access Some HIV-infected people cannot participate in clinical drug trials and may not have other opportunities for treatment. Under this system, experimental drugs are distributed to them.

Factor VIII A component of the blood system that causes it to clot. The shortage of this element is the source of hemophilia.

false negative The result of a blood test where the blood sample contains too few antibodies or antigens to show a positive result. A person with this test result could be thought not to be carrying the virus, even though it is present.

fellatio The act of stimulating a male penis with the tongue or mouth during sexual activity.

fisting The insertion of the hand into the rectum or vagina during sexual activity.

Fluconazole A drug approved for use against candidiasis and cryptococcal meningitis.

Food and Drug Administration (FDA) The federal agency charged with approving new drug treatments for use by the public.

Foscavir An antiviral agent approved for use against CMV retinitis, CMV colitis, and strains of herpes simplex and zoster.

full-blown AIDS A case of HIV infection that meets the requirements of CDC's case definition.

fungus Mushrooms, yeasts, and molds fall into this class of microbes. PWAs are vulnerable to a host of fungi that otherwise would be fought off by the body.

Ganciclovir An antiviral drug approved for treatment of CMV retinitis.

gay Specifically refers to a man who finds other men sexually attractive. It can also be used to generally refer to gay men and lesbians as a group.

genitalia The external sex organs of the body. In the female, these are the vulva, the inner and outer lips of the vagina, and the clitoris. In the male, the penis, the scrotum, and the testicles are included.

giardiasis This infection of the small intestine is caused by a common protozoan passed by person-to-person contact, or by contaminated food or water.

gonorrhea   A sexually transmitted disease.

hairy leukoplakia   A white lesion that shows on the side of the tongue. It may be related to Epstein-Barr viral infection.

harm reduction   Strategies aimed at assisting people who use drugs to do so more safely, by helping individuals manage their drug use and their personal health, and by placing abstinence from drugs at one end of a continuum of behaviors. Harm reduction strategies have grown in acceptance with the spread of HIV and the realization by some health care providers that there must be services for active drug users as well as for people seeking to end drug use.

helper T-cells   Also known as T4 and CD4, they are a set of T-cells (helper, killer, or suppressor cells) that prompt antibody response and other immune functions.

hemoglobin   The component of red blood cells that carries oxygen.

hemophilia   A disorder of the blood system found in some males, in which they do not have a sufficient amount of the clotting factor.

hepatitis   An illness causing inflammation of the liver, accompanied by fevers and jaundice.

Herpes Simplex Virus I (HSV I)   This virus causes sores or blisters around the mouth; they can be transmitted to the genitals. The virus can be set into action by trauma, stress, infection, or immune suppression.

Herpes Simplex Virus II (HSV II)   This virus causes sores or blisters on the anus or genitals. They may be in a latent state in nerve tissue, become active, and produce symptoms. HSV II may be transmitted to an infant during birth from an infected mother.

Herpes Varicella-Zoster Virus (HVZ)   This is the virus that causes chicken pox in children and may manifest in adults as herpes zoster, also called shingles. Shingles are painful blisters that pattern themselves on the skin along nerve paths, frequently on the face and trunk of the body.

heterosexual intercourse   Sexual activity between a male and a female.

high-risk behavior   The preferred term for referring to actions that place one in danger of being exposed to HIV. In the early years of the epidemic, "high-risk groups" were described as being gay men, IV drug users, their sexual partners, and others, but the evolution of language to discuss the virus has placed the emphasis on behavior that can be changed or influenced, rather than on groups of people whose sexuality or drug use makes them a target of other discrimination. High-risk behavior includes unprotected sexual intercourse and sharing of needles in IV drug use.

HIV or HIV-1   Human Immunodeficiency Virus, the retrovirus that causes AIDS.

HIV-2   A virus found in West Africa in 1985, similar to HIV. The new virus was originally seen in prostitutes who showed no symptoms of it; a few cases have been verified in the United States. There has recently been pressure to test U.S. blood supplies for this virus, but little is known about it at the present time.

HIV antibody screening test   Refers to the two tests for the HIV antibody— ELISA and the Western blot. This term is infrequently used compared to the grossly inaccurate term "AIDS test."

HIV negative   A test result that does not show the presence of antibodies to HIV. This result does not mean that a person does not have HIV, however, as it may take as long as six months for the body to produce antibodies. During this period, the person can still transmit the virus to others and not show any symptoms.

HIV positive   A test result that shows the presence of antibodies to HIV. This result does not mean that the person has AIDS or will develop AIDS.

homophobia   A bias against homosexuals and homosexuality.

homosexual intercourse   Sexual activity between two people of the same gender.

horizontal transmission   The passing of HIV through blood or semen.

host   A cell or an organism that provides a home for the growth of a virus or a parasite.

HTLV-III   Human T-Lymphotropic Virus—Type III. U.S. scientists first used this term to refer to the virus that causes AIDS.

HTLV-III/LAV   Human T-Lymphotropic Virus—Type III/Lymphade-nopathy-Associated Virus. Two very similar viruses that are considered a primary cause of AIDS. Despite the confusion it causes, the virus that causes AIDS is referred to by several different names in the medical and scientific literature.

iatrogenic   Caused by the activities of a physician.

immune   Resistant to a disease, possibly because of the presence of antibodies.

immune boosters or immune modulators   Substances that enhance the body's natural defenses against infection and disease. A course of immune boosters has been found helpful to some HIV-positive individuals who are trying to prolong the period of time before the onset of full-blown AIDS.

immune system   The body fights off infections, viruses, bacteria, and other foreign matter through its immune, or defense, system. The body then uses these defenses again when called on to fight the same threat.

immunodeficient   An immune system that is not functioning or is suppressed in some way, making one vulnerable to infection and disease.

incidence   The number of cases of a disease occurring in a particular period of time.

incubation period   The period of time it takes for something, such as a disease, to develop in the body after infection or exposure has taken place.

infection   A bodily condition in which an infectious agent enters, multiplies, and produces a negative effect.

infectious   Can be transmitted by infection.

informed consent   A method of protecting people who are, for instance, possibly being tested for HIV, or entering a drug trial. Participants must indicate that they understand some basic information about the procedure by signing a consent form.

institutional review board   A group composed of doctors, scientists, and people with HIV/AIDS who ensure that a clinical drug trial or research program is safe and that the rights of participants are protected.

intercourse   Sexual activity where a man places his penis into a woman's vagina (heterosexual activity) or into another person's (male or female) rectum (homosexual or heterosexual activity).

interleukin-2   A lymphokine that is important to immune response and results in the expansion and proliferation of T-lymphocytes.

intravenous drugs   Chemical substances used in the body by means of inserting a syringe or needle into a vein.

in vitro   A scientific study conducted in an artificial environment, such as one created in a test tube.

in vivo   A scientific study conducted in a living organism, such as an animal or a human being.

IVDU   Intravenous drug user.

Kaposi's sarcoma (KS)   A rare form of cancer usually found in older men, until the arrival of the HIV epidemic. The cancer is most widely recognized by purple spots on the skin, resulting from tumors in the walls of blood vessels. However, the lesions can occur inside the body as well.

KS-OI   Kaposi's sarcoma (KS) and opportunistic infections was an early name used by CDC officials for what was eventually called AIDS.

KY   A water-based lubricant of the sort that can be safely used with condoms.

LAS (Lymphadenopathy Syndrome)   Chronically enlarged lymph nodes often found in HIV infection.

latency A period during which an organism is in the body but is not causing an apparent effect. HIV can remain latent for long periods of time.

LAV Lymphadenopathy-Associated Virus, a retrovirus in a person with enlarged lymph nodes who may have engaged in high-risk behavior. LAV is believed to be the same virus as HTLV-III.

LAV-HTLV-III Another of the names used for the virus that causes AIDS.

lesbian A woman who finds other women sexually attractive.

lesion A term used to refer to the infected part or sore in a skin disease.

leukocytes White blood cells.

leukopenia A low level of leukocytes in the blood.

lymph A yellowish fluid carrying lymphocytes. Lymph comes from fluids in tissues and is collected from all parts of the body and put back into the blood system.

lymph nodes The specific sites of the immune system throughout the body. The nodes are small organs that filter lymph fluid and where lymphocytes are found. Antigens in the body are filtered by the lymph system or the spleen and attacked by the immune system.

lymphadenopathy Swollen lymph nodes caused by an infection. Influenza, mononucleosis, lymphoma, or HIV may be the cause.

lymphatic system A network running throughout the body to transport lymph to the immune system and into the blood system.

lymphocytes These cells are produced in the lymph tissue.

lymphokines Substances released into the bloodstream by the T-cells to direct immune response.

lymphoma Cancer of the lymph nodes.

macrophage A cell that scavenges particulate matter in the system, especially in the form of infectious bacteria. Macrophages may be reservoir sites for HIV.

malabsorption Deficient intake of nutrients from the intestinal tract. HIV infection can cause the absorbing villi lining of the intestines to become atrophied. Malabsorption can lead to malnutrition, causing further immune suppression.

malaise A nonspecific condition of discomfort.

malignant Cancerous.

mandatory testing Refers to required HIV antibody testing.

meningitis Infection of the membranes that surround the brain.

menstrual blood   The bloody discharge that is passed from a female's body during her menstrual period.

metastasis   The spread of cancer in the body.

microbe   A living organism of microscopic size. Microbes include fungus, protozoa, and bacteria.

molecule   The smallest particle of a substance that can exist on its own.

monogamy   A continuing sexual relationship with one partner.

morbidity   How frequently a disease is appearing in a population.

MRI (Magnetic Resonance Imaging)   A diagnostic procedure that informs about the internal tissues and organs of the body.

multi-drug resistant tuberculosis (MDR-TB)   Recent strains of tuberculosis that are impervious to two or more of the thirteen commonly-used antibiotics employed to treat the disease.

Mycobacterium Avium Intracellulare (MAI)   A bacillus that causes infection of the internal organs. About 50 percent of PWAs show signs of MAI at the time of death.

needle exchange   The practice of providing clean syringes to intravenous drug users, in an effort to reduce the incidence of transmission of HIV.

neonatal   The period of the first few weeks of life after birth.

nonoxynol-9   A chemical in some spermicides, lubricants, and condoms that reduces the risk of HIV infection.

oil-based lubricants   Ordinary hand lotions, baby oil, Crisco, Vaseline, and mineral oil are oil-based lubricants that may be used in sexual intercourse but can cause condoms to break.

opportunistic infections   A general term for the variety of diseases and infections that can surface and become problematic when the immune system is depressed as the result of HIV infection. The infections would not have an effect in a healthy person.

oral sex   Stimulation of a sex partner's genitals with the mouth or tongue; the placing of the penis in a partner's mouth.

oral-anal sex   The use of the tongue or mouth to stimulate the anus of a sexual partner.

orphan drug   A medication indicated for a rare disease. The Orphan Drug Act of 1983 gives tax breaks to pharmaceutical companies, as well as a monopoly, as an incentive to develop drugs useful for up to 200,000 people.

p-24 antigen test   Used to monitor the immune status of an infected person.

pandemic An epidemic disease of widespread proportions.

parallel track A method of providing experimental drugs to patients who cannot participate in the regular drug trials and have no other opportunities for treatment.

parasite A plant or animal that feeds off another living thing. Not all parasites cause disease, but some (especially food-borne parasites) can be life-threatening to people with HIV/AIDS.

partner notification A public health practice of contacting the sexual partners of a person infected with an STD to notify them of their own risk of transmitted infection.

passive immunotherapy In this treatment, blood from an HIV-positive asymptomatic person is processed to deactivate the virus and then transfused to HIV-infected recipients.

pathogen Any microorganism or material that produces diseases.

Patient Zero A term referring to Air Canada steward Gaetan Dugas. Dugas was established by public health researchers as the person who had sex with many of the first gay men diagnosed with what became known as AIDS.

Pelvic Inflammatory Disease (PID) Painful infection of the fallopian tubes in a woman. It is commonly transmitted by sexual intercourse and sometimes occurs following abortion. PID is not part of the CDC diagnostic framework for AIDS, but has been characterized as a common component of HIV/AIDS in women.

perinatal Any event that takes places at or around the time of birth.

PGL (Persistent Generalized Lymphadenopathy) Chronic noncancerous lymph node enlargement.

phagocyte A type of cell that destroys foreign matter in the system, including bacteria.

placebo A substance administered in a drug investigation to measure the efficiency of a specific drug. A placebo is inactive and can cause a change called the "placebo effect" in a patient, due to the expectations of the recipient.

platelets Cellular fragments that circulate and play an important role in blood clotting.

Pneumocystis carinii **pneumonia (PCP)** A parasitic, fungal pneumonia common in persons with AIDS. It is the most life-threatening of the opportunistic infections.

prevalence The number of cases of a disease at a given time.

prognosis Medical outlook.

prophylaxis Any treatment intended to prevent disease and preserve health.

proteins One of the major components of cells. Proteins are made up of amino acids.

protocol A set of rules for a clinical trial. The protocol describes what types of patients will participate, the schedule of tests and procedures, drugs and dosages, and the length of time the study will be conducted.

protozoa One-celled animals, some of which cause disease in humans.

quarantine The often involuntary isolation of persons with infection. Cuba has quarantined persons with HIV infection.

radiation A form of treatment for cancer using high-level radiation such as x-rays.

recombinant human alpha interferon A drug approved for use against Kaposi's sarcoma.

rectum The end of the intestinal tract; the section of the intestine through which bowel movements, or stools, pass. It is also the interior site of anal intercourse.

red blood cells The component of the blood that carries oxygen to the cells.

retinitis Inflammation of the retina that can lead to blindness. It is caused in AIDS by infection with CMV.

retrovirus HIV is a retrovirus. This group of viruses contains the genetic material RNA and copies it into DNA inside an infected cell. The DNA that results from this process is then included in the genetic structure of the cell as a provirus. Proviruses are then passed to each infected cell's offspring cells. In the case of HIV, the problem that this presents is that, in order to kill the virus, the cell must also be killed.

reverse transcriptase An enzyme in retroviruses that can copy RNA into DNA. This process is necessary to the life cycle of HIV.

rimming Stimulation of the anus with the tongue.

risk factors Generally refers to behaviors or practices that place one at risk for HIV transmission. The most common risk factors are IV drug use and unprotected sexual intercourse. Previously, use of blood or blood products was also a risk factor.

rubber A common expression for a condom.

safe sex A general term to describe sexual practices and attitudes that protect a person from transmitting or receiving HIV. Also describes any sexual activity that does not involve the exchange of body fluids.

salmonellosis (*Salmonellae*) Bacteria that are usually food- or waterborne and multiply in the small intestine. *Salmonella* infection is about 20 times more common in persons with immune system problems than in persons with healthy immune systems; recurrent incidences of it in HIV-positive people are grounds for a diagnosis of AIDS.

semen   The fluid that a male ejaculates from the penis during orgasm.

seroconversion   When a person's antibody status (seronegative) changes to positive.

serologic test   A class of laboratory tests performed on the serum portion of the blood, which is the clear, liquid portion of blood.

seronegative   This test result reflects a negative result for the HIV antibody test.

seropositive   This test result reflects a positive result for the HIV antibody test.

seroprevalence   A number that would express the frequency or absolute number of people in a given group (city, state, clinic) with positive results for the HIV antibody test.

serum   The clear, fluid portion of the blood that contains antibodies.

sharing needles   Using a syringe to inject drugs after it has been used by someone else, or passing it to another person after using it yourself. A small amount of blood accumulates in the syringe when it is used, and, if infected, this blood can transmit HIV to another user.

shigellosis   (*Shigella*) An acute infection of the bowel, caused by the *Shigella* organism. It is very common in persons with immune system problems.

shingles   See Herpes Varicella-Zoster Virus (HVZ).

SIDA   The acronym for AIDS in Spanish and French.

side effects   Unwanted or unexpected actions or responses caused by a drug. Experimental drugs are studied for both short-term and long-term side effects.

spermicide   A chemical that kills sperm and other organisms on contact. Spermicides are used on condoms, in lubricants, and in contraceptive jellies and foams.

spleen   An organ in the abdomen that plays an important role in the immune system.

STD   A sexually transmitted disease. More than 25 different infections are now classified as STDs, including gonorrhea, syphilis, and herpes simplex. Most STDs can be treated.

straight   A heterosexual person.

subcutaneous   Beneath the skin, as in a subcutaneous injection.

sulfonamides   A type of antibiotic drug.

suppressor T-cells A type of T-cell that stops antibody production and some other immune responses.

symptoms Changes in the body or body functions that are indicative of disease.

T4 See CD4.

T-helper cells, or T-lymphocytes The immune system uses these white blood cells to fight infection. There are three types of cells: helper, killer, and suppressor. They are mainly found in the blood and lymph system and are targeted by HIV. Many clinics stop monitoring T-cell counts after they fall to 200 from the normal level of 1,000 or more. Recent reports show that many AIDS-linked infections and deaths occur at levels below 50.

thrush The fungus *candida* causes this infection in the throat, mouth, and/or esophagus. It manifests as white patches.

thymus An organ in the chest cavity where T-cells develop. The thymus is inert in adults.

titer This measurement is used in the laboratory to find the concentration of a particular component in a solution.

T-lymphocytes See T-helper cells.

toxicity The extent to which a substance is harmful or poisonous to the body.

toxoplasmosis This disease is caused by infection with the protozoan *Toxoplasma gondii*. Inflammation of the brain is a frequent result. The protozoan is passed in the feces of infected cats.

treatment IND (investigational new drug) This program offers experimental treatment to patients without satisfactory alternative treatments.

tuberculosis (TB) An acute or chronic infection that is being seen more frequently in HIV-positive people and poor people. It is caused by an airborne pathogen, passed through inhalation, thus contributing to its spread in crowded physical situations, such as overcrowded housing or shelters. While TB was once believed to be all but wiped out in this country, case numbers have been rising in recent years.

underground A general term to refer to self-help activities by PWAs and HIV-positive people that either bring untested or unapproved drugs into the country from other sources, or manufacture them outside official laboratory environments.

unprotected sex Sexual activity without a condom or dental dam.

vaccine A substance made of the antigenic components of an infectious organism. The resulting substance prompts an immune response, but not the disease itself, when it is put into the body. A person is subsequently protected against infection by that organism.

vagina The organ in mature females that leads from the vulva to the uterus.

vaginal intercourse The insertion of the penis into the vagina.

vaginal secretions Fluids found in the vagina.

vaginitis Infectious and inflammatory diseases of the vagina, usually caused by bacteria. Although not part of the CDC diagnostic framework for AIDS, vaginitis has been characterized as a common component of HIV/AIDS in women.

vertical transmission The passing of disease or infection to a child through infection of the placenta.

viral culture A method for growing viruses in the laboratory.

virology The study of viruses.

virus This organism causes infectious disease and needs living cells (a host) to reproduce. A virus may take over the cell's normal functioning and cause it to behave in ways determined by the virus.

vulva The inner and outer lips of the vagina and the clitoris in a female.

wasting Involuntary weight loss that is a common symptom of HIV infection. Weight loss indicates progression of HIV disease and can occur at any stage of the infection. It can result from malabsorption of nutrients and is thus associated with malnutrition, which can contribute to immune suppression.

water-based lubricant A substance without oil or grease that is used in sexual intercourse because it does not weaken a condom.

watersports An expression to describe sexual activities involving urine.

Western blot This laboratory procedure detects antibodies to HIV. The Western blot test is more difficult than the ELISA test and is used as a back-up for ELISA results that show positive.

works A slang expression for syringes used for injecting drugs.

zoster See Herpes Varicella-Zoster Virus (HVZ).

Index

ABA. *See* American Bar Association.
Abbott Laboratories, 33
Abrams, Donald I., 206
Acer, David, 50, 149–151
Acquired Immune Deficiency Syndrome. *See* AIDS
ACT UP, 15, 37, 38, 39, 40, 42, 52, 172
The ACT UP/NY Women and AIDS Book Group, 221
Active Lipid. *See* AL-721
Acyclovir, 63
ADA. *See* American Dental Association; Americans with Disabilities Act
Adolescents and HIV/AIDS, 98–101, 212–213, 215
Aerosolized pentamidine, 63
African Americans
    and AIDS, 231
    and community response to AIDS, 11–12
    and percent infected, 9–10, 98, 99
AIDS (Acquired Immune Deficiency Syndrome), 218, 224
    among adolescents, 98–101
    and the church, 224
    curriculum, 216
    deaths from (U.S.), 92
    definitions, 5–6, 43, 56–57, 58
    distinguished from HIV, 56–57
    early history in U.S., 1, 113–126
    first named, 29, 119–120
    full-blown, 59
    history, 212, 222
    and hospitals, 210

    human rights cases, 218
    inaccurate terminology for, 57
    legal issues, 209, 211
    local services, 218
    and the media, 213
    public opinion on, 106–107
    related diseases, 90–92
    scientific issues, 224, 225–226
    state statistics, 92–94
    U.S. statistics, 83–92
    and volunteerism, 211–212
    and women, 94–97, 135–136, 209, 214, 221
    and the workplace, 148–149
    world statistics, 81–83
    See also HIV
AIDS, 214
AIDS: Health Services in Five Communities, 219
AIDS: Profile of an Epidemic, 218
AIDS: The Burdens of History, 223
AIDS: The Spiritual Dilemma, 225
AIDS: The Ultimate Challenge, 213
AIDS: Trading Fears for Facts: A Guide for Teens, 212
AIDS: What Does it Mean to You?, 212
AIDS Action Council, 172
AIDS and Substance Abuse, 224
AIDS and the Health Care System, 223
AIDS and the Law: A Basic Guide for the Nonlawyer, 208–209
AIDS and the Law: A Guide for the Public, 211
AIDS and the Law Legal Docket, 209
AIDS and Women: A Sourcebook, 209

AIDS Answers for Teens, 215
AIDS Awareness Day, 40
The AIDS Benefits Handbook, 207–208
The AIDS Caregivers Handbook, 206
AIDS Clinical Trial Group (ACTG),
    16, 63, 153, 157
AIDS Clinical Trials Information
    Service (ACTIS), 188–189, 203
AIDS Coalition to Unleash Power. *See*
    ACT UP
AIDS Crisisline, 203
AIDS dementia complex, 5
AIDS Demographics, 222
*AIDS Education: Gaps in Coverage Still
    Exist,* 219
*AIDS Education: Programs for
    Out-of-School Youth Slowly
    Evolving,* 219
*AIDS Education: Public School Programs
    Require More Student Information
    and Teacher Training,* 219
*The AIDS Epidemic: Private Rights and
    the Public Interest,* 223
AIDS Funding, 206
AIDS/HIV Treatment Directory, 206
AIDS Housing Opportunities
    Act, 13
AIDS in the Mind of America, 209
AIDS Information Sourcebook, 208
AIDS Medical Foundation (AMF), 53
AIDS National Interfaith Network,
    172
*AIDS Practice Manual: A Legal and
    Educational Guide,* 208
*The AIDS Reader: Documentary History
    of a Modern Epidemic,* 222
*The AIDS Reader: Social, Political,
    Ethical Issues,* 223
AIDS Reference and Research Collection,
    209
AIDS Technical Assistance Hotline,
    203
AIDS Treatment News, 36, 215–216
AIDS Treatment Resources (ATR),
    172–173
AIDSQUEST ONLINE, 235
AIDS-related complex. *See* ARC
AIDSTRIALS, 235
AIDSWALK, 44
Alabama Department of Health, 194
Alaska Department of Health, 194

Alcohol, Drug Abuse, and Mental
    Health Administration
    (ADAMHA), 189
AL-721 (Active Lipid), 63
Altman, Dennis, 209
Alyson, Sasha, 221–222
AMA. *See* American Medical
    Association
*America Living with AIDS: Transforming
    Anger, Fear, and Indifference into
    Action,* 152
American Bar Association (ABA), 173
American Civil Liberties Union AIDS
    Project, 173, 209
American Civil Liberties Union
    National Prison Project,
    173–174
American Dental Association (ADA),
    43, 174, 215
American Foundation for AIDS
    Research (AmFAR), 38, 53, 174,
    229–230
American Medical Association
    (AMA), 42, 174–175
American Nurses Association, 42
American Public Health Association
    (APHA), 175
American Red Cross, 29, 30, 175
Americans with Disabilities Act
    (ADA), 13, 158
AMF. *See* AIDS Medical Foundation
AmFAR. *See* American Foundation
    for AIDS Research
Amphotericin-B, 63
Ampligen, 63
And the Band Played On, 215
Andrulis, Dennis P., 210
Answers about AIDS, 230–231
Antibiotic, 63
Antibody, 58
Antibody-positive (term definition),
    62
Antigen, 58
Antiviral drug, 63
Antivirals, 8, 64
APHA. *See* American Public Health
    Association
ARC (AIDS-related complex), 58
Arizona Department of Health, 195
Arkansas Department of Health, 195
Ashe, Arthur, 49

Association for the Care of
Children's Health (ACCH),
175–176
Asymptomatic (term definition), 58
Athey, Jean Garrison, 215
ATN Publications, 176
AZT (Zidovudine or
Azidothymidine), 8, 34, 37, 42,
43, 46, 47, 50, 64, 214
AZT Federal Hotline, 203

Bactrim, 64
Baker, Ronald A., 206
Baltimore, D., 27
Barre, Françoise, 50
Bateson, Mary Catherine, 210
Baxter v. City of Belleville, Illinois, 160
Bayer, Ronald, 210
Bergalis, Kimberly, 7, 12, 45, 49, 50,
149–151
Berrigan, Daniel, 224–225
Black People Get AIDS, Too, 231
Blake, Amanda, 49
Blood Transfusion Risks and Benefits,
231
Blood transfusions and donors, 28,
29, 54, 122–123, 231–232
screening, 33
B'nai B'rith International, 176
Body fluids, 58
Body Positive, 176
Bogard v. White, 160–161
Borrowed Time, 226
Brandt, Edward, 31
Brickner, Philip W., 222
Broder, Samuel, 50
Brown, Lawrence D., 222
Buchanan, Pat, 31
Buler v. Southland Corporation, 161
Burris, Scott, 11
Burroughs Wellcome, 34, 50
Bush, George, 13, 37, 39, 45, 52, 53

California Department of Health, 195
California Prostitutes Education
Project (CAL-PEP), 176–177
Callen, Michael, 50, 225
Campbell, Bobbi, 32
CARE Act. *See* Ryan White
Comprehensive AIDS Resource
Emergency Act

Cartland, Cliff, 210
Case definition, 58
Case histories, 3, 5, 6, 8
Casual contact, 58
CDC. *See* Centers for Disease Control
CD8, 59
CD4, 59. *See also* T4 cells
Center for Population Options
(CPO), 177
Center for Women Policy Studies
(CWPS), 177
Centers for Disease Control (CDC),
1, 5–6, 28, 29, 34, 35, 40, 43, 58,
59, 189–190
hotlines, 203–204
recordings, 203–204
surveillance case definition, 66–80
*Chalk v. U.S. District Court of
California, Orange County
Superintendent of Schools,*
161–162
Chemotherapy, 64
Chermann, Jean Claude, 33
Child Welfare League of America
(CWLA), 177–178
Children, HIV among, 4, 5, 10, 45,
46, 97–98, 123, 210, 214
The Church with AIDS, 224
Cikins, Warren I., 211
Circle of Hope, 227
CIS/INDEX, 216
Clarke, Loren K., 222
Clinical trial, 64
Colorado Department of Health, 195
Community Programs for Clinical
Research on AIDS (CPCRA),
16–17
Community response to AIDS, 11–12,
155, 213, 218–219
*Community-Based AIDS Prevention:
Studies of IV Drug Users and Their
Sexual Partners,* 218–219
Compassionate use, 64
Compound Q, 64
Computer databases, 235–237
Condoms, 41, 44, 46, 59, 104
Conference of State and Territorial
Epidemiologists, 31
*Confronting AIDS: Directions for Public
Health, Health Care, and Research,*
216–217

Congressional Information Service (CIS), 216
Documents on Demand, 237
Connecticut Department of Health, 195
Connor, Steve, 225
Correctional facilities. See Prisons
COSSHMO. See National Coalition of Hispanic Health and Human Service Organizations
Courage To Care: Responding to the Crisis of Children with AIDS, 210
Covering the Plague: AIDS & the American Media, 213
Cox, Elizabeth, 225
CPO. See Center for Population Options
Crimp, Douglas, 222
Crisis at the Front Line: The Effect of AIDS on Public Hospitals, 210
Criteria for Evaluating an AIDS Curriculum, 216
Cunningham, Ann Marie, 227
CWPS. See Center for Women Policy Studies

Dalton, Harlan, 211
Dancing against the Darkness: A Journey through America in the Age of AIDS, 227
Databases, 235–237
Day Without Art, 40
D.C. Government, Office of AIDS Activities, 196
ddC (Dideoxycytidine), 46, 64
ddI (Dideoxyinosine or Didanosine), 8, 43, 46, 64
Defense Health Care: Effects of AIDS in the Military, 219–220
Delaney, Martin, 34
Delaware Division of Public Health, 195
Dementia complex. See AIDS dementia complex
Dental dam, 59
Dentists. See Health care workers
The Denver Principles, 132–134
Department of Veterans Affairs. See U.S. Department of Veterans Affairs (VA)

Design Industries Foundation for AIDS (DIFFA), 178
Dextran sulfate, 64
Didanosine. See ddI
Dideoxycytidine. See ddC
Dideoxyinosine. See ddI
Digeronimo, Theresa Foy, 212
Dinkins, David, 39, 45, 46
Discrimination cases, 160–166
Doe v. Dolton Elementary School District No. 148, 162
Doe v. Westchester County Medical Center, New York State Department of Health, 166–167
Does AIDS Hurt?, 214
Doherty, Diane, 215
Don't Forget Sherrie, 232
Double blind, 64
Drug Abuse: Research on Treatment May Not Address Current Needs, 220
Drug Abuse: The Crack Cocaine Epidemic, 220
Drug Treatment, 220–221
Drug use
    and growth of prison populations, 102
    and HIV/AIDS, 2, 3, 11, 101–102, 136–139, 154–155, 217–218, 220–221, 224
    hotline, 204
    See also Intravenous drugs
Drug-Exposed Infants: A Generation at Risk, 220
Dugas, Gaetan, 50–51

Early Care for HIV Disease, 206
Education issues, 17–18, 108–109, 154, 219
Eidson, Ted, 206
ELISA (enzyme-linked immunosorbent assay), 62
Ending the Silence: Voices of Homeless People Living with AIDS, 226–227
Endocarditis, 4
Enzyme-linked immunosorbent assay. See ELISA
Epidemic of Fear, 209–210
Erythropoietin, 65
Estate of Behringer v. Princeton Medical Center, 166
Estate of Campanella v. Hurwitz, 163

Expanded access, 65

Factor VIII, 59
Facts about AIDS for the Dental Team, 215
Faggots, 52
Failure of U.S. Health Care System To Deal with HIV Epidemic, 39, 217
Falco, Mathea, 211
False negative (term definition), 62
FDA. *See* Food and Drug Administration
"Fear of Disclosure," 54
Federal programs related to HIV/AIDS, 188–194
Fee, Elizabeth, 223
Fernandez, Joseph, 41
Films and videos, 229–235
Florida, 44
Florida Department of Health and Rehabilitative Services, 196
Fluconazole, 65
Food and Drug Administration, 38, 43, 65, 153–154, 190
    Anti-Infective Drugs Advisory Committee, 37
Forsyth, Elizabeth, 212
Fortunato, John E., 225
Foscavir, 65
The Foundation Center, 206
Fox, Daniel M., 223
Funders Concerned about AIDS, 178
Funding (U.S.), 84–86

Gaffney, Martin, 41–42
Gallo, Robert, 27, 32, 34, 40, 51, 53, 225–226
Ganciclovir, 65
Gay Men's Health Crisis (GMHC), 28, 52, 178
Gay Men's Health Crisis (GMHC) et al. v. Sullivan, Sec'y. HHS, 168
Gays, 9
    bathhouses and, 32, 33
    and behavioral changes, 35
    and blood donor screening, 33
    and community response to AIDS, 11
    and leveling of new infections, 10
Georgia Department of Infectious Diseases, 196

Glaser, Elizabeth, 226
Global AIDS Policy Coalition, 81, 179
Glover v. Eastern Nebraska Community Office of Retardation, 167
GMHC. *See* Gay Men's Health Crisis
Goldsby, Richard, 210
Good Intentions: How Big Business and the Medical Establishment Are Corrupting the Fight against AIDS, 214
Gostin, Lawrence O., 223
Government and AIDS, 13–14
Government Document Cataloging Service (GDCS), 238
Graubard, Stephen R., 223
Grieco, Michael H., 206
Grief, 213
Griggs, John, 211–212
Grmek, Mirko D., 212
Guidelines for the Development of a National AIDS Prevention and Control Programme, 221

Haitians, 30, 34
Halleron, Trish, 207
Halston, 49
Haring, Keith, 51
Harvard School of Public Health, 35
Hawaii Department of Health, 196
Health care access, 15–16, 87–88, 152–153
Health Care Financing Administration (HCFA), 153, 190
Health care system and HIV/AIDS, 210, 217, 223
Health care workers, 7, 39, 41, 42, 43, 44, 47, 50
    C. Everett Koop on, 44
Health Omnibus Programs Extension (HOPE) Act, 158
Health Policy Advisory Center (Health/PAC), 179
Health Policy and the Disadvantaged, 222
Health Resources Services Administration (HRSA), 153, 190–191
Healy, Bernadine, 42
Heckler, Margaret, 30, 32, 34
Hein, Karen, 212
Helms, Jesse, 42, 43, 47, 53
Hemophilia, 59, 121–123

Hernandez, Ralph, 136–137
Heterosexual intercourse and HIV
    infections, 2, 123–124
High-risk behaviors, 59–60. *See also*
    Risk factors and reduction
Hispanics
    and community response to AIDS,
        11–12
    and percent infected, 10, 98, 99
*History of AIDS: Emergence and Origin of
    a Modern Pandemic,* 212
HIV (Human Immunodeficiency
    Virus), 60
    among adolescents, 98–101
    antibody screening test, 62
    and antivirals, 8
    and body fluids, 7
    distinguished from AIDS, 56–57
    effect on children, 4, 5, 21, 45, 46,
        97–98, 123, 210, 214
    geographic patterns, 11
    global patterns of spread, 82
    and holistic approaches, 9
    and homelessness, 5, 10, 19–20, 45,
        139–143, 222
    and immune modulators, 8
    inaccurate terminology, 57
    infected health care workers,
        7, 39, 41, 42, 43, 44, 47, 50,
        149–151
    and modes of transmission, 83
    and nature of virus, 3
    and numbers currently infected,
        1, 9–10
    and predicted numbers to be
        infected, 2
    and progression of disease, 4
    public opinion on, 106–107
    and related illnesses, 4, 90–92
    as retrovirus, 3
    and social disenfranchisement in
        U.S., 2
    social effects of, 2, 210, 223
    state statistics on, 92–94
    and sub-Saharan Africa, 2
    symptoms, 4
    testing, 88–90
    transmission of, 6–7
    treatments, 8–9, 153–154
    and tuberculosis, 4–5, 90–92
    U.S. statistics on, 83–92

    and women, 94–97, 135–136
    and the workplace, 148–149
    world statistics on, 81–83
    See also AIDS
HIV Disease in Correctional Facilities,
    217
HIV negative (term definition), 62
HIV positive (term definition), 62
Holistic health measures, 9
Homelessness and HIV, 5, 10, 19–20,
    45, 139–143, 222
HOPE Act. *See* Health Omnibus
    Programs Extension Act
Horne, George Kenneth, Jr., 28, 51
Hospitals. *See* Health care system and
    HIV/AIDS
Hotlines, 203–204
Houston, 35
How To Find Information about AIDS,
    207
HTLV-III (Human T-Lympho
    tropic Virus-Type III), 32,
    34, 60
Hudson, Rock, 12, 34, 36, 49, 51
Human Immunodeficiency Virus.
    See HIV
Human Rights Campaign Fund
    (HRCF), 179
Hyde, Margaret O., 212

*Iacono v. Town of Huntington Security
    Division, et al.,* 163–164
Idaho Bureau of Communicable
    Disease Prevention, 196
IHPP. *See* Intergovernmental Health
    Policy Project
Illinois Department of Health, 196
*Illness as Metaphor and AIDS and Its
    Metaphors,* 224
Images: Crisis on AIDS, 232
Immigration and AIDS testing, 13
Immune boosters (immune
    modulators), 65
Immunodeficient (term definition),
    60
In the Absence of Angels, 226
Indiana State Board of Health,
    197
The Indomitable Spirit, 228
Information centers, 66, 191–192,
    203–204, 235–238

Institute of Medicine, National Academy of Sciences, 37, 216–217
Institutional review board, 65
Interferon, 8, 53, 60. *See also* Recombinant human alpha interferon
Intergovernmental Health Policy Project (IHPP), 179–180
Interleukin-2, 27
International Conference on Acquired Immune Deficiency Syndrome, 34, 37, 42, 47
Intravenous drugs, 60
Investigational new drug. *See* Treatment IND
Iowa Department of Public Health, 197
IVDU, 60

Jackson, Michael, 54
James, John S., 36, 215–216
Job Corps and HIV/AIDS, 100
John, Elton, 54
Johnson, Earvin "Magic," 12, 45, 47–49, 52, 212–213

Kansas Department of Health and Environment, 197
Kaposi's sarcoma (KS), 5, 28, 29, 51, 60, 115–119. *See also* Recombinant human alpha interferon
Kelly, Sharon Pratt, 46
Kentucky Department for Health Services, 197
Kingman, Sharon, 225
Kinsella, James, 213
Kirp, David L., 213
Klein, Michael, 228
Know about AIDS, 212
Koch, Edward, 38
Koop, C. Everett, 28, 37, 44, 52, 57, 226. *See also* Surgeon General's Report on the Acquired Immune Deficiency Syndrome
Koop: The Memoirs of America's Family Doctor, 226
Kramer, Larry, 37, 52, 226, 229
Krim, Mathilde, 53

KS. *See* Kaposi's sarcoma
Kübler-Ross, Elisabeth, 213

Lambda Legal Defense and Education Fund, 180
LAS (Lymphadenopathy Syndrome), 60
LAV (Lymphadenopathy-Associated Virus), 31, 53, 60
Leadership, Legislation, and Regulation, 39, 217
Learning AIDS: An Information Resources Directory, 207
Learning by Heart: AIDS and Schoolchildren, 213
Leckelt v. Board of Commissioners of Hospital District 1, et al., 167
Legal cases
    discrimination in, 160–166
    miscellaneous, 167–169, 218
    and testing, 166–167
Legislation (federal), 157–159
LEGISNET, 236
A Letter from Brian, 232–233
Liberace, 49
Lingle, Virginia A., 207
Living with AIDS, 223
Local AIDS Services: The National Directory, 218
Los Angeles, 35
Louisiana Department of Health and Hospitals, 197
Lymphadenopathy Syndrome. *See* LAS
Lymphadenopathy-Associated Virus. *See* LAV

McCormack, Thomas, 207–208
McDermott, Jim, 139
McKenzie, Nancy F., 223
Maine Department of Human Services, 197
Malinowsky, H. Robert, 208
Mandatory testing, 62
Mapplethorpe, Robert, 53
Martinez, Robert, 47
Martinez v. School Board of Hillsborough County, Florida, 163–164
Maryland Department of Health and Mental Hygiene, 198
Mason, Belinda, 45, 53, 152
Massachusetts, 44

Massachusetts Department of Public
  Health, 198
Media and AIDS, 14
Media network, 208
Medicaid, 15–16, 153
Meningitis, 4
Miami, 35
Michigan Department of Health,
  198
Military
  AIDS testing in, 13, 34, 36
  and HIV/AIDS, 104–105, 219–220
Minnesota Department of Health,
  198
Minorities. *See* African Americans;
  Hispanics; National Minority
  AIDS Council; National Native
  American AIDS Hotline; Office
  of Minority Health;
  Racial/ethnic groups and
  HIV/AIDS
Mississippi Department of Health, 198
Missouri Department of Health, 198
Mitzutani, S., 27
Mixon v. Grinker, 168
Mobilizing against AIDS, 213
Monette, Paul, 226
Monkeys, 47
Montagnier, Luc, 31, 42, 50, 51, 53
Montana Department of
  Health—AIDS Program, 199
*Morbidity and Mortality Weekly Report
  (MMWR),* 28, 30, 113, 114
Morgan, D. A., 27
Moulton, Jeffrey M., 206

NAMES Project AIDS Memorial
  Quilt, 38, 54, 180, 228
NAPWA Link, 236–237
National AIDS Hotline, 191, 204
National AIDS Information
  Clearinghouse (NAIC), 66,
  191–192, 204, 237
National AIDS Program Office, 192
National AIDS Research Foundation,
  35
National Association of PWA's
  (NAPWA), 181. *See also* NAPWA
  Link
National Cancer Institute (NCI),
  42, 50

National Cancer Institute AIDS
  Information, 204
National Coalition for the Homeless,
  226–227
National Coalition of Advocates for
  Students, 216
National Coalition of Hispanic
  Health and Human Service
  Organizations (COSSHMO), 181
National Commission on AIDS
  (NCOA), 17, 39, 52, 53, 54, 136,
  152, 192, 217–218
National Conference of State
  Legislatures (NCSL), 181–182
National Council of Churches
  (NCC), 182
National Council of La Raza (NCLR),
  182
National Endowment for the Arts, 53
National Gay and Lesbian Task Force
  (NGLTF), 182
National Gay Rights Advocates,
  182–183, 208
National Hemophilia Foundation,
  183
National Institute of Allergy and
  Infectious Diseases (NIAID),
  16–17, 63, 192
National Institute of Drug Abuse, 204
National Institute of Justice, 103
National Institutes of Health (NIH),
  40, 41, 50, 153, 154, 157,
  192–193
National Lawyers Guild AIDS
  Network, 183, 208
National Leadership Coalition on
  AIDS, 183–184
National Library of Medicine
  (NLM), 193
National Minority AIDS Council
  (NMAC), 184
National Native American AIDS
  Hotline, 204
National Native American AIDS
  Prevention Center, 184–185
National Network of Runaway and
  Youth Services, 185
National Organizations Responding
  to AIDS (NORA), 185
National Pediatric HIV Resource
  Center (NPHRC), 185–186

National School Boards Association, 186
National Sexually Transmitted Diseases Hotline, 204
NCI. *See* National Cancer Institute
NCOA. *See* National Commission on AIDS
NCSL. *See* National Council of State Legislatures
Nebraska Department of Health, 199
Needle exchanges, 37–39, 45, 60, 93–94
Needles
  clean, 59
  sharing, 61
Nevada State Health Division, 199
New England Journal of Medicine, 34, 47
New Hampshire Public Health Service, 199
New Jersey Division of AIDS Prevention and Control, 199
New Mexico Department of Health, 199
New York City, 5, 10, 11, 28, 29, 35, 38, 39, 41
New York State, 30, 46
New York State Department of Health, 199
Newark, N.J., 35
Newsletters, 215–216
Nichols, Eve K., 213
NIH. *See* National Institutes of Health
Nixon, Bebe, 228
Nixon, Nicholas, 228
No Nos Enganemos, 233
NORA. *See* National Organizations Responding to AIDS
The Normal Heart, 52, 229
North Carolina Division of Epidemiology, 200
North Dakota Department of Health, 200
Nourse, Alan E., 214
Nussbaum, Bruce, 214

Office of Minority Health, 193
Ohio Department of Health, 200
Ojos Que No Ven/Eyes That Fail To See, 234
Oklahoma Department of Health, 200
O'Malley, Padraig, 223

Opportunistic infections, 60
Oregon State Health Division, 200
Organizations, 171–188
Osborn, June, 54
Osborn, M. Elizabeth, 229

Palmer, Laura, 226
Pan American Health Organization, 218
Parallel track, 65
Passive immunotherapy, 65
Pasteur Institute, 31, 33, 53
Paul F. Cronan v. New England Telephone Company, 162
PCP. *See Pneumocystis carinii* pneumonia
Peavey, Fran, 227
Pediatric AIDS Coalition, 186
Pediatric AIDS Foundation, 186–187
Pennsylvania Department of Health, 200
People v. 49 West 12 Tenants Corporation, 164
People with AIDS. *See* Persons with AIDS
People with AIDS, 228
People with AIDS Coalition, 50
Perinatal (term definition), 60
Perinatal transmission, 123
Perry, Gerald J., 208
Persistent Generalized Lymphadenopathy. *See* PGL
Persons with AIDS (PWAs), 14–15, 53, 84, 132–134, 223, 224–228
  social treatment of, 109–110
  See also Underground
Petrow, Steven, 227
PGL (Persistent Generalized Lymphadenopathy), 60
Philip Morris Co., 42
Photographers + Friends United Against AIDS, 228
Photographic collections, 228
Pisaneschi, Janet, 207
Placebos, 65
Plays, 229
Pneumocystis carinii pneumonia (PCP), 5, 8, 28, 29, 54, 61, 114–117, 118–119
Pneumonia, 4. *See also Pneumocystis carinii* pneumonia (PCP)

Poetry, 228
Poets for Life: Seventy-Six Poets Respond to AIDS, 228
Poff v. Caro, 164
Poiesz, B. J., 27
Policy. *See* Public policy issues
Popovic, Mikulas, 34
Porter, Irving, 139–140
Porter v. Axelrod, 168
"Positive," 54
Potts, Malcolm, 222
Praunheim, Rosa, 54
Prego, Veronica, 39–40
Presidential Commission on the Human Immunodeficiency Virus, 218
Prevention issues, 108–109
"Prevention Point," 41
Prisons and HIV/AIDS, 102–104, 123–124, 144–148, 217
Private Acts, Social Consequences: AIDS and the Politics of Public Health, 210
Project Inform (PI), 34, 187, 204
Protocol, 65
p-24 antigen test, 63
Public opinion on HIV/AIDS, 106–107
Public policy issues, 152, 217, 221, 222
 access to health care, 15–16, 87–88
 approval of new treatments, 16–17
 care systems, 19–22
 education, 17–18, 108–109, 154
 prevention, 17–18
 research, 16–17
 testing and confidentiality, 18–19
Puerto Rico, 11, 201
PWA Coalition, 54, 187
PWA Prison Project, 187
PWAs. *See* Persons with AIDS

Quackenbush, Marcia, 214
The Quilt: Stories from the NAMES Project, 228
Quilt project. *See* NAMES Project AIDS Memorial Quilt

Racial/ethnic groups and HIV/AIDS, 98, 99
Rask, Grethe, 54
Ray family, 44

Ray v. School District of DeSoto County, 164–165
Raytheon Company v. Fair Employment and Housing Commission, Estate of Chadbourne, 165
Reagan, Ronald, 12, 13, 36, 37, 52
Reagan administration, 33, 35
Recombinant human alpha interferon, 65
Reference books, 206–209, 216–217
Religious institutions and AIDS, 14
Report of the Presidential Commission on the HIV Epidemic, 13
Report of the Presidential Commission on the Human Immunodeficiency Virus Epidemic, 218
Reports from the Holocaust: The Making of an AIDS Activist, 226
Research. *See* AIDS Medical Foundation; American Foundation for AIDS Research; Community Programs for Clinical Research on AIDS; Gallo, Robert; Montagnier, Luc; National AIDS Research Foundation; Public policy issues
Research, the Workforce and the HIV Epidemic in Rural America, 217
Retroviruses, 3, 27, 31, 61
Reverse transcriptase, 27, 61
Rhode Island Department of Health, 201
Richardson, Diane, 214
"Rights and Reactions: Lesbian and Gay Rights on Trial," 54
Risk factors and reduction, 61, 125–126. *See also* High-risk behaviors; Safe sex
Robert Wood Johnson Foundation (RWJ), 187–188
Robinson, Max, 49
Rolston, Adam, 222
Rural areas and HIV/AIDS, 105, 217
Rural Drug Abuse: Prevalence, Relation to Crime, and Programs, 221
Ruscetti, F. W., 27
Ruskin, Cindy, 228
Russell, Letty M., 224
Ryan White: My Own Story, 227
Ryan White Comprehensive AIDS Resource Emergency (CARE) Act, 13, 84–85, 158–159

Safe sex, 61. *See also* Unprotected sex
San Francisco, 30, 32, 33, 35, 41
San Francisco AIDS Foundation, 188
Saridakis, Spero, 41
Sarngadharan, M. G., 34
Schmoke, Kurt, 137
Schwartz, Linda, 215
Science, 31
The Science of AIDS, 224
Scientific American, 224
*The Search for the Virus: The Scientific
    Discovery of AIDS and the Quest for
    a Cure*, 225
Seeing through AIDS, 208
Seroconversion, 61
Serologic test, 63
Seronegative (term definition), 63
Seropositive (term definition), 63
Seroprevalence, 63
    in prisons, 103
Service Employees International
    Union, AFL-CIO, 188
Sex, Drugs, and AIDS, 215
Sexually transmitted diseases (STDs),
    61
A Shallow Pool of Time, 227
Sharpe, Phyllis, 135–136
Shilts, Randy, 215
SIDA, 61
Side effects, 66
Siegel, Larry, 224
"SILENCE=DEATH," 54
Silverman, Mervyn, 32, 33
Simple Acts of Kindness, 211–212
Social response to AIDS, 11–12, 215,
    221–222
Social Security, 20, 153, 193
Someone Was Here, 227–228
Sontag, Susan, 224
*Sorrow Built a Bridge: Friendship and
    AIDS*, 224–225
South Carolina, 11
South Carolina Department of
    Health, 201
South Dakota Department of Health,
    202
S.P., et al. v. Sullivan, 169
State AIDS coordinators, 194–203
Statistics
    states, 92–94
    U.S., 83–92, 222

world, 81–83
STDs. *See* Sexually transmitted diseases
Students with AIDS, 34, 36, 54, 213
Substance abuse. *See* Drug use
Sulfonamides, 66
*Surgeon General's Report on Acquired
    Immune Deficiency Syndrome*, 37,
    126–132, 219
Surveillance case definition, 66–80
Surviving AIDS, 225
*Surviving and Thriving with AIDS, Volume
    I: Hints for the Newly Diagnosed*, 225
*Surviving and Thriving with AIDS,
    Volume II: Collected Wisdom*, 225

T. v. A Financial Services Co., 165–166
Taylor, Elizabeth, 35
T-cells (T-lymphocytes), 27, 61. *See
    also* T4 cells
    helper, 59
    suppressor, 61
*Teenage Drug Use: Uncertain Linkages
    with Either Pregnancy or School
    Dropout*, 221
Teenagers. *See* Adolescents and
    HIV/AIDS
Temin, H. M., 27
Tennessee Department of Health
    and Environment—Disease
    Control, 201
Terl, Alan H., 208–209
Testing, 88–90, 211
    and legal cases, 166–167
    See also Mandatory testing; p-24
    antigen test; Serologic test;
    *subheadings under Immigration,
    Military, Public policy issues, U.S.
    State Department*
Texas Department of Health, 201
T4 cells, 3, 34.
    counts of, 6, 43
    See also CD8; CD4
*Thinking AIDS: The Social Response to
    the Biological Threat*, 210
*Thomas Bradley v. Empire Blue Cross
    and Blue Shield*, 167–168
*Thomas v. Atascadero Unified School
    District*, 166
Tighe, John Charles, 206
'Til Death Do Us Part, 234
Tilleraas, Penny, 227

T-lymphocytes. *See* T–cells
Toward a National Policy on Drug and AIDS Testing, 211
Toxicity, 66
Trapani, Margi, 207
Treatment IND (investigational new drug), 66
Treatments, 8, 153–154
Troubled Adolescents and HIV Infection, 215
Tuberculosis, 4–5, 46, 62, 90–92
  in prisons, 104
The Twin Epidemics of Substance Use and HIV, 217–218

Under the Safety Net: The Health and Social Welfare of the Homeless in the United States, 222
Underground, 66
U.S. Conference of Mayors AIDS/HIV Program, 188, 218
U.S. Department of Health and Human Services, 153, 154, 193, 218–219
U.S. Department of Veterans Affairs (VA), 190
U.S. General Accounting Office, 219
U.S. Public Health Service, 35, 36, 154, 194
U.S. State Department
  AIDS testing, 13
University Publishing Group, 209
Unprotected sex, 62. *See also* Safe sex
Utah Bureau of HIV/AIDS Prevention, 202

VA. *See* U.S. Department of Veterans Affairs
Vermont AIDS Program, 202
Villarreal, Sylvia, 214
Virgin Islands Department of Health, 202
Virginia Department of Health, 202
Virus, 62
Virus Hunting: AIDS, Cancer, and the Human Retrovirus, 225–226

Wachter, Oralee, 215
War on Drugs, 21
Washington, D.C., 11
Washington Department of Social and Health Services—Office on AIDS, 202
Wasting, 62
Watstein, Sarah, 209
The Way We Live Now: American Plays & the AIDS Crisis, 229
West Virginia Department of Health, 202
Western blot, 63
What Is AIDS?, 234
What You Can Do To Avoid AIDS, 212–213
White, Ryan, 12, 34, 38, 49, 54, 134–135, 227. *See also* Ryan White Comprehensive AIDS Resource Emergency (CARE) Act
Whitmore, George, 227–228
WHO. *See* World Health Organization
Wiggins v. Maryland, 169
Wisconsin Division of Health AIDS/HIV Program, 202
Women, AIDS & Activism, 221
Women and HIV/AIDS, 10, 94–97, 135–136, 209, 214
Women in Love, 52
Wood, M. Sandra, 207
Woodruff, John O., 215
Workplace and HIV/AIDS, 148–149
World Health Organization (WHO), 40, 81, 194, 221
Wyoming Division of Health and Medical Services
  AIDS Prevention Program, 203

Yale AIDS Law Project, 211
You Can Do Something about AIDS, 221–222
You Can Protect Yourself and Your Family from AIDS, 210

Zidovudine. *See* AZT
Zwickler, Phil, 54